TIME

Inside The Red Border

A history of our world,
told through the pages
of TIME magazine

Contents

A giant facsimile of the June 6, 1932, cover with Japan's Emperor Hirohito looms over an entrance to the TIME and *Fortune* pavilion at the 1933 World's Fair in Chicago (red border colorized)

A Rough Draft Of History, One Cover at a Time

By Richard Stengel

Managing Editor, TIME magazine

U.S. Representative Joseph Cannon, a former Speaker of the House, was on the first cover of TIME, March 3, 1923

A preliminary sketch, left, by Boris Artzybasheff for the April 30, 1956, cover with Soviet leader Nikita Khrushchev, drawn on a previous cover template. The final cover, above.

THE TIME COVER IS THE MOST IMPORTANT REAL ESTATE in journalism. The iconic red border grabs you by the lapels and says, "Pay attention." That border divides the world into everything outside it and everything inside; everything inside is important, meaningful, urgent—and everything outside, well, not so much. The red border is a visual drum roll that has the effect of heightening everything inside it so that the image and the line get enhanced power and relevance and focus. It started as a visual flourish and ended up as one of the most recognizable signatures in the world. Each week, the TIME cover fuses word, art and design to become a part of history.

The red border didn't exist when TIME was born in 1923. For the first four years of our history, there was just an elegant filigree to the left and right of the black-and-white charcoal portraits of the magazine's cover subjects. But the magazine was languishing on the newsstand. In 1930, according to *The Man Time Forgot,* Isaiah Wilner's biography of Briton Hadden, who founded the magazine with Henry Luce, TIME's advertising chiefs went to newsdealers for advice, and one of them said, "What you need on the cover is pretty girls, babies or red and yellow." The girls and babies just didn't fill the bill, and yellow seemed too garish. One day, sitting in Hadden's office, a friend of his named Philip Kobbe took a red crayon and drew a border around the cover of the current issue. Everyone loved it.

The red border debuted on the first issue of 1927, gracing a portrait of Leopold C. Amery, the British Secretary of State for the Colonies. Few remember Amery, but the red border stuck. In fact, the business side soon upgraded the paper stock so it would better accept color, and the cost was soon recouped by the additional revenue earned from selling color ads on the inside and back covers.

Through much of our history, the cover image was almost always a portrait of an individual. "Names make news," Luce said, and his conception of TIME was that we would write about the news through the people who made it. This seems pretty unexceptional today, but in the 1920s and '30s, it was a new and revolutionary notion. For Luce, history didn't make the man; the man—and woman—made history.

The first full-color portrait, an oil painting of Walter P. Chrysler, appeared in January 1929. Within 10 years, there were color photographs on the cover. But by 1939, TIME began to take a different direction. For the next 25 years, TIME featured distinctive painted cover portraits by three artists: Boris Artzybasheff, Ernest Hamlin Baker and Boris Chaliapin—the ABCs as they were known in the office. This era was the golden age of the TIME cover.

BAKER WAS A COLGATE UNIVERSITY GRAD who started drawing caricatures when he was in college. Both of the Borises were Russians who had been displaced by the Russian Revolution. Artzybasheff escaped as a deckhand on a steamer and jumped ship in New York. Chaliapin was the son of the one of Russia's greatest opera singers. In terms of style, Baker was the most straightforward and realistic, yet his covers often had a sweetness and optimism about them. Chaliapin's pictures were moody, more impressionistic and often lyrical. Artzybasheff's portraiture was extremely realistic, but his images, especially the backgrounds, were often surreal, displaying an imagination that was wild and surprising. From 1939, when Baker did his first cover, until 1970, when Chaliapin executed the last of his, the three men painted more than 900 covers.

Within a few years, these portraits added another feature. Because some of the subjects were not well known to readers, the artists started painting elaborate backgrounds filled with objects and iconography that put the person in context. One of the first of these was a 1941 portrait of the dissident Lutheran pastor Martin Niemoller of Germany; his face was flanked by a swastika and a cross. The backgrounds came to be symbolic landscapes with images and objects that helped identify the subject. They were as rich in their own way as the portraits. For many readers, the background came to be a kind of weekly puzzle helping them decipher the main image.

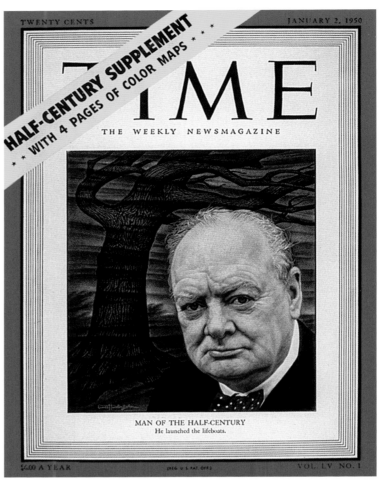

WINSTON CHURCHILL | January 2, 1950

Portrait by Ernest Hamlin Baker

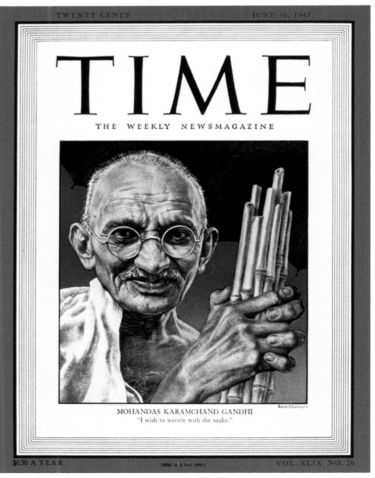

MOHANDAS GANDHI | June 30, 1947

Portrait by Boris Chaliapin

HEDDA HOPPER | July 28, 1947

Portrait by Boris Chaliapin

HUMPHREY BOGART | June 7, 1954

Portrait by Ernest Hamlin Baker

ADOLF HITLER | May 7, 1945

Portrait by Boris Artzybasheff

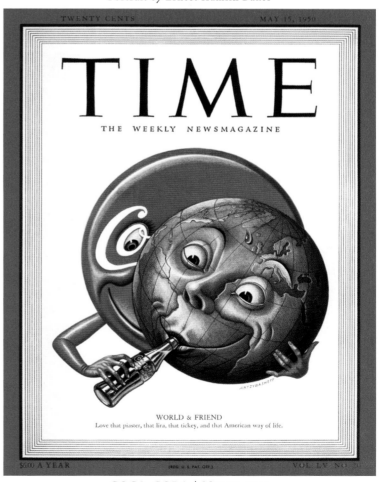

COCA-COLA | May 15, 1950

Illustration by Boris Artzybasheff

MARTIN LUTHER KING JR. | January 3, 1964
Portrait by Robert Vickrey

I have two portraits from this period hanging in my office. One is Baker's wonderful rendering of Jackie Robinson, showing the beaming Brooklyn Dodger surrounded by giant baseballs. It is a happy image, with a sunny Robinson radiating optimism and confidence. It's hard not to smile while looking at it. The other is Artzybasheff's brilliant portrait of designer Buckminster Fuller with a head shaped like his greatest invention, the geodesic dome. It is so clever, so brilliantly executed and so much fun. It is irresistible.

By 1940 the filigree was gone. In the 1950s the logo began to be superimposed on the cover image rather than sitting above it. This created more of a pure poster effect. I've always conceived of the TIME cover as a poster, something that catches your eye and informs at the same time. Like posters, it is meant to be bold, clean, immediately understandable. To use Horace's definition of great art: the TIME cover is *dulce et utile*—it teaches while delighting.

In the mid-'60s, TIME's editors began moving the covers away from portraiture. They did not abandon it altogether but used more graphic images and bigger headlines to tackle social and societal issues. The iconic 1966 cover "Is God Dead?"—which simply used bold red type on a black background—was powerful, visually arresting and modern. One of my favorite covers from this period is Roy Lichtenstein's 1968 "The Gun in America," published a week after the assassination of Robert Kennedy. Just four issues before, Lichtenstein's brilliant portrait of Kennedy, in the middle of his campaign for President, depicting him as a comic-book superhero, had been the cover of the magazine.

THE RED BORDER REMAINED UNCHANGED until the late 1970s, when the magazine introduced a corner "flap"—a graphic version of a page corner being turned down. The idea was to feature a second big story. We also introduced a more compact logo that, like so many things of the '70s, seems a little less than lofty today. Elegance should be a virtue of the TIME cover, and the classic logo, as well as the one today, preserves that.

The first time we changed the color of the border was for the edition we rushed to press in the wake of Sept. 11, 2001—an issue dominated by a single article and pictures telling the story of the terrorist attacks on U.S. The border was black. It was an echo of the time LIFE magazine changed its iconic red title box from red to black for its cover on the assassination of John F. Kennedy. We've since altered it three more times: a green border to commemorate Earth Day, a silver border for the 10th anniversary of 9/11 and a silver border for Barack Obama's second Person of the Year cover, in 2012.

On occasion, we've created three-dimensional objects for the cover, like George Segal's sculpture for Machine of the Year in 1983

THE BEATLES | September 22, 1967
Portrait by Gerald Scarfe

THE SEARCH FOR GOD | April 8, 1966

ALEC GUINNESS | April 21, 1958

Portrait by Ben Shahn

GUNS | June 21, 1968

Illustration by Roy Lichtenstein

JOHN LINDSAY | November 1, 1968

Photo collage by Romare Bearden

and Christo's globe for Planet of the Year in 1988. While these are genuine works of art, they work less well on a magazine cover, which struggles to capture three dimensions on a flat surface.

When I arrived at TIME in the early 1980s and began work as a staff writer, I'd see the cover for the first time on Monday mornings like our millions of readers. Sometimes I was pleased, sometimes disappointed, but it seemed like a mysterious and almost magical process that I could never be part of. A few years later, I was sometimes called on to participate in what became a tradition: a gathering of writers and editors and art and photo editors in a conference room on Friday night to look at cover options that were created by the art director. This process had its pluses and minuses. The virtues of it were that you got people's first reactions and could get a sense of what was working and what was not. It also made more people feel included in the cover decisionmaking process. The downside was that it could be pretty arbitrary as well as demoralizing for the art director, and the opinions were just that, opinions.

WHEN I BECAME MANAGING EDITOR, I slowly began to change the process. I've always cared a great deal about design, and I have a fairly well-defined aesthetic. I wanted covers to be not a visual compromise but a bold, singular vision that would cut through the hurly-burly of the newsstand. I spend more time thinking about and working on the cover each week than any other part of my job. The cover was the single most important decision I would have to make for every issue, and I wanted the process to reflect that. We didn't have the resources we once had to work on two or three cover stories a week, so the burden was that we had to choose both a story and an image to focus on. I'd work with our art director—first Arthur Hochstein, later D.W. Pine—to come up with a handful of images, often by several artists or photographers, that would make a striking and arresting image. We'd refine that over the course of the week, getting to the point that there was often only one option. With the arrival in 2009 of Kira Pollack as director of photography, we were even more proactive in planning and scheduling photo shoots not only for cover portraits but also images like the dueling wife and husband (with babe in arms) for "The Chore Wars" in 2011, the unweaned 3-year-old boy for our attachment-parenting story in 2012 and the child in a corner with a bullhorn for "The Power of Shyness," also in 2012.

Under Hochstein, we came up with some memorable images: the ten-gallon hat over a pair of cowboy boots for "The End of Cowboy Diplomacy" in 2006 and, the same year, the Weegee photograph of the backside of an elephant for a Republican

JESSE JACKSON | April 6, 1970
Portrait by Jacob Lawrence

BILL CLINTON | April 20, 1992
Photograph by Steve Liss

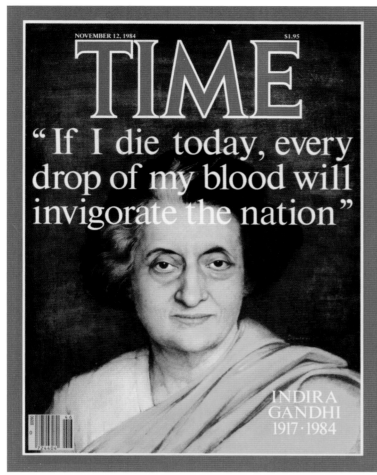

INDIRA GANDHI | November 12, 1984

Portrait by Mario Donizetti

MICHAEL JACKSON | March 19, 1984

Portrait by Andy Warhol

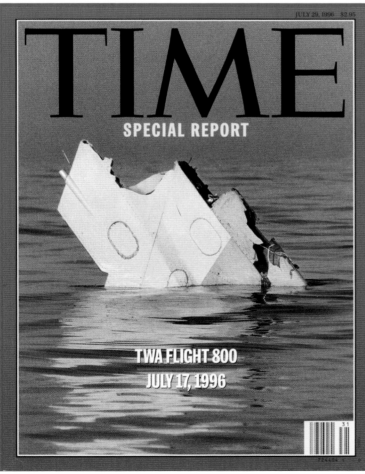

TWA FLIGHT 800 | July 29, 1996

Photograph by Jon Levy

EVOLUTION | March 14, 1994

Photo-illustration by Matt Mahurin

Party scandal involving underage congressional interns. Because I think a magazine should look both recognizable and fresh, we became known for doing striking images and graphics on a white background. Under Pine, who succeeded Hochstein in 2010, we've moved to a different style, with symbolic images that can hold big, bold and graphic type. The image supports a big line—New Jersey Governor Chris Christie with "The Boss" boldly superimposed, for example, or a man in a bow tie looking through binoculars with a backdrop of cumulus clouds for "Rethinking Heaven."

ULTIMATELY, IT IS THE WORDS THAT ARE the sell. I love it when the type forms either a triangle or an inverted triangle and seems to be a solid graphic image all by itself. We've continued to use great artists. In June 2013, the Chinese dissident Ai Weiwei designed what may be one of the most beautiful covers ever, "How China Sees the World," a dazzling red and white Chinese paper cutting that takes up every square centimeter of the cover real estate.

Under Pollack, we have done many memorable cover shoots, including Nadav Kander's dreamlike portrait of Obama for the 2012 Person of the Year; Martin Schoeller's photograph of Mark Zuckerberg, our 2010 Person of the Year; and an image of Steve Jobs by Marco Grob for the cover that marked the introduction of Apple's iPad to the world.

Of all the cover decisions I've made, the one I lost the most sleep over was the graphic, haunting portrait by Jodi Bieber of a young Afghan girl whose nose was sliced off by the Taliban. It was one of those images that you could both not look at and not look away from. It was so strong that I could barely examine it myself, but I thought the grim reality was something that millions of people should see.

In this book, we have assembled a small selection of the more than 4,500 covers published by TIME over the past nine decades to tell the history of the period. Along with the covers are excerpts from their accompanying stories. Until 1982, bylines were a rarity and TIME spoke as a single entity, despite the fact that many prominent writers worked for the magazine. Where records exist, we have now lifted the veil of anonymity to reveal the contributions of writers like John McPhee, James Agee and John Hersey, among the many who gave voice to TIME.

Over 90 years, the cover has captured Presidents and Popes, heroes and villains, science and medicine, ideas and trends, scandal and catastrophe. The cover itself has become a touchstone in our culture. I get many letters every week telling me the cover subject is either worthy or not worthy of putting inside that red border. We try to live up to that iconic red frame. Every week, the goal is to create a cover that is both timely and timeless.

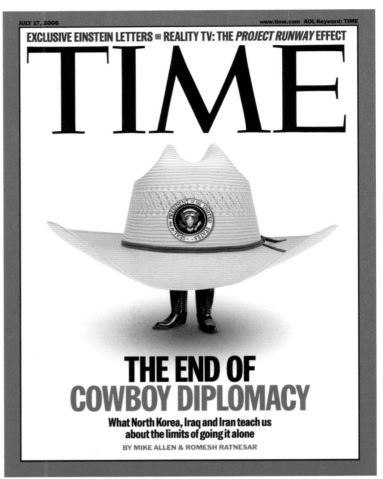

DIPLOMACY | July 17, 2006

Photo-illustration by Arthur Hochstein

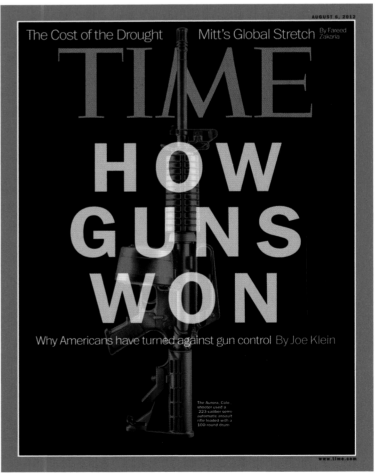

GUN CONTROL | August 6, 2012

Photo-illustration by Bartholomew Cooke

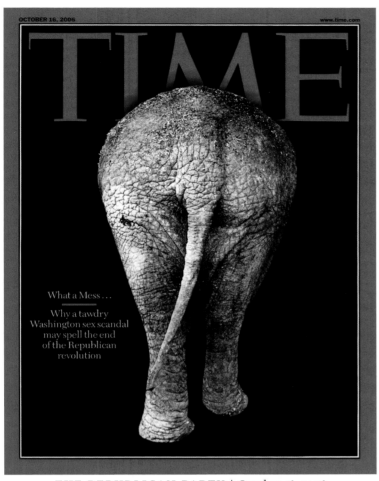

THE REPUBLICAN PARTY | October 16, 2006

Photograph by Weegee

THE IRAQ WAR | July 30, 2007

Photo-illustration by Arthur Hochstein

BARACK OBAMA | December 31, 2012

Photograph by Nadav Kander

CHINA | June 17, 2013

Art by Ai Weiwei

Though in office just over 1,000 days, Kennedy inspired a nation with his exuberance— and the power of the new medium of television

Photograph by Gerald French

☐The Presidents

ALWAYS THE GENTLEMAN, PRESIDENT WARREN HARDING CAME to office in 1921 with modest ambitions and a mild vision for his office. "If I felt that there is to be sole responsibility in the Executive for the America of tomorrow, I should shrink from the burden," he said at his Inauguration. True to his words, Harding's time in office was marked by the minor role he played. "To be a 'good fellow,' handshaker and amiable 'regular guy' and still occupy the President's chair is, in the national mind, the realization of the highest American idealism," TIME reported then.

In the 90 years since, the constitutional role for the President has not changed on paper. As Harry Truman said, "The presidency is exactly as powerful as it was under George Washington." But the means and exercise of that power have swung like a great pendulum through times of war and peace, domestic strife and economic prosperity. Just a decade after Harding's death in office, Franklin Roosevelt remade the presidency in ways that would have shocked many of the Founding Fathers. With the support of Congress, he claimed and wielded new powers over the banks, new controls over agricultural production and the power to create the social safety net that anchored the New Deal.

By the time of John Kennedy, those powers had grown even further: he had the clear ability to rally the American public through the new medium of television, and he was willing to use the Internal Revenue Service to target political groups that opposed him. This swing toward the empowered and unaccountable Executive reached its farthest point with Richard Nixon, who not only gained power from Congress to impose price controls and decoupled the dollar from the gold standard but also wielded the police and spying power of the presidency outside the control of the law to counter his political enemies. As a result of the latter and the Watergate break-in, Congress and the Judicial Branch reasserted themselves in a true test for the country. Swearing in Gerald Ford after Nixon's resignation, Chief Justice Warren Burger grabbed the hand of Senator Hugh Scott, a Pennsylvania Republican, to celebrate the success of the American system. "Hugh," said Burger, standing in the White House, "it worked. Thank God, it worked."

The debate over presidential powers continued into the next century, as the country was tested by another attack, on Sept. 11, 2001. In its wake, Congress gave the President broad new powers to combat terrorism, and George W. Bush seized upon them in ways that are still debated. At one point, in 2004, his FBI director and his Attorney General threatened to resign with other senior Justice Department officials over a classified surveillance program that they had determined was in violation of the law. Faced with the threat, Bush agreed to alter the program, but the debate over the scope and secrecy of government surveillance powers did not go away. Barack Obama, who won office opposing much of Bush's approach to the war on terrorism, found himself after his re-election facing outrage among his supporters for secret surveillance policies leaked by a young intelligence contractor.

Throughout this time, the power of the presidency did not reside solely in the actions Presidents took by order or veto. With the dawn of the era of mass communications and transcontinental flight, they found themselves occupying a much more public position, expected to respond to every major event and to travel the world to defend and promote the American project. In 1928, senior aides to Calvin Coolidge complained to TIME of the radio host Will Rogers' mimicking the President's voice to sell Dodge automobiles. Franklin Roosevelt used fireside chats to talk directly to the American people for more than a decade. Television helped bring in the age of Kennedy, and Ronald Reagan, a veteran of the big screen, became a master of the medium. Then, decades later, the Internet helped organize millions of Americans around Obama's two elections. With each technological innovation, the White House's ability to set the national conversation only increased.

Franklin Roosevelt was the first President to fly on a plane while in office, and in short order, globetrotting became a key part of the job description. Truman signed the National Security Act of 1947, which created the U.S. Air Force, on board a plane. By 1959, Dwight Eisenhower was being hailed as a truly world leader, having been received by throngs in Ankara, Karachi, Kabul, New Delhi, Tehran, Athens, Madrid and Casablanca on one of his voyages. "I saw at close hand the faces of millions," he reported on his return. The expectations proved a great burden to Kennedy. Reporters for TIME once found him in shorts, hugging his legs high over the Atlantic Ocean, suffering from the acute back pain that afflicted him, particularly on long trips. Today, frequent tours abroad are no longer remarkable, and Obama has used them to launch global campaigns.

But for all that, the politics of the office remain largely unchanged. Eisenhower called himself a "born optimist," much like nearly every President before and since. "I was not brought up to run from a fight," announced Truman, who also said he would "tell the people the facts"—phrases neatly paraphrased by Bill Clinton and a half-dozen others. They were men who invariably described themselves as defenders of freedom and free enterprise and of the better days ahead. In their view, as Reagan put, it is always "morning in America." And in their care, the American experiment has survived to continue to test that promise. —MICHAEL SCHERER

Warren Harding
March 10, 1923
Portrait by William Oberhardt

After two years in office, Harding saw corruption scandals threatening to overwhelm his achievements. Five months after this issue came out, he would be dead.

He is not a superman like [Theodore] Roosevelt or [Woodrow] Wilson; he never pretended to be, and he should not be judged according to such lofty standards. He is important and successful as the embodiment of the American idea of humility exalted by homely virtues into the highest eminence. He is the actuality of the schoolboy notion that anybody has a chance to be President. Mr. Harding has no personal enemies. Almost everybody in Washington likes him and admits he is a "good fellow." And to be a "good fellow," handshaker and amiable "regular guy" and still occupy the President's chair is, in the national mind, the realization of the highest American idealism. No one realizes this more completely and shrewdly than Harding.

Calvin Coolidge
January 16, 1928
Portrait by S.J. Woolf

Enjoying the fruits of an economic boom, he was able to restore public confidence in the White House after the Harding scandals. But then there was radio ...

Time was when court jesters got their ears stoutly boxed for following up a timely prank with an impertinence. Last week, though the technique had changed, the intent was the same when "those close to the President" pronounced Funnyman Will Rogers in bad taste. Having just served his country by amusing President [Plutarco Elías] Calles of Mexico at Ambassador [Dwight] Morrow's behest, Funnyman Rogers, home again in California, performed in a nationwide radio program to advertise Dodge automobiles. During his piece, Funnyman Rogers announced that the broadcasting would switch to Washington, where President Coolidge "would say a few words." The "few words" that followed were typically Rogersian but the voice that spoke them so closely aped President Coolidge's voice that many a dull-witted radio owner switched off his instrument under the impression that he had heard the President actually endorse Dodge automobiles.

Herbert Hoover
March 26, 1928
Portrait by S.J. Woolf

Profiled during his first campaign, Hoover would be elected on his reputation as a public servant. But the economic collapse led to his defeat for re-election in 1932.

The central fact militating against Candidate Hoover is that many people cannot understand what he stands for. He is no forthright protagonist of an ideal or program. He puts forth no clear-cut political or social theory except a quiet "individualism," which leaves most individuals groping. Material wellbeing, comfort, order, efficiency in government and economy—these he stands for, but they are conditions, not ends. A technologist, he does not discuss ultimate purposes. In a society of temperate, industrious, unspeculative beavers, such a beaverman would make an ideal King-beaver. But humans are different. People want Herbert Hoover to tell where, with his extraordinary abilities, he would lead them. He needs, it would seem, to undergo a spiritual crisis before he will satisfy as a popular leader. Until then, his detachment, his impatience with questions not concrete, his zeal for his own job, will continue to be interpreted by many as political cowardice or autocratic overbearing.

FIFTEEN CENTS   NOVEMBER 29, 1943

TIME

THE WEEKLY NEWSMAGAZINE

Wide World

THE PRESIDENT
Ahead might be a world Thanksgiving.
(U.S. at War)

VOLUME XLII   (REG. U. S. PAT. OFF.)   NUMBER 22

Franklin Roosevelt
November 29, 1943

Not since Lincoln has a President so transformed the office. In his four terms, he battled back the Great Depression, remade the federal government as a social safety net and led the country into World War II.

Yet associates still marvel at his Gargantuan appetite for work, his ability to relax in the midst of it, his endless gay optimism. As it has to everyone else, the strain of war has wrenched, strained and hacked at his basic traits of character. But in the President's case the grind has only polished what was already polished, only toughened what was already steel-strong. He still relishes jokes and wisecracks. He can still drop off for a cat nap anywhere, anytime. He still looks forward to a nightly old-fashioned or two in his study before dinner as a high point of his day. He has grown almost impervious to political criticism. He rarely becomes angry at all— and then it is usually when somebody snipes at him through one of his children. —HUBERT KAY

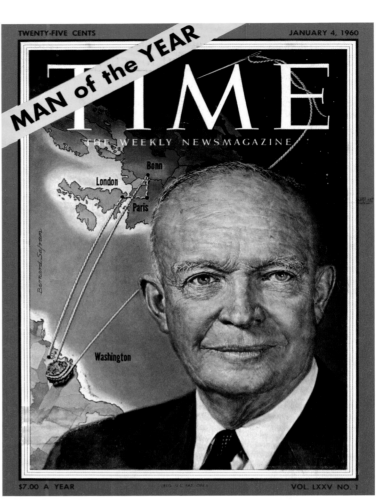

Harry Truman
January 3, 1949
Portrait by Ernest Hamlin Baker

Truman said the death of Roosevelt felt like a "bull or load of hay" falling on him. But FDR's Vice President soon found his bearings, overseeing the end of the war and the beginning of an new era.

Harry Truman succeeded in dramatizing himself; to millions of voters he seemed a simple, sincere man fighting against overwhelming odds—fighting a little recklessly perhaps, but always with courage and a high heart. Few men have been able to communicate their personality so completely. He never talked down to his audience. He showed no shadow of pompousness. He introduced his wife as "my boss," sometimes as "the madam." "I would rather have peace than be President," he cried. He never had to remind his audience that he had been a Missouri farmer, a man who could stick a cow for clover bloat and plow the straightest furrow in the county, a small-time businessman who could still twist a tie into a haberdasher's knot. When he stumbled over a phrase or a name, he would grin broadly and try again. Newsmen snickered and politicians winced. But his audiences smiled sympathetically. They knew just how he felt. "Pour it on, Harry," they cried, "Give 'em hell!" —A.T. BAKER

Dwight Eisenhower
January 4, 1960
Portrait by Bernard Safran

A Cold War leader at a time of economic boom and falling national debt, Eisenhower approached the end of his two terms as President riding a wave of popularity.

Ike's faults are those that his countrymen can share and understand, and in his virtues he is more than anything else a repository of traditional U.S. values derived from his boyhood in Abilene, Kans., instilled in him by his fundamentalist parents, drilled into him at West Point, tempered by wartime command, applied to the awesome job of the presidency and expanded to meet the challenges of the cold war. Returning to Abilene in 1952, Dwight Eisenhower spoke of his mother and father. "They were frugal," he said, "possibly of necessity, because I have found out in later years that we were very poor. But the glory of America is that we didn't know it then." In a 1959 speech, he again drew on his memories, going back to his days as an Army subaltern, newly married to Mamie Geneva Doud, when he scrimped to buy a tiny insurance policy. "Well," he said, "I gave up smoking readymade cigarettes and went to Bull Durham and the papers. I had to make a great many sacrifices ... Yet I still think of the fun we had in working for our own future." Fiscal responsibility was more than a nostalgic, negative notion with Ike. He saw it as the basis of a positive philosophy of government. —CHAMP CLARK

In 1948 everyone expected Thomas Dewey to win, but Truman took the popular vote and 28 states to his rival's 16 (a third candidate won four)

Photograph by W. Eugene Smith

In a televised address during his showdown with Moscow, Kennedy informed the nation of the presence of Soviet nuclear missiles in Cuba

Photograph by Ralph Crane

TWENTY-FIVE CENTS · JANUARY 5, 1962

MAN of the YEAR

TIME

THE WEE...AZINE

$7.00 A YEAR · VOL. LXXIX NO. 1

John Kennedy
January 5, 1962
Portrait by Pietro Annigoni

After his first year in office, a Gallup poll showed 78% of the public approved of Kennedy's job performance—an astronomical number for a time of relative peace.

He was fascinated by the perquisites of his office and his sudden access to the deepest secrets of government. He explored the White House, poked his head into offices, asked secretaries how they were getting along. He propped up pictures of his wife and children in office-wall niches, while Jackie rummaged through the cellar and attic, charmed with the treasures she found there and already determined to make the White House into a "museum of our country's heritage." The Kennedy "style" came like a hurricane. For a while, the problems of the world seemed less important than what parties the Kennedys went to, what hairdo Jackie wore. Seldom, perhaps never, has any President had such thorough exposure in so short a time. —ED JAMIESON

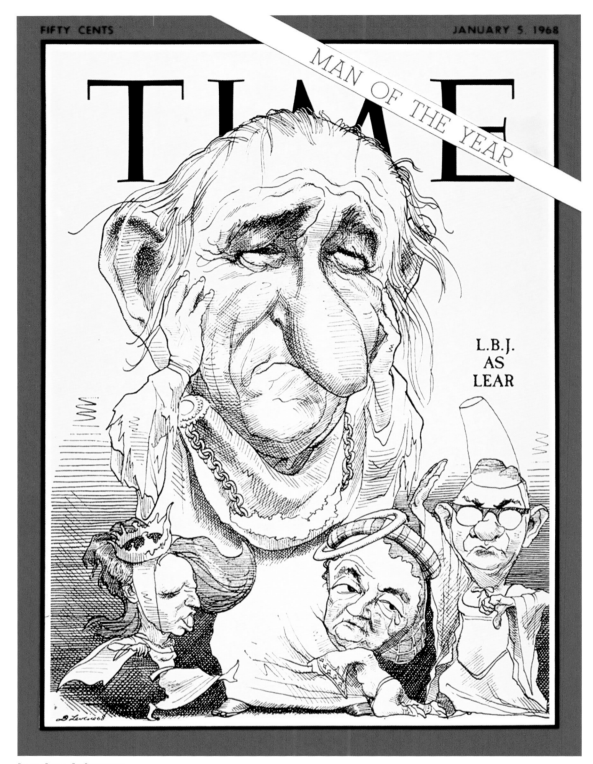

Lyndon Johnson

January 5, 1968

Caricature by David Levine

At the end of his presidency, Johnson faced a deteriorating war in Vietnam and a civil rights struggle at home. Three months after this story ran, he announced he would not seek re-election.

Johnson has had less to say about the job than many of his predecessors. But once, in the early days of his presidency, when aides warned him against risking his prestige by fighting for a civil rights bill because the odds were 3 to 2 against its passage, he asked quietly: "What's the presidency for?" That brief remark spoke volumes about his desire to use the office not simply as a springboard for self-aggrandizement but for the nation's progress. Unlike Ike, who set up military lines of command and delegated considerable responsibility, Johnson wants to be in on everything. His night reading often a five-inch-thick stack of memos and cables, covers everything from the latest CIA intelligence roundup to a gossipy report on a feud between two Senators. "Not a sparrow falls," says a former aide, "that he doesn't know about." —RONALD KRISS

Richard Nixon
January 3, 1972
Sculpture by Stanley Glaubach

He was hailed for good reasons. But Watergate was yet to come, and his downfall would be swift and brutal, testing the constitutional system and reawakening the courts and Congress as checks on the presidency.

In 1971 President Nixon helped cool national passions. He made his bid for a historic niche on the issues of war and peace and in the business of keeping his nation economically solvent. Perhaps his major accomplishment was simply helping the U.S. to catch up. On the war, on China, on welfare reform, on devaluation, he moved the country to abandon positions long outdated and toward steps long overdue. In doing so, he also destroyed some once sacrosanct myths and shibboleths. The result in the U.S. was a greater sense of reality and of scaled-down expectations; given the temper of the times he inherited, that was mostly to the good. The ultimate judgment of his presidency will depend on how he manages to live within the new reality he himself tried to define—and on whether history accepts his definition. —ED MAGNUSON

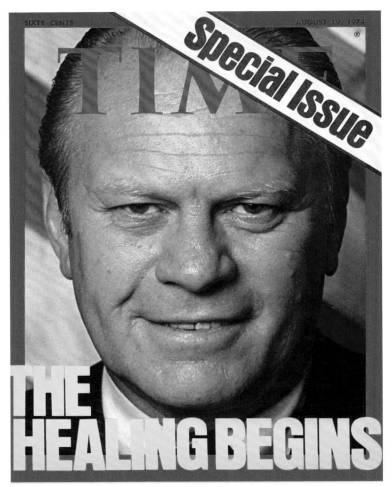

Gerald Ford
August 19, 1974
Photograph by David Hume Kennerly

Ford's sudden promotion to Commander in Chief came at a time of national crisis, and he approached the job focused on healing the wound that had been left by his predecessor.

In their two-hour meeting that afternoon, Ford was characteristically simple and direct. "I need you," he told [Secretary of State Henry] Kissinger, stressing that they had known each other for years and that they could probably get along without any trouble. Said Kissinger: "It is my job to get along with you and not your job to get along with me." The two made plans for messages to go out to all nations, assuring them of the continuity of U.S. foreign policy. That night, after watching Nixon's resignation speech on television with his family at home, Ford stepped outside ... to speak to reporters and about 100 cheering neighbors. "This is one of the most difficult and very saddest periods, and one of the saddest incidents I've ever witnessed," he said. It was obvious to all that he meant it. "Let me say that I think that the President of the United States has made one of the greatest personal sacrifices for the country and one of the finest personal decisions on behalf of all of us as Americans by his decision to resign." Ford announced that Kissinger, whom he called "a very great man," had agreed to say on as Secretary of State. "I pledge to you tonight" Ford concluded, "as I will pledge tomorrow and in the future my best efforts in cooperation, leadership and dedication to what is good for America and good for the world." —LANCE MORROW

Jimmy Carter
May 5, 1980
Portrait by Daniel Schwartz

Carter's single term ended with economic and global crises. His problems came into sharpest relief just before the 1980 campaign with the failure of a rescue mission for kidnapped diplomats in Iran.

The supersecret operation failed dismally. It ended in the desert staging site, some 250 miles short of its target in the capital city. And for the world's most technologically sophisticated nation, the reason for aborting the rescue effort was particularly painful: three of the eight helicopters assigned to the mission developed electrical or hydraulic malfunctions that rendered them useless. For Carter in particular, and for the U.S. in general, the desert debacle was a military, diplomatic and political fiasco. A once dominant military machine, first humbled in its agonizing standoff in Viet Nam, now looked incapable of keeping its aircraft aloft even when no enemy knew they were there, and even incapable of keeping them from crashing into each other despite four months of practice for their mission. That was embarrassing enough, but the consequences of the mission that failed were far more serious; they affected everything from the future of Jimmy Carter to the future of U.S. relations with its European allies and Japan. While most of Carter's political foes tactfully withheld criticism, his image as inept had been renewed. Already hurt by mounting economic difficulties at home, the President now had a new embarrassment abroad. The failure in the desert could prove to be a blow to his re-election hopes. —ED MAGNUSON

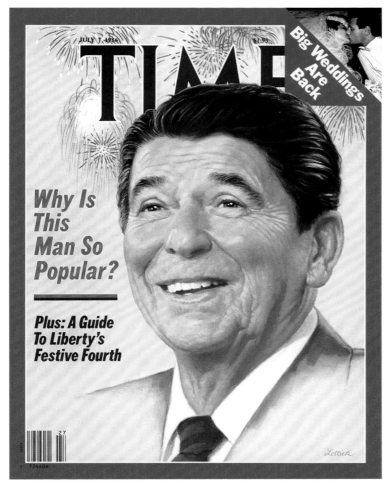

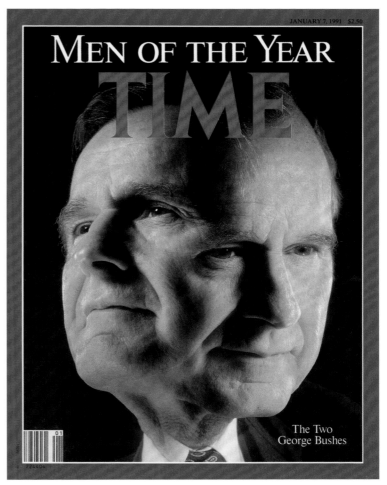

Ronald Reagan
July 7, 1986
Portrait by Birney Lettick

He led the nation during one of the great economic booms of the 20th century and enjoyed the highest second-term approval ratings— and for a longer period—than any other President up to that point.

Ronald Reagan is a sort of masterpiece of American magic—apparently one of the simplest, most uncomplicated creatures alive, and yet a character of rich meanings, of complexities that connect him with the myths and powers of his country in an unprecedented way. Sleight of hand: during a meeting of the Economic Policy Council last year, the Secretary of State and the Secretary of Agriculture started lobbing grenades at each other over a proposal to sell grain to the Soviet Union. Others entered the argument. Voices rose, arms waved. Through it all, Ronald Reagan sat silently, apparently concentrating on picking the black licorice jelly beans from the crystal jar on the table in front of him. Occasionally, he would look up. Once, as he did so, he caught the eye of an aide sitting opposite him at the back of the room. The President winked. The tumult gradually subsided. When it was peaceful again, Reagan looked up, turned to Treasury Secretary James Baker, and said, "What's the next item, Jim?" It had been a very private wink, but it seemed to its one witness to go beyond the walls of the White House, out over the Rose Garden and well outside the Beltway that surrounds the nation's capital. It was as if Ronald Reagan had winked at America, sharing the people's amused disdain for the sort of thing that goes on in Big Government. —LANCE MORROW

George H.W. Bush
January 7, 1991
Photograph by Gregory Heisler

Bush had two competing story lines: success overseas ousting Iraqi forces from Kuwait and economic strain at home. American ambivalence presaged his loss less than two years later.

He often paused in the hideaway office beside his bedroom before a favorite painting of Abraham Lincoln conferring with his generals during the Civil War. "He was tested by fire," Bush would muse, "and showed his greatness." And to one friend, Bush wondered aloud how he might be tested, whether he too might be one of the handful of Presidents destined to change the course of history. On Aug. 1 he found out. It was about 8 p.m. in Washington and Bush had gone upstairs for the evening, when an aide brought an urgent message from the White House Situation Room. Iraq had invaded Kuwait. At first, most diplomatic and intelligence analysts believed Saddam Hussein would confine his thrust to long-disputed border areas. But as Bush followed the latest reports ... Iraqi tanks churned into the Kuwaiti capital, forcing the royal family to flee. It was a full-blown takeover. Next morning the world was waiting to hear what Bush had to say about that blatant act of aggression. At 8 ..., he invited reporters in for a brief exchange. "We're not discussing intervention," Bush insisted. "I'm not contemplating such action." He stammered a bit, as he often does when he is tired—or when he does not believe what he is saying. This time it was both. As Bush would later recall, he had made an "almost instantaneous" judgment that the U.S. must intervene. —DAN GOODGAME

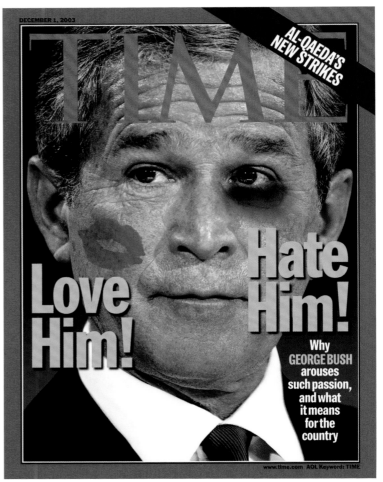

Bill Clinton

August 24, 1998

Photograph by Nigel Parry

After a rocky first term, Clinton easily won re-election with a booming economy and weak opponent. But a personal scandal would return Clinton to crisis mode and a confrontation with Congress.

From its very first days this scandal has divided the nation between those who want to leave Clinton alone and those who want him to pay, between those who think everyone lies about sex—that he has been persecuted just because he is President—and those who think this fate goes with the job. Presidents aren't like kings, but they aren't supposed to be like the rest of us either. The office confers a mystic expectation, a combination of Roosevelt's brains and Johnson's clout and Reagan's grace, that helps Presidents persuade Congress and the people to follow their lead. The agony of Clinton's choice was that his best chance for survival demanded that he declare himself less than we expect a President to be and more like the rest of us after all.

The moment Clinton confesses to anything, he loses some magical powers; his decisions during the past seven months have already cost him some actual powers as well. The shrapnel from this scandal is now embedded in the polity, the culture and the law, and it will take more than the passage of time to dig it out. The wreckage spreads across the whole field of battle: his moral authority, his ability to respond to a crisis, his room to negotiate with a Congress that might soon be his judge, and his ability to get the advice he needs. —NANCY GIBBS AND MICHAEL DUFFY

George W. Bush

December 1, 2003

Photomontage with an image by Brooks Kraft

Defined by the terrorist attacks on Sept. 11, 2001, Bush's presidency unfolded as a series of principled stands that sharply divided the nation. Those divisions consumed much of his second term.

George Bush is the son of a President who couldn't convince the country that he stood for anything. He succeeded a President whose survival depended on the public's capacity to divorce what it thought of his personal values from what it thought of his public ones. Bush has done the opposite of both. He has wrapped his presidency in who he is and what he believes. So it's no surprise that the theme of Bush's first presidential ad of the campaign is essentially: I, George Bush, am the war against terrorism. "Some are now attacking the President for attacking the terrorists," the ad suggests darkly. But for many, it's not so much Bush's policies or programs that make them adore or despise him, but the very way he carries himself—their sense of George Bush as a man. To some, the way that Bush walks and talks and smiles is the body language of courage and self-assurance, and of someone who shares their values. But to others, it is the swagger and smirk that signals the certainty of the stubbornly simpleminded. —JOHN F. DICKERSON AND KAREN TUMULTY

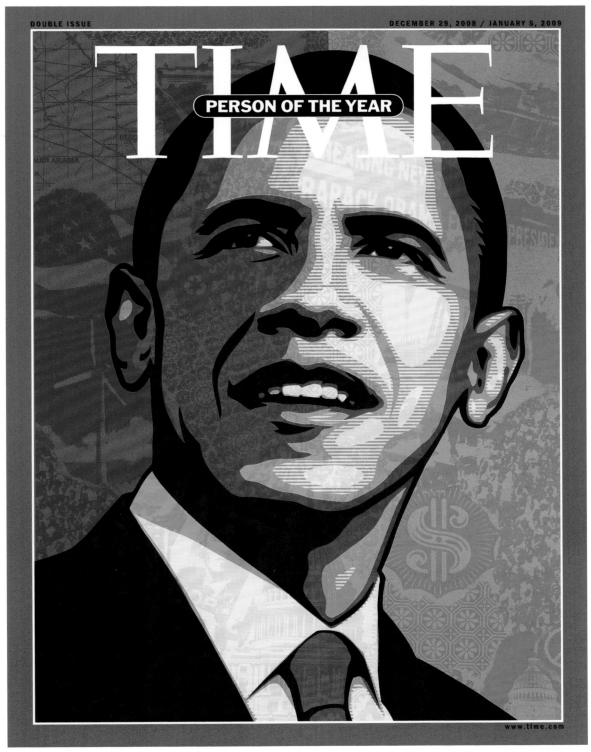

DOUBLE ISSUE

DECEMBER 29, 2008 / JANUARY 5, 2009

TIME

PERSON OF THE YEAR

www.time.com

Barack Obama

December 29, 2008

Portrait by Shepard Fairey

After a celebrated campaign, he would assume office in the middle of the most severe economic crisis since the Great Depression. His response, and the frustrations that followed, would define his first term.

Crisis has a way of ushering even great events into the past. As Obama has moved with unprecedented speed to build an Administration that would bolster the confidence of a shaken world, his flash and dazzle have faded into the background. In the waning days of his extraordinary year and on the cusp of his presidency what now seems most salient about Obama is the opposite of flashy, the antithesis of rhetoric: he gets things done. He is a man about his business—a Mr. Fix It going to Washington ... We've heard fine speechmakers before and read compelling personal narratives. We've observed candidates who somehow latch on to just the right moment. Obama was all these when he started his campaign ... But while events undermined those pillars of his candidacy ... Obama has kept on rising. —DAVID VON DREHLE

America's First Ladies: Forces in Their Own Right

Being the unelected conjugal partner in the White House requires deft circumspection. In a 1939 cover story on Eleanor Roosevelt, TIME described the First Lady's modus operandi as follows: "She operates quite apart from the President, behind and beneath what is commonly called 'politics.' Stories that she influences his policies and appointments are as untrue as stories that he tries to edit her conduct. She is a one-woman show in herself, requiring the full-time services of three able assistants to stage everything she feels she must." America's First Ladies have always had to manage both public appearance and inevitable influence. Some abdicated any role; others found beautifying the White House—or the countryside—to be their way of pressing their husbands' policies, making the presidency more intimate. But the most successful wives have always managed to be heard, even if not in public. East Wing is East and West Wing is West, but the twain do definitely meet.

APRIL 17, 1939 | *Photograph by Thomas D. McAvoy*

JANUARY 14, 1985 | *Portrait by Aaron Shikler*

JANUARY 23, 1989 | *Photograph by Gregory Heisler*

JANUARY 20, 1961 | *Portrait by Boris Chaliapin*

AUGUST 28, 1964 | *Portrait by Boris Artzybasheff*

OCTOBER 20, 1997 | *Photograph by Patrick Demarchelier*

JUNE 1, 2009 | *Photograph by Platon*

□The World At War

D-Day, June 6, 1944: the complex military operation was planned by hundreds but was the responsibility of one man, Dwight Eisenhower

Photograph from Camerique/Getty Images

FIFTEEN CENTS JANUARY 1, 1945

TIME

THE WEEKLY NEWSMAGAZINE

MAN OF THE YEAR

He took more than Hitler gave him.

(World Battlefronts)

VOLUME XLV (REG U S PAT OFF) NUMBER 1

N THE 2,192 DAYS FROM GERMANY'S LIGHTNING INVASION OF
Poland to the Japanese surrender on board the U.S.S. *Missouri* in Tokyo Bay, from
Sept. 1, 1939 to Sept. 2, 1945, the planet was convulsed by a war like no other in
human history. It absorbed existing rivalries and magnified them into a ferocious contest
of national wills, with enormous civilian populations churning out tanks and planes
and armaments, all somehow emerging as an epic battle between good and evil. And
somehow good prevailed. But that outcome was not always clear. The mechanization of

death—both the way battles were conducted and the way people were systematically killed—made huge progress in the six years of the war, if *progress* is a word to be applied to such appalling destruction. The pitiless Axis onslaught was avenged with the Allies' vicious firebombing of German and Japanese cities. And Japan's capitulation came as a result of the U.S.'s winning the race to master atomic weaponry, which promised even more destruction.

The war was won not just by arms. With the massive numbers of men drafted to serve in the military, huge numbers of women—on both sides of the conflict—entered the workforce to power the emerging military-industrial complexes. And civilian involvement was not limited to labor. Millions of ordinary citizens died in the attacks on cities. Indeed, the entire Japanese homeland prepared to turn itself into an imperial human shield to face down the American invaders, emulating the individual kamikaze pilots who were driving bomb-laden planes into U.S. ships to defend nation and Emperor.

The human toll remains unfathomable, with as many as 70 million people dead and every continent except Antarctica touched by a conflict that took to land, sea and air. Estimates of the dead do not include the warfare that came before Sept. 1, 1939—the miasma of angry confusion and bitter confrontation left over from the Great War of 1914 through '18 and the legacy of colonialism and the mutual envy of empire builders. These included the Japanese encroachment on China, the Spanish civil war, the Italian occupation of Ethiopia. Those precursor conflicts would have added hundreds of thousands, perhaps millions, to the toll. But the horrors of World War II were sufficient unto themselves. The six-month battle of Stalingrad alone may have resulted in the deaths of a million people.

TIME's foremost contribution to the coverage of the cataclysm was to name it. When Adolf Hitler launched his blitzkrieg invasion of Poland on Sept. 1, 1939—which happened to be a Friday, at that time, the magazine's weekly deadline—TIME declared that "World War II" had broken out, saying so on the first line of its cover story, which featured the commander of the Polish defense forces. Critics claimed that the designation was premature. But TIME nevertheless introduced its readers to a section called World War. It would be months before other newspapers and magazines followed suit with the name. In the next six years,

TIME's coverage would grow even as the news from the various fronts became more dismaying and then more compelling after the U.S. was drawn into the conflict with the Japanese surprise attack on Pearl Harbor, Hawaii, on Dec. 7, 1941.

Prescience in anticipating a global conflict was one thing. But few were prepared for the horrors of the war itself. Details of conditions in occupied Europe trickled out to paint a nefarious portrait of the Nazi regime, and the tales of the brutal Bataan death march after the fall of the Philippines enraged Americans. But the full extent of Germany's genocidal policies would not emerge until after Europe was liberated. The drama instead focused on the massive movement of forces on the face of the earth: Germany and Japan's explosive conquests; the reeling response from Britain, propped up by the U.S.; the lumbering but eventually irresistible resurgence of Joseph Stalin's Soviet Union and its Red Army, which would take Berlin; the U.S.'s island-hopping conquest of the western Pacific, bloody atoll by bloody atoll. The stories of the commanders—Dwight Eisenhower, Douglas MacArthur, Bernard Montgomery, Erwin Rommel, George Zhukov, Isoroku Yamamoto—were epics within the epic. Announcing the Man of the Year in its Jan. 1, 1945, issue, the magazine said the D-Day "invasion was the greatest gamble, the most complex operation in the history of war. The design of it was the product of hundreds of brains. The responsibility of it fell on the shoulders of one man—Dwight David Eisenhower." It was a time for titans.

The military pursuit nevertheless demanded the sacrifice of ordinary lives from countless ordinary families. Graveyards for the military dead are everywhere in Europe and Asia. The war took young men to parts of the world they never knew existed to die for a cause that was yet unclear. To those who believe in western democracy, that sacrifice bore fruit with the establishment of free societies and economies in Europe and Asia. Nazism and belief in racial and cultural purity were ousted from political power. Meanwhile, the Holocaust gave impetus to the creation of a Jewish homeland. But others saw all that as the overreach of the American empire. Opposed by a Soviet one, a new kind of world war would emerge—cold and bipolar and full of nuclear anxieties. It would last for nearly half a century, defined by a realpolitik set in place by the awful memory of how many lives could be lost in unrelenting global conflict. —HOWARD CHUA-EOAN

DWIGHT DAVID EISENHOWER

JANUARY 1, 1945 | *Portrait by Ernest Hamlin Baker*

FIFTEEN CENTS (IN CANADA, 20c) (Reason: Tariff)   March 13, 1933

TIME

The Weekly Newsmagazine

ADOLF HITLER
His keynote: "Rebirth or Bolshevism!"
(See FOREIGN NEWS)

Volume XXI   Number 11

Circulation Office, 350 East 22nd Street, Chicago.   (Reg. U. S. Pat. Off.)   Editorial and Advertising Offices, 135 East 42nd Street, New York.

Circulation this issue more than 400,000

Adolf Hitler
March 13, 1933
Portrait by Jerry Farnsworth

Under the cloak of democracy, the National Socialist Party and its demagogic leader swept to power with elections in Germany and immediately started a campaign of political repression.

Exulted Chancellor Hitler: "The National revolution is on its way and will continue!" … The Hitler Cabinet had to launch last week a juggernaut of super-suppressive measures & decrees for which they needed an excuse. What excuse could be better than the colossal act of arson which had just sent a $1,500,000 fire roaring through the Reichstag Building … gutting completely the brown oak Reichstag Chamber and ruining its great dome of gilded copper and glass?

The Reichstag fire was set by Communists, police promptly charged. Over a nationwide radio hookup the Minister of Interior for Prussia, blustering Nazi Captain Hermann Wilhelm Göring, cried: "The Reichstag fire was to have been the signal for the outbreak of open civil war! … From all these horrors we have saved the Fatherland!" —LAIRD S. GOLDSBOROUGH

Neville Chamberlain
October 17, 1938
Portrait by S.J. Woolf

Instead of going to war, the British Prime Minister chose to appease Hitler by allowing him to annex the sections of Czechoslovakia that the Germans had forcibly occupied.

In the Middle Ages the leaders of Christendom, although frankly convinced that infidel leaders incarnated the very devil, found it best to make deals and trades with them for peace. The Christians, to their surprise, found the infidels in the main to be honest traders, although still devils and fair game for the next crusade. Was the Munich Agreement dismembering Czechoslovakia a trade between the two devils and their opposite numbers? Was it even a trade?

So vast were the issues broached at Munich that no man can say with firm assurance whether history will record it as a first great stride on the road to peace, or as a first great slip toward world war. Any man could see last week, however, that in itself the Munich Agreement was not a trade. To give a man a quarter to watch your car because you believe he will slash the tires unless you do is not a trade. At Munich it was impossible to call the police, as Neville Chamberlain would have done in the Municipality of Birmingham, if Adolf Hitler had offered to slash tires. There are no international police.

Heinrich Himmler
April 24, 1939
Portrait by Ernest Hamlin Baker

Of Hitler's henchmen, Himmler was the most feared, with the Gestapo watching and listening in on everything in order to stamp out dissent and eliminate the enemies of the Nazis.

To the anxious question of "Will there be war in Europe?" the right answer early this week could be given only by those who knew what was in the mind of Adolf Hitler. Among the few Nazi higher-ups who should have known the Führer's mind (who as usual kept all he knew discreetly to himself) was a man named Heinrich Himmler ... Reichsführer of the Schutzstaffel (the famed, black-uniformed SS Guards), and Inspector of the dread, notorious Gestapo (State Secret Police). From the founder and ruler of the Third Reich's State Secret Police there can be few State secrets ... If nothing intervenes, Greater Germany will vociferously acclaim the 50th birthday of its creator and Führer this week ... Clustered around Herr Hitler on a reviewing stand are to be the familiar, conspicuous figures of the Nazi hierarchy—fat, strapping Field Marshal Hermann Wilhelm Göring, mousy little Propaganda Minister Dr. Paul Joseph Goebbels, coarse, Jew-baiting Julius Streicher, Nazi Deputy Leader Rudolf Hess, Labor Front Leader Dr. Robert Ley. Inspector Himmler will be there too, but the weak, fleshy-chinned, owlish Gestapo chief, looking more like an Austrian Gymnasium teacher than a leader of men, will be the least conspicuous of them all.

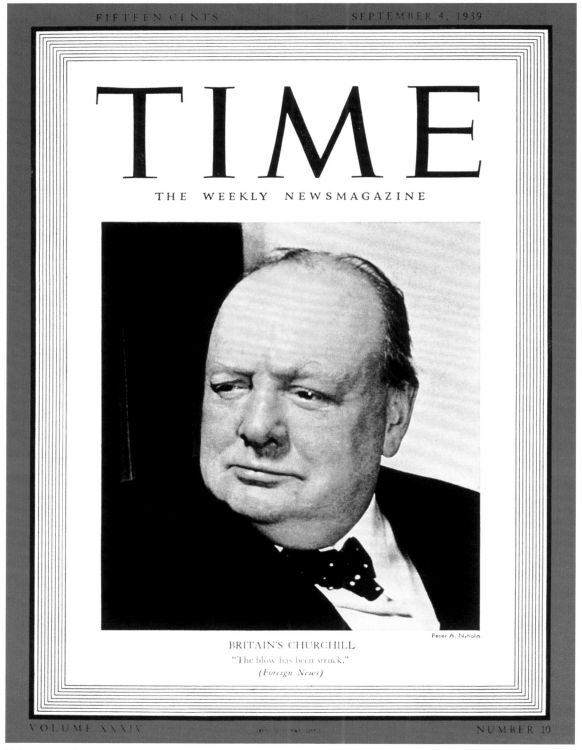

FIFTEEN CENTS   SEPTEMBER 4, 1939

TIME

THE WEEKLY NEWSMAGAZINE

BRITAIN'S CHURCHILL
"The blow has been struck."
(Foreign News)

Peter A. Nyholm

VOLUME XXXIV   NUMBER 10

Winston Churchill
September 4, 1939
Photograph by Peter A. Nyholm

A loud critic of Chamberlain's policies, Churchill would join the war cabinet after Germany invaded Poland on Sept. 1, 1939. In May 1940, Chamberlain resigned, and Churchill became Prime Minister.

When the vote came [Churchill] walked out the door on the Government side of the House, thereby signifying his assent to the granting of war powers to the Government. Implicit in Prime Minister Chamberlain's speech ... was an acknowledgement that Churchill had been right. For six bitter, hog-ridden years he had pounded on his argument as tenaciously as Cato the Elder demanding the destruction of Carthage: that a rearmed and rearming Nazi Germany was a menace to Britain, to the Empire, to free speech, to Parliament. To Britons newly enraged by the German-Soviet Pact, he had been terribly justified ... Churchill expected no cheers for his foresight. He rushed off to have dinner with Harold Nicolson, M.P. ... and then hurried to his country home ... to run his six secretaries ragged and hang on the telephone putting in calls all over Europe.

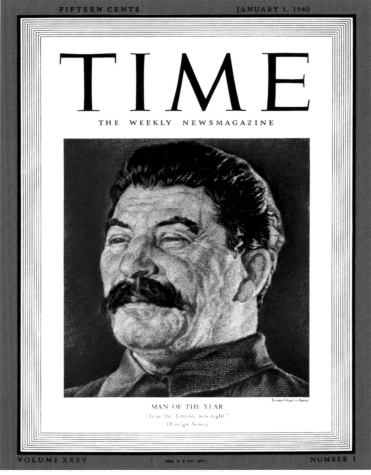

Edward Smigly-Rydz

September 11, 1939

Portrait by Ernest Hamlin Baker

TIME *coined the term* World War II *in its cover story in the issue featuring the commander in chief of Poland, which would be overwhelmed by Nazi forces.*

World War II began last week at 5:20 a.m. (Polish time) Friday, September 1, when a German bombing plane dropped a projectile on Puck, fishing village and air base in the armpit of the Hel Peninsula. At 5:45 a.m. the German training ship *Schleswig-Holstein* lying off Danzig fired what was believed to be the first shell: a direct hit on the Polish underground ammunition dump at Westerplatte. It was a grey day, with gentle rain.

Joseph Stalin

January 1, 1940

Portrait by Ernest Hamlin Baker

The Soviet ruler's nonaggression pact with Hitler gave Germany the freedom to invade Poland—with territorial gains for Moscow. But Hitler would betray Stalin and invade Russia on June 22, 1941.

Without the Russian pact, German generals would certainly have been loath to go into military action. With it, World War II began. From Russia's standpoint, the pact seemed at first a brilliant coup in the cynical game of power politics. It was expected that smart Joseph Stalin would lie low and let the Allies and the Germans fight it out to exhaustion, after which he would possibly pick up the pieces. But little by little, it began to appear that Comrade Stalin got something much more practical out of his deal ... But if, in the jungle that is Europe today, the Man of 1939 gained large slices of territory out of his big deal, he also paid a big price for it. By the one stroke of sanctioning a Nazi war and by the later strokes of becoming a partner of Adolf Hitler in aggression, Joseph Stalin ... not only sacrificed the good will of thousands of people the world over sympathetic to the ideals of Socialism, he matched himself with Adolf Hitler as the world's most hated man. —ROBERT NEVILLE

Hermann Göring
April 1, 1940

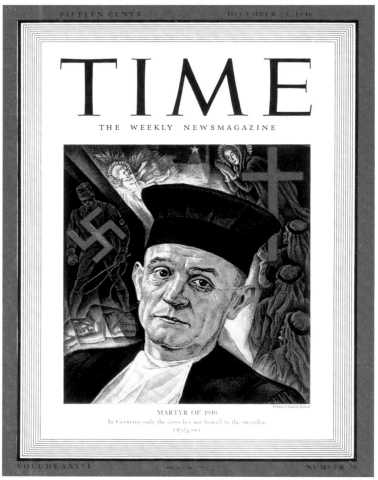

Martin Niemoller
December 23, 1940
Portrait by Ernest Hamlin Baker

The air marshal of the Third Reich was an architect of Germany's terrifying blitzkrieg stratagems, Hitler's heir apparent and a bigger-than-life example of Nazi hubris.

A former Hitler supporter, Niemoller survived the war to provide the famous quote about political inaction with the final line "Then they came for me—and there was no one left to speak out for me."

Göring is the one Nazi leader the German people understand and like. They worship Hitler in a mystical sort of way. They love Göring and call him "wiser Hermann." "Our Hermann." To the German people Göring is the embodiment of the satiation of all their own more normal appetites. They love sport. Göring is Reich's Master of the Hunt, lives in the middle of a 100,000-acre game preserve, imports falcons from Iceland to pursue that medieval sport. He plays tennis in the garden behind his palace in Berlin, wearing a hairnet to keep his long reddish hair from falling away from the balding area. He skis in a fur cap, rides in all kinds of costume. He has himself photographed at all his sports except swimming. Because of his sensitiveness about his hyper-developed mammary glands, other guests were excluded from a Baltic beach where Hermann and his wife went bathing. But he displays no such squeamishness in regard to his guests' sensitivities. All of them are expected to frolic with his lion cub, Caesar, and distinguished visitors at Karinhall are invited to watch his prize cattle breed. —CHARLES WERTENBAKER

Not you, Herr Hitler, but God is my Führer. These defiant words of Pastor Martin Niemoller were echoed by millions of Germans. And Hitler raged: "It is Niemoller or I." So this second Christmas of Hitler's war finds Niemoller and upwards of 200,000 other Christians (some estimates run as high as 800,000) behind the barbed wire of the frozen Nazi concentration camps. Here men bear mute witness that the Christ—whose birth the outside world celebrates unthinkingly at Christmas—can still inspire a living faith for which men and women even now endure imprisonment, torture and death as bravely as in centuries past ... At Sachsenhausen Pastor Niemoller has been placed on a regime of half rations, double heavy labor, solitary confinement. Rock-breaking, roadbuilding, ditch-digging, harsh treatment are fast wearing him out. He has not been beaten, but has told his wife on the rare visits she is permitted that he has seen others beaten unconscious. "When I write the address, 'Concentration Camp, Sachsenhausen,'" said one daughter, "then I am always very proud." —SAMUEL G. WELLES JR.

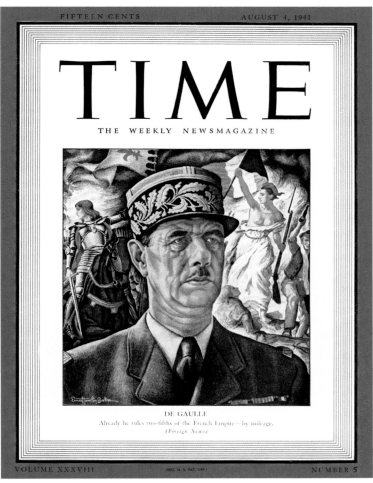

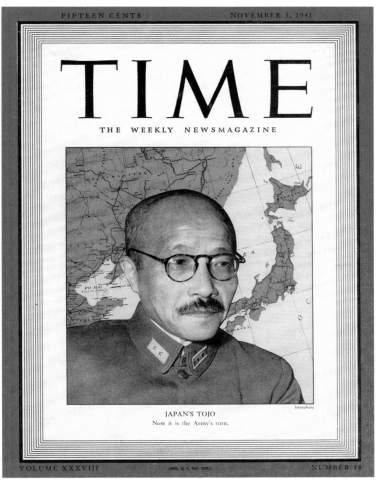

Charles de Gaulle
August 4, 1941
Portrait by Ernest Hamlin Baker

*With much of France ruled by the pro-German Vichy,
de Gaulle used France's colonial empire in Africa as a base for
his Free French.*

In France a handful of defeatist politicians surrendered
to Germany in the belief that Britain was doomed. They
assured Frenchmen everywhere that this was the case,
and most Frenchmen believed them. General de Gaulle
went to England to rally the French Empire to the cause
of fighting on. A good many oldsters in charge of colonial
administration, convinced that all was lost, refused to respond.
Many younger leaders wanted to fight, but doubted Britain's
and De Gaulle's will or ability to fight on. By the time they
decided on resistance many had been replaced by Vichy men ...
Free France knows it is struggling for France's freedom, and
it is this knowledge that binds De Gaulle's men to his cause
with fanatical loyalty. This loyalty has overcome De Gaulle's
lack of personal magnetism; it has overcome his political
inexperience. His supporters include Socialists, Monarchists
and Republicans. He insists that he is not leading a political
movement, that he is merely leading a military movement
to restore France's freedom, that when that is accomplished
he will render account to the chosen representatives of the
French people. —CHARLES WERTENBAKER

Hideki Tojo
November 3, 1941

*Tojo was vilified by TIME and other U.S. news organizations—
caricatures that would increase in the popular press after
Pearl Harbor, which he did not plan but oversaw.*

Fortnight ago a bald little Japanese general nicknamed
The Razor became Premier of Japan. Hideki Tojo's
sparse mustache looks as if it might blow off in a
stiff breeze and his tortoise-shell spectacles have a slightly
cockeyed, precarious perch on his nose. Nevertheless the world
press shuddered with apprehension that The Razor might
be the raging snickersnee that the Japanese Army had been
crying for, that Japan's months of indecision would now be
resolved by mad swipes at Siberia, at Singapore, or at both ...
Japan has a Navy only slightly below parity with the combined
U.S. Pacific and Asiatic Fleets, an Air Force of perhaps 4,000
combat planes. Japan is said to have 2,000,000 men in arms,
4,500,000 in reserve, for whom weapons may not be available ...
Russia may still have dozens, perhaps hundreds, of long-range
bombers in Vladivostok, within 600 miles of inflammable
Tokyo. And Japan must consider possible U.S. interference ...
Japan's best military bet would probably be an all-out attempt
to finish the Chinese War. Japan has never risked more than
1,000,000 men against Generalissimo Chiang Kaishek. A
force of 2,000,000 hurled at China, first cutting off the Burma
Road, might end the war. But Japan would then have to forget
about Siberia. —WILDER HOBSON

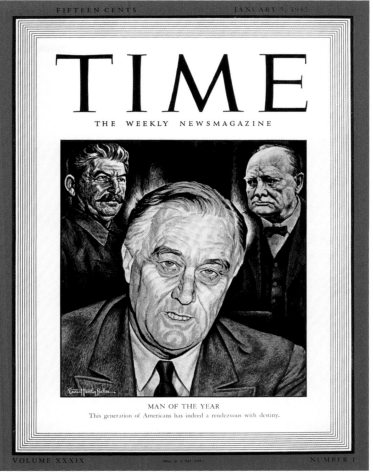

Isoroku Yamamoto
December 22, 1941
Portrait by Arthur Szyk

The admiral was key to the planning and execution of the attack on Pearl Harbor. He would be killed in April 1943, when U.S. forces learned his whereabouts and shot his plane out of the sky.

Isoroku Yamamoto is not the grinning, bowing, breath-sipping little man with horn-rimmed glasses, eager mustache and super-buck teeth which U.S. cartoonists have selected as Mr. Japan. He is not a monster who enjoys killing babies and takes rape after dinner instead of coffee. He is, instead, a hard-bitten professional man with a sixth sense—hatred. He hates, and all his colleagues hate, the U.S. and British attitude toward Japan, and especially toward Japan's Navy. He has heard for years the U.S. Navy's boast that the Japs would be a pushover ... He has long hated, and did much to fight, the imputation of inferiority which Britain and the U.S. made in insisting on maintaining ... The Admiral is an adversary who does not want underrating. *Yamamoto* means Base of a Mountain, and the Admiral is solid. He is deliberate, positive, aggressive. His passion for winning has made him the bridge, poker, chess, and go champion of the Japanese Navy. Once an American asked him how he learned bridge so quickly. He explained: "If I can keep 5,000 ideographs in my mind, it is not hard to keep in mind 52 cards." —JOHN HERSEY

Franklin Roosevelt
January 5, 1942
Portrait by Ernest Hamlin Baker

Even as the U.S. struggled to emerge from the Great Depression, the American President saw his country yanked into World War II by the Japanese attack.

At the close of 1940 the two great figures locked in the world struggle were Winston Churchill and Adolf Hitler. In midsummer of 1941, Stalin and Churchill perhaps shared the position of being Hitler's chief opponents. By the time that 1941 ended, Franklin Roosevelt stood out clearly as Hitler's major adversary. Stalin, Churchill, Chiang Kaishek, whatever their individual stature, had their future dependent on the help that the U.S.—and Franklin Roosevelt—alone could give ... In his own right and on his own record, President Roosevelt stood out as a figure of the year and of the age. His smiling courage in the face of panic, his resourcefulness in meeting unprecedented threats to the nation's economy and morale, his sanguine will place him there. The intensity of his feeling for what America can be and therefore will be—a feeling that awakened the country to master its creeping paralysis—these qualities prepared the nation for its struggle in the depth of depression. On a far greater scale, for a far greater cause, against a worldwide sense of hopelessness, those same qualities were called into play when the Japanese on a sunny December morning descended from the sky on Pearl Harbor. —ROBERT CANTWELL

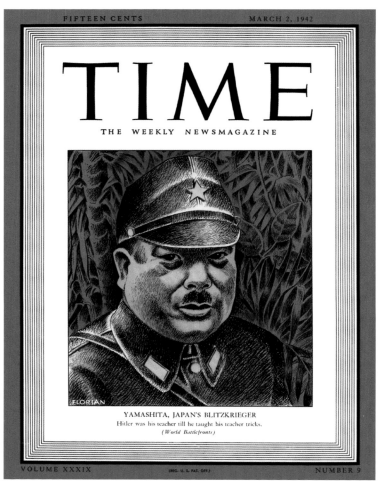

Tomoyuki Yamashita

March 2, 1942

Portrait by Florian

Seen as a proponent of Germany's fighting style, Yamashita was the commander of the brutal conquest of the British colonies of Malaya and Singapore.

In Germany Yamashita had been excited by the Luftwaffe's function as heavy artillery mounted on hawks' wings. He had acquired licenses to build Stukas and light attack bombers. He had also got the rights for the 800-horsepower B.M.W.-132 radial motor, and for certain precision instruments made by Patin and Telefunken ... The result is the Air Force which so far has had its way in the southwest Pacific. It is not the Air Force of the brutal, aimless, bootless raids of Chungking. It has been as smooth as a team of riveters tossing white-hot rivets into tiny buckets, or driving them cleanly home. In Malaya this Air Force confused and broke the British, made their calm confidence look like childish complacency ... That Air Force actually taught its teacher, Adolf Hitler, some tricks. In skillful use of the torpedo bomber, it excelled anything the Germans had devised. In speed of maintenance, fueling and supply far from home base, it suggested the solution of problems which had seemed formidable to the Germans. In widespread yet effective dispersion of effort, it gave the Germans something to ponder. —JOHN HERSEY

Chester Nimitz

May 18, 1942

Portrait by Robert S. Sloan

Sprinkled with derogatory references to the Japanese, TIME's story was a paean to the admiral who began to turn the tide in the Pacific war in America's favor.

It was, in truth, the greatest battle in the history of the U.S. Pacific Fleet. It was fought below the equator, in the Coral Sea off Australia's northeast coast. For five days, smudged with belching smoke screens and roaring with bomb bursts, a U.S. naval force and Army bombers from land bases took turns tearing into a heavy Jap task force, invasion-bound ... For the Jap the going was too tough. His fleet was badly shot up, largely by one of the greatest concentrations of air power ever sent against a naval force ... Punished until he could stand no more, he turned tail, while 500 airplanes, U.S. and Japanese, roared through the bright subtropical sun over his uneasy head. The U.S. aircraft had the edge. They burst through the Jap fighters again & again, rained bombs and aerial torpedoes at the surface craft ... The battle ended in a nightmare of retreat, with U.S. aircraft hacking at the enemy every step of the way back to the questionable shelter of the islands trailing off the east coast of New Guinea. —ROY ALEXANDER

Erwin Rommel

July 13, 1942

Portrait by Boris Artzybasheff

The German commander's efficiency in Africa had become legendary, taking Hitler's troops within striking distance of the Allied strongholds of Cairo and Alexandria in Egypt.

He had performed no miracle. At every stage of the battle [of Tobruk] he had merely fought intelligently, fought hard, seen what the next thing was to do, done it today, instead of tomorrow. He had merely shown what can be accomplished by common battle sense and the energy to begin the next tough job before its predecessor is finished ... When Hitler decided in 1940 to put Rommel in charge of the Afrika Korps and send him to strengthen the stumbling Italians in Libya, Rommel began to train the kind of army that could fight a successful desert war ... Once his men were in Africa, Rommel made them as comfortable as possible. Each man got his own green bivouac tent, with a floor, and a pack containing a camp stove, solid fuel, eye lotion, mouthwash, body powder, washing sets, flashlight, billfolds. Rations included beer, coffee, tinned and fresh meat, lemons, potatoes, onions. Hospitals were never short of anything. At the rest camps in the rear there were beer gardens, brass bands, playing grounds, movies ... Rommel never tells his men that the British are pushovers. He tells them that the British are tough—and that they, the thin, hard young elite of Germany, must be tougher. —JOHN STOCKLY

James Doolittle

November 23, 1942

Portrait by Ernest Hamlin Baker

Assigned to Africa, Doolittle had earlier in the year planned and led the daring attack on the Japanese home islands, the first time the U.S. had struck back at the empire since Pearl Harbor.

In April the public heard that Tokyo had been bombed. Not until five weeks later did President Roosevelt, decorating the crews of 16 B-25s, reveal that Jimmy Doolittle had prepared and commanded the raid on Japan. (Doolittle said that "somebody else" thought it up ...) According to Air Forces apocrypha, Jimmy announced after he was on his way: "I was a lieutenant colonel when I took off, I'm a colonel now, and when we get over Tokyo I'm gonna look down and say: 'This is from Brigadier General Doolittle, you bastards, and how do you like that?'" When he landed [in China], actually unaware that he had been promoted, Doolittle was met by famed Brigadier General Claire Chennault. Chennault took a star from one of his shoulders, pinned it on Brigadier General Doolittle's ... The sour, belated news that some of his men were captives of the Japanese ... and that many of his planes had crashed after dropping their bombs did not cloud Jimmy Doolittle's fame. Nor did it tinge the devotion of the Tokyo flyers who returned with or followed him to the U.S. —JOHN OSBORNE

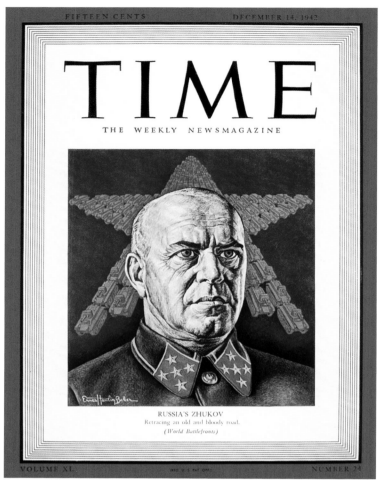

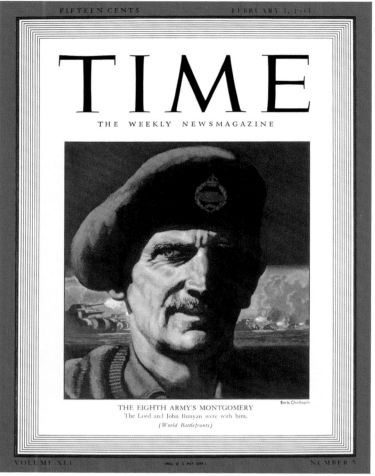

Georgy Zhukov
December 14, 1942
Portrait by Ernest Hamlin Baker

An ideologically committed communist, Zhukov was essential to the defense of the Soviet Union—and the master of the eventual drive west to destroy Nazi Germany.

The Germans are losing the war in Russia, which means that they are losing World War II ... On the frozen plains of Rzhev before Moscow, on the Don and in the Volga corridor at Stalingrad, in the snows and floods of the Caucasus, the Russians are on the offensive. But, as of this week, the Russian offensives alone are not defeating the Germans ... Time is defeating the Germans. Old victories and old defeats are defeating the Germans: the Red Army's stands, retreats and counterattacks; the Wehrmacht's losses at Smolensk, Rzhev and Moscow; the men and weapons spent, the weeks forever lost at Sevastopol; the spaces of the Ukraine, the Kuban plains and the upper Caucasus, conquered but nonetheless expensive to their conquerors; and, finally, the pit of Stalingrad. No one of these great battles, sieges or marches in the greatest campaign of history exhausted or defeated the German Army. But in the aggregate they saved Russia and they saved the Red Army. —JOHN OSBORNE

Bernard Montgomery
February 1, 1943
Portrait by Boris Chaliapin

Rommel's nemesis was the redoubtable Englishman who, after the victory at the second battle of El Alamein on the Egyptian coast, was key to routing the Germans from North Africa.

The Road is a ribbon along the fair, azure sea. It wanders past graves inscribed "This is hallowed ground. They died in the service of their country." It twists up arid escarpments. It streaks, hot and straight, for miles across the desert sands ... At the Road's end last week stood a wiry man with pale, piercing eyes, hawk's nose and cadaverous cheeks. General Sir Bernard Law Montgomery had traversed half the continent of Africa, leading a victorious army on the heels of a beaten one. To his troops he had proclaimed: "Nothing has stopped us ... Nothing will." This week he was in Tripoli and driving on ... The tanks went in at dawn. While a bitter wind swirled the sands of the Sahara the infantry waited in slit trenches for their signal. Faces and clothes were grimed with the dust. They were in full battle kit. Their weapons glinted in the bright sun. These were Montgomery's shock troops. They had done the job before at El Alamein where the long trek had started. They were eager to do it again for the harsh, implacable man whom they adored. —DUNCAN NORTON-TAYLOR

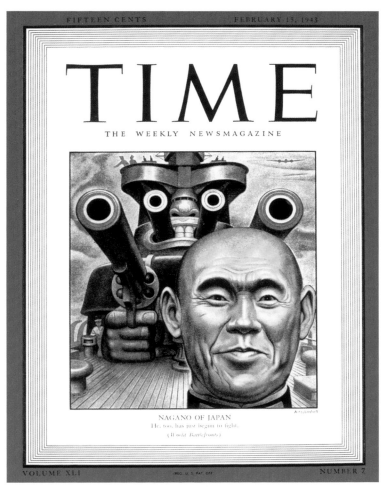

Osami Nagano

February 15, 1943
Portrait by Boris Artzybasheff

The chief of the Japanese Imperial Navy's general staff oversaw the empire's Pacific war strategy, which was devised by military hard-liners.

The man responsible for plans was ... Chief of Staff Osami Nagano. He must orient his plans, whatever they may be, to the situation in which Japan now finds herself. It is an excellent defensive position. To the east there is a stretch of Pacific across which the U.S. would hesitate to send an all-out amphibian invasion, knowing what carrier and land-based forces were able to do to such an invasion when the Japs tried to take Midway. To the north there is a temporary security which rests on the virtual certainty that Russia would not be willing to let the U.S. move on Japan over her soil—at least until after the defeat of Hitler. To the west, the mass of China could well base hostile air and land forces, but China is of limited use to Japan's enemies until they own Burma, and the stalemated minor campaign there indicates that that is not now a danger. To the south there lies a great arc of air and naval bases, one sector of which is threatened at the Solomons ... The logic of this defensive pattern imposes on Admiral Nagano an ironclad duty: he must, either by defensive or offensive measures, make the southern arc secure. —JOHN HERSEY

Karl Doenitz

May 10, 1943
Portrait by Boris Artzybasheff

The mastermind behind the Third Reich's terrifying U-boat campaign against Allied ships, Doenitz would briefly lead Germany after the fall of Berlin to the Soviets in 1945.

The outlook, after more than three and a half years of war, was still not good for the Allies. Germany was building subs faster than they were being sunk; Allied shipbuilding was just beginning to hold its own. The balance was close, and there were factors weighing heavily in Nazi Germany's favor. What Adolf Hitler could not do by land to stop the Allies' march toward Europe's borders, Grand Admiral Karl Doenitz, CINC of the German Navy, was working hard to do by sea in the Atlantic moat where the first defense of Europe lay ... Grand Admiral Doenitz had not been CINC for long. Only three months ago he replaced Erich Raeder as the head of Hitler's Navy, and the shift in command was a tip-off on the Nazis' future strategy. For Karl Doenitz was a submariner from away back. A submariner he remained, in personal command of the U-boat fleet ... Sooner than most, he had recognized that Germany's hope on the high seas, in this war as in the last, lay in the slender, lonely little craft effectively typed "torpedo carriers." When he took the supreme command, he pledged: "The entire German Navy will henceforth be put into the service of inexorable U-boat warfare." —PERCIVAL KNAUTH

Benito Mussolini

June 21, 1943

Portrait by Ernest Hamlin Baker

Bellicose under siege, Mussolini would be deposed in July 1943 and had to be rescued by the Nazis, who set him up in a rump regime in northern Italy.

Mussolini has wrapped a toga of self-righteousness about his sub-Napoleonic figure. More than two decades as the father of 20th-century Fascism have taught him how to play upon the childlike sentiment of millions of his people. While the Allies paused in Tunisia he cunningly launched a hate-the-U.S. campaign which was ridiculous but effective ... Into minds dulled by years of propaganda and on to nerves chewed raw by this winter's bombings, Mussolini rubbed wholly fabricated atrocity stores: U.S. airmen, "bloodthirsty flying gangsters," have been bombing only churches, hospitals and nurseries; fiendish pilots have been dropping lipsticks, ladies' purses, flashlights, pens, pencils, cough drops and candy which explode in innocent and eager Italian hands. There have been broadcasts, press stories and faked newspictures of those supposedly maimed or killed ... The vigor of his campaigns against the U.S. was in direct ratio to his fears that U.S. troops might be welcomed with flowers, that his people as a whole might display the same Latin logic as that of the Italian soldier in Tunisia who said to his captors: "All right, laugh, but we're going to America. You're only going to Italy." —JOHN OSBORNE

George Patton

July 26, 1943

Portrait by Boris Chaliapin

The American commander led an assault on Sicily against Italian and German troops, saying to his men, "Keep punching. God is with us. We shall win."

Many of the men in the boats had been seasick on the packed ships. Now, on the way to the flaming shore, they were sicker than ever. They held their heads in their hands. They moaned. They vomited. A shore light picked out one of the boats. The faces in the light were pale and green. One of the men growled: "Why don't they shoot out that goddam searchlight?" ... Red balls flew toward, over and among the boats. The Italians on the shore had depressed their *ack-ack* guns. A soldier, crouching, head down, said: "Shooting at the boats. Jeezus!" ... Gunboats with blue lights, standing in toward the shore as guides for the landing craft, began to hail the first comers: "Straight ahead. Go straight ahead. You'll see the light on your right. Land there. Look out for mines. Good luck ..." The naval ensigns commanding the boats cut their underwater exhausts, gave their engines the gun, roared toward the nearing shore. Toward some of the boats the red balls converged in multiple lines. For some, other things went wrong. They struck sandbars or reefs. Ramps stuck. Men jumped too late or too soon. Some, on orders, leaped with their equipment into the water, sank to their chins or lower. Some drowned ... "Get inland! Keep moving!" —JACK BELDEN

George Marshall

January 3, 1944
Portrait by Ernest Hamlin Baker

The chief of staff of the Army, he had originally planned the D-Day invasion for 1943. It finally launched in June 1944 under Dwight Eisenhower, supreme commander of the Allied forces.

The American people do not, as a general rule, like or trust the military. But they like and trust George Marshall. This is no more paradoxical than the fact that General Marshall hates war. The secret is that American democracy is the stuff Marshall is made of ... Hired by the U.S. people to do a job, he will be as good, as ruthless, as tough, as this job requires. There his ambitions stop. "He has only one interest," said one of his intimates, "to win this damned war as quick as he can, with the fewest lives lost and money expended, and get the hell down to Leesburg, Va., and enjoy life ..." His mind, which works with an earthbound simplicity that is the precise opposite of Hitler's "intuition," cut through all the cross currents in this planetary war. The pattern that emerged was simple and inescapable: first, while checking the Japanese advance, to clean Hitler out of Africa, then push him up on the Continent, and finally hit him with everything at once, from all possible directions.

Ernie Pyle

July 17, 1944
Portrait by Boris Chaliapin

The syndicated American journalist and his reports from the front were overwhelmingly popular. He was killed amid fighting on an island near Okinawa in April 1945.

More than anyone else, he has humanized the most complex and mechanized war in history. As John Steinbeck has explained it: "There are really two wars and they haven't much to do with each other. There is the war of maps and logistics, of campaigns, of ballistics, armies, divisions and regiments—and that is General Marshall's war ... Then there is the war of homesick, weary, funny, violent, common men who wash their socks in their helmets, complain about the food, whistle at Arab girls, or any girls for that matter, and lug themselves through as dirty a business as the world has ever seen and do it with humor and dignity and courage—and that is Ernie Pyle's war. He knows it as well as anyone and writes about it better than anyone."

Douglas MacArthur

October 30, 1944

Portrait by Boris Artzybasheff

Having fled the U.S. commonwealth of the Philippines after the Japanese invaded in December 1941, MacArthur promised, "I shall return." He kept his promise.

Last week, on the flag bridge of the 10,000-ton, 614-ft. light cruiser *Nashville,* stood a proud, erect figure in freshly pressed khaki. Douglas MacArthur had come back to the Philippines, as he had promised … He had slept well, eaten a hearty breakfast. Now with his corncob pipe he pointed over the glassy, green waters of Leyte (rhymes with 8-A) Gulf, where rode the greatest fleet ever assembled in the Southwest Pacific. Around him were hundreds of transports, shepherded by an Australian squadron and MacArthur's own Seventh Fleet, reinforced with jeep carriers from Admiral Chester Nimitz' vast armada of seagoing airdromes. On the horizon loomed the majestic battleships of Admiral William F. Halsey's Third Fleet—some of them ghosts from the graveyard of Pearl Harbor. Beyond the horizon steamed the greatest concentration of water-borne air power in war's history— Vice Admiral Mitscher's fast carrier task groups … There was not a Japanese surface craft in sight. Only one enemy plane ventured out to attack. It dropped one bomb harmlessly into the sea. —ROBERT CANTWELL

Omar Bradley

December 4, 1944

Portrait by Ernest Hamlin Baker

One of the chief planners of the D-Day invasion, Bradley was key to throwing the Nazis out of France and driving into Germany just as the Soviets rushed toward Berlin.

Bradley was the line smasher as well as quarterback for the Allied operations (as he is now). He did not fumble, and he invariably capitalized on the errors of the enemy … Eisenhower has a pleasant and sense-making way of telling his commanders what his general strategic objectives are, then letting them devise their own tactics. It was Bradley who designed the breakthrough to the west side of the Normandy peninsula, cutting off Cherbourg, and the breakthrough at Saint-Lô which began the battle of France. For the latter, he had an unheard-of number of heavy bombers laying down a tactical preparation (causing some U.S. casualties), and he had not only regiments but divisions attacking in column. Bradley also designed the Argentan-Falaise pincers, and the scythelike sweeps to the Seine which ruined the German Seventh Army. His rush to the German border was a bid to knock out German resistance once & for all, before his supply lines snapped. He was philosophical about not winning that one: nobody can win them all. —WALTER STOCKLY

FIFTEEN CENTS   APRIL 23, 1945

TIME
THE WEEKLY NEWSMAGAZINE

THE PRESIDENT OF THE UNITED STATES
He followed a great leader.
(U. S. at War)

VOLUME XLV   (REG. U. S. PAT. OFF.)   NUMBER 17

Harry Truman
April 23, 1945
Portrait by Boris Chaliapin

The death of FDR thrust Harry Truman into the White House just as the two fronts of the war were reaching a climax. How would the new President deal with the crises?

Upon what sort of man had this cosmic load fallen? After their first shocked incredulity at the news that Franklin Roosevelt was dead, almost the next words of most U.S. citizens were: "What's Harry Truman like?" ... During the campaign, when the possibility of his becoming President was often discussed, some political pundits labeled him the "Democratic Coolidge" ... One thing can be said with certainty: he will be a great change from Franklin Roosevelt ... With almost complete unanimity, Harry Truman's friends—in Washington and across the land—agreed last week that he "would not be a great President." By this they did not mean that he would not be a good President. But he would not be a bold, imaginative, daring leader, carrying the U.S. people through reforms and upheavals and crises and flights of idealism as Franklin Roosevelt did.

FIFTEEN CENTS   MAY 7, 1945

TIME

THE WEEKLY NEWSMAGAZINE

VOLUME XLV   (REG. U. S. PAT. OFF.)   NUMBER 19

The End of Hitler

May 7, 1945

Portrait by Boris Artzybasheff

The Soviets won the race to Berlin and, as the German capital was ransacked, Hitler vanished, reportedly dead from suicide or some sudden malady. TIME *produced the first of its X covers.*

Fate knocked at the door last week for Europe's two fascist dictators. Mussolini, shot in the back and through the head by his partisan executioners, lay dead in Milan ... Adolf Hitler had been buried, dead or alive, in the rubble of his collapsing Third Reich. Whether or not he had suffered a cerebral hemorrhage (as reported from Stockholm), or had "fallen in his command post at the Reich chancellery" ... or was a prisoner of Gestapo Chief Heinrich Himmler, Adolf Hitler as a political force had been expunged. If he were indeed dead, the hope of most of mankind had been realized. For seldom had so many millions of people hoped so implacably for the death of one man. —WHITAKER CHAMBERS AND MARSHALL SMITH

As many as 240,000 people died as the immediate result of the atomic bombings of Hiroshima and Nagasaki in August 1945

Photograph from Popperfoto/Getty Images

Japan Defeated

August 20, 1945

Illustration by Boris Artzybasheff

On Truman's orders, the cities of Hiroshima and Nagasaki were devastated by atomic attacks.
And with the imminent entry of the Soviet Union into the Pacific war, Japan chose to surrender.

The greatest and most terrible of wars ended, this week, in the echoes of an enormous event—an event so much more enormous that, relative to it, the war itself shrank to minor significance. The knowledge of victory was as charged with sorrow and doubt as with joy and gratitude. More fearful responsibilities, more crucial liabilities rested on the victors even than on the vanquished ... In what they said and did, men were still, as in the aftershock of a great wound, bemused and only semi-articulate ... But in the dark depths of their minds and hearts, huge forms moved and silently arrayed themselves: Titans, arranging out of the chaos an age in which victory was only the shout of a child in the street ... With the controlled splitting of the atom, humanity, already profoundly perplexed and disunified, was brought inescapably into a new age. —JAMES AGEE

The Superpowers

СВОБОДА

ПЕРЕД, К ПОБЕДЕ КОММУНИЗМА !

Б-2-ВВ

A Soviet rocket being
paraded past portraits of
Lenin, Marx and Engels
through Red Square in
Moscow to celebrate
May Day in 1963

*Photograph from
Associated Press*

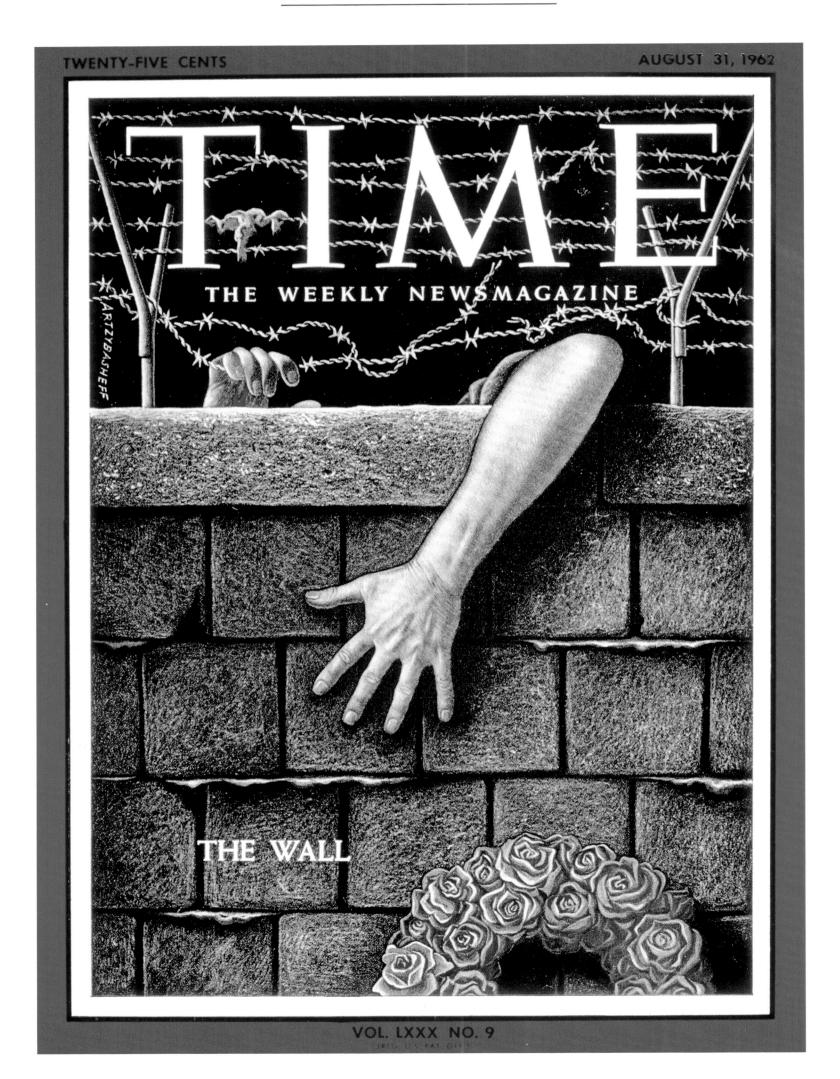

FOR THOSE WHO HAD SURVIVED WORLD WAR II, IT WAS HARD TO imagine. But the troops were hardly home before it became clear that the contest between the victors in the fight against Nazi Germany and imperial Japan would have even higher stakes than the war itself. Two superpowers emerged in Washington and Moscow, with greater military strength and global reach than any powers before them. From the Americas to Europe, from Africa to Asia, the foundations of human society and the very existence of mankind would ultimately be in play.

At first it seemed the Cold War might be just a contest of ideas, a competition over the best way to constitute government. Among those who had been persecuted by the fascists—and had made enormous sacrifices to defeat them—were the followers of the 19th century political philosopher Karl Marx, who had predicted the ultimate demise of capitalism in favor of a communist pooling of property, labor and social goods. Variants emerged everywhere, with different degrees of totalitarian control over political and economic power, but eventually they were led by Joseph Stalin's mighty, genocidal Soviet Union.

On the other side were the adherents of the political and economic liberalism that had grown out of the European Enlightenment of the 17th and 18th centuries. Here too there were variations in constitutional structures: some, like France and Sweden, embraced a degree of socialist state control over the economy, and several retained, then ultimately relinquished, vast colonial dictatorships. But most Western democracies rallied behind the leadership of the strongest and most stable of World War II's victors, the U.S.

Strategically, the stakes were anything but theoretical. World War II had driven a technological revolution in warmaking, fueling the invention of fission and fusion bombs that could kill on a previously unimaginable scale. Once Moscow emerged as a nuclear power, the two sides began an arms race to gain strategic advantage and carved up the global map into spheres of influence that could determine the results of the competition through control of geography, people and resources. The physical symbol of this division was the Berlin Wall, which separated the Western enclave of the city from the Communist-ruled part of Germany. As TIME described it, "Seldom in history have blocks and mortar been so malevolently employed or so richly hated in return." With both sides armed to the teeth and facing each other across contested borders worldwide, the real possibility of an apocalyptic, nuclear World War III became clear to people everywhere.

Facing annihilation or subjugation, the Cold War contestants occasionally risked turning it hot. In Asia, Africa and Latin America, overt and covert proxy wars in the West's former colonies took tens of thousands of lives. Militarily, the wars between right- and left-wing forces in Korea and Vietnam weakened the U.S.; the post-invasion insurgency in Afghanistan contributed to the Soviet Union's terminal decline.

As each side sought advantage over the other, vast spying networks and perceived threats emerged at home. TIME itself became involved in a prominent case when one of its best writers, Whittaker Chambers, admitted to being a former communist spy and identified a diplomat, Alger Hiss, as a co-conspirator—a charge Hiss denied to his death.

TIME emerged from World War II as influential, in its way, as the country it called home. In capitals around the world, the TIME bureau was said to be second only to the U.S. embassy in influence. That was partly because of the breadth of the magazine's readership and its nearly unique access to the individuals at the heights of power. But it was also because, somewhat audaciously, TIME presumed to be the voice of the new power that bestrode the world.

So when in 1948 TIME declared George Marshall, the architect of the West's postwar resurgence, Man of the Year, we began by declaring America's arrival as a superpower. "It was in 1947," we wrote, "that the U.S. people, not quite realizing the full import of their act, perhaps not yet mature enough to accept all its responsibilities, took upon their shoulders the leadership of the world." Then, two months later, on the 100th anniversary of the publication of The Communist Manifesto, it put Marx on the cover and suggested he was the leading contender for our Man of the 20th Century, making clear that we recognized that the looming Cold War contest might be close. Against those "who rule Russia and all Communist parties throughout the world," TIME wrote, "stands capitalist democracy, which has certainly not fulfilled the shiny, steam-driven dreams of some of its early prophets."

As the contest continued, TIME became less equivocal in its embrace of America's message to the world but remained the definitive arbiter of events as the contest played out, from the arms race and spy scandals at home and abroad to the proxy wars in Asia and Latin America and the diplomatic maneuvering as China became a nascent superpower. TIME chronicled what would prove to be the sources of the West's ultimate victory against Communism: superior alliances and diplomatic strategies; open political and economic competition, which seemed undisciplined or fractious but proved resilient and efficient over the long term; and the foundational insight that individual liberty, modestly constrained, is better at delivering for the common good than the totalitarian pooling of people's interests. —MASSIMO CALABRESI

THE BERLIN WALL
AUGUST 31, 1962 | *Illustration by Boris Artzybasheff*

George Marshall

January 5, 1948

Portrait by Ernest Hamlin Baker

Recognizing the strategic importance of the Secretary of State's plan to resurrect the war-ravaged countries of Europe, TIME linked the retired general to the U.S.'s new leadership role in the world.

On June 5 [1947], standing under the elms in the Harvard Yard, George Marshall, in almost casual terms, announced the beginning of the program that was to become the Marshall Plan. Then & there the U.S. at last set out to seize the initiative from Russia in the cold war … To a growing sense of realism in U.S. foreign policy, the speech added a much-needed note of resolution: "One of the primary objectives of the foreign policy of the United States is the creation of conditions in which we and other nations will be able to work out a way of life free from coercion … We shall not realize our objectives, however, unless we are willing to help free peoples … against aggressive movements that seek to impose on them totalitarian regimes …"

Whatever the rewards world leadership might return in the long run, they would not be reaped until the hold of want and oppression on the world's throat was broken. The country's decision to break it was the vastest gamble in peacetime history. George Marshall's estimate—"calculated risk"—meant in soldier's language that it could be won, if all went well, if the most powerful nation in the world threw all its physical and moral strength into the fight. —DUNCAN NORTON-TAYLOR

Karl Marx

February 23, 1948

Portrait by Ernest Hamlin Baker

The lasting power of Marxism and the spreading challenge it posed to Western democracy were treated with respect and thoughtful analysis in the early days of the Cold War.

Barring the unlikely appearance, before 2000, of an extraordinarily effective saint or major prophet, the Man of the Century will be a German intellectual, devoted to children, caviar and Aeschylus. He does not look the part. His scholarly forehead, his small, sparkling eyes, his massive and majestic beard set him apart from other 20th Century heroes. The black-rimmed eyeglass, which he carries on a thin ribbon around his neck, is a gentle anachronism. Above all, his dates seem wrong. For it was at the height of the Victorian era, when the atom appeared almost as indestructible as Britain's dominion of the waves, that Karl Heinrich Marx died. But that was a technicality. In the historic sense (as distinguished from the merely biological), Karl Marx has only just begun to live. —HENRY A. GRUNWALD

TWENTY CENTS · FEBRUARY 7, 1949

TIME

THE WEEKLY NEWSMAGAZINE

民主統一

CHINA'S MAO TSE-TUNG
The Communist Boss learned tyranny as a boy.

$6.50 A YEAR · (REG. U.S. PAT. OFF.) · VOL. LIII NO. 6

Mao Zedong

February 7, 1949
Portrait by Ernest Hamlin Baker

Capturing the extraordinary rise of the charismatic Mao (spelled in TIME's previous style), the magazine bemoaned the revolutionary takeover of China but painted a vivid picture of its leader.

U.S. visitors to Yenan described Mao as a heavy-set man (5 ft. 8 in., 200 lbs.) with the humor, the strength and often the manner of a Chinese peasant. He frequently sat with his feet propped on the table, and in warm weather he unceremoniously stripped to the waist. Once, in Yenan in the presence of General Lin Piao, president of the Red Academy, he took off his trousers for comfort while studying a military map. He smokes incessantly and tends his own tobacco patch. In 1938, the Party Central Committee gave him a $5 monthly raise so he could buy more cigarettes. Between noisy puffs, he chews melon seeds or peanuts. Until recently, when his doctors made him slow up, he used to wash down his heavy meals with kaoliang (grain liquor). Since then Mao has become something of a hypochondriac. —HENRY A. GRUNWALD

G.I. Joe
January 1, 1951
Illustration by Ernest Hamlin Baker

TIME *focused attention on the front lines of the fight against communism in Korea, quoting a British officer on the qualities of the American fighting man.*

Your chaps have everything it takes to make great soldiers—intelligence, physique, doggedness and an amazing ability to endure adversity with grace. The thing they lack is proper discipline. They also would be better off with a little more training in the art of retreat. I know they like to say that the American soldier is taught only offensive tactics, but if Korea has proved nothing else it has proved the absolute necessity of knowing how to retreat in order. Your marines know how, but your Army men just don't. In our time, you know, we were able to make quite a thing of the rearguard action." —HENRY A. GRUNWALD

Joe McCarthy
March 8, 1954
Portrait by Ernest Hamlin Baker

With a detailed look at the Senator's home life, TIME *flaunted its access to Joe McCarthy, the rabble-rousing red baiter—and at who his next victims might be.*

By the evening of Thursday, Feb. 25, 1954, Senator Joe McCarthy, after a fortnight of mounting frenzy, had built the smallest of molehills into one of the most devastating political volcanoes that ever poured the lava of conflict and the ash of dismay over Washington. Joe, the stoker, was still disorganized but quick-witted, charging in and out of his Senate office, snatching up telephones, rushing to the Senate floor to answer quorum calls, dictating statements to reporters. As he dashed about, his office staff lost track, believed a rumor that he had emplaned for New York. Then Joe stomped in from the corridor, stuffed a briefcase, said "Come on" to a waiting reporter and hurried out. —HENRY LUCE III

The Hydrogen Bomb
April 12, 1954

TIME *took a scientific approach to the experimental explosion of the first hydrogen bombs, 750 times more powerful than the ones used against Japan.*

For four years the hydrogen bomb grew in secret and silence, stirring like a quickened fetus in the guarded laboratories. Few qualified physicists, U.S. or foreign, cared to talk about it. They knew that their science would soon give monstrous birth, but they had been warned to keep quiet. When the pictures of the bomb's fury hit the public last week, not many laymen remembered that the scientists long ago predicted what was likely to happen …

Few scientists feel cheerful about the H-bomb. It looks like too ready a tool of destruction. They have only one reassuring opinion. At the present state of the art, they say, there is no chance that even the most monstrous bomb will get out of control, set fire to the ocean's hydrogen and turn the earth into a short-lived star. The H-bomb's ingredients must be pure and carefully selected, but the ocean is a mess of many nonreactive elements. Less than one-ninth of it is hydrogen, and the safe kind of hydrogen at that. —LOUIS BANKS

Fidel Castro

January 26, 1959
Portrait by Boris Chaliapin

Chronicling the bloody executions that punctuated Castro's overthrow of Fulgencio Batista's grotesque regime, TIME *was skeptical any good would result from the uprising. The missile crisis would come in 1962.*

Castro showed a natural flair for publicity. Rebel beards, originally grown for lack of shaving gear, gave the revolt a trademark. Astigmatic from birth, Castro was seldom caught with his spectacles on. "A leader does not wear glasses," he said ... Castro led a revolution against personal government and for restoring a rule of law; since the date of his victory, he has built a government based largely on his personality, while his men have violated his country's basic law. If he can summon maturity and seriousness, the bloody events of last week may yet turn out to be what Puerto Rico's Muñoz Marin thinks they are: "A bad thing happening in the midst of a great thing." If not, the seeds of hate sown in the execution ditches will sprout like the Biblical tares. —RICHARD ARMSTRONG

Francis Powers
May 16, 1960

Nikita Khrushchev
September 8, 1961
Photographs by Carl Mydans and J.R. Eyerman

The capture of an American spy pilot alive and of a high-flying spy plane with surveillance films intact was a tactical and propaganda victory for Nikita Khrushchev.

After taking off from his base in Turkey on April 27, said Khrushchev, Powers flew across the southern boundary of the U.S.S.R. to Peshawar in Pakistan. From there, on May 1, he took off on a reconnaissance flight that was supposed to take him up the Ural Mountains to Murmansk on the Kola Peninsula to a landing in Norway. Soviet radar tracked him all the way, and over Sverdlovsk, on Khrushchev's personal order, he was shot down at 65,000 ft. by a Soviet ground-to-air rocket. Pilot Powers, said Khrushchev, declined to fire his ejection seat because that would have blown up his plane, its instrumentation and possibly Powers himself. Instead, he climbed out of his cockpit, parachuted to earth and was captured, while his plane crashed near by.

Khrushchev spared no cloak-and-dagger touches. He brandished what he called a poisoned suicide needle that Powers was supposed to use to kill himself to avoid capture. Said Khrushchev: Powers refused to use it—"Everything alive wants to live" ... Khrushchev waxed in sarcasm as he reported that Powers had carried a conglomeration of French francs, Italian lire and Russian rubles, plus two gold watches and seven gold rings. "What was he going to do?" asked Khrushchev scornfully. "Fly to Mars and seduce Martian women?"

Khrushchev had vowed not to resume unilateral nuclear testing. But he did, blaming NATO for its aggressive policies toward the Soviets, destroying any hopes that John Kennedy had for test-ban talks.

Conceivably, the Russians may have made a major technological breakthrough on some new nuclear device that is so important that testing outweighs all other factors; some American scientists feel that with luck, hard work and unlimited testing, the U.S. could develop within five years the first crude version of a neutron bomb, which would kill by neutrons but leave buildings more or less unharmed. Khrushchev recently warned U.S.'s John McCloy, President Kennedy's adviser on disarmament, that the Russians were working on the neutron-bomb idea themselves.

What kind of a bomb did Moscow explode last week? There were few clues. In fact, Moscow was not even admitting that an explosion had occurred. It was Washington that detected the test, on its secret worldwide network of nuclear observation posts. From the White House came a terse statement of the bare known facts:

"The Soviet Union today has conducted a nuclear test in the general area of Semipalatinsk in Central Asia. The device tested had a substantial yield in the intermediate range. It was detonated in the atmosphere." —EDWARD HUGHES

William Westmoreland
February 19, 1965
Portrait by Boris Chaliapin

With continuing Viet Cong attacks and apprehension that China would enter the conflict, the commander of American forces in Vietnam pondered the U.S.'s counterinsurgency strategy.

Westmoreland remains an optimist. "I think the job can be done," he says. "In no manner do I underestimate the magnitude of the problem, but I am realistically hopeful that we can move out in a successful way." How long will it take? Warns Westmoreland: "It could be a long, drawn-out campaign. In Malaya it took twelve years."

Sometimes even twelve months seems an impossibly long time for the Americans involved in the dirty jungle war. For the 10,000 or so who lived in Saigon before the dependents moved out ... there were ... roomy villas with two or three servants, broad tree-lined boulevards and a delightfully Gallic tang to the city.

But the life had a darker side. At the American Community School, pupils were told not to put their hands in their desks without checking first for booby traps, and those roomy villas were often ringed with barbed wire to ward off terrorists. A year ago, five Americans died, 100 were wounded in a week when the Viet Cong bombed a ballpark and a movie house.

For those further afield, the comforts are fewer, the dangers greater. Amoebic dysentery is endemic. Few amusements are available. Four U.S. soldiers went on a fishing trip near Quinhon last month, were later discovered murdered; three had been weighted with rocks and dumped in watery graves. —RONALD P. KRISS

Ho Chi Minh
July 16, 1965
Portrait by Boris Artzybasheff

Facing off against Westmoreland was North Vietnam's leader, who had already outlasted the French and the Japanese. He died in 1969, six years before the fall of Saigon—now Ho Chi Minh City.

Hanoi last week was ready for total war. So was Ho Chi Minh, the goat-bearded god of Vietnamese Communism and, at 75, Asia's oldest, canniest Red leader. North Viet Nam's Ho was making his last and most steely stand, and his young country seemed ready to win or die with him. Since February, U.S. air strikes into North Viet Nam have pounded Ho steadily: in more than 4,050 sorties, jets and prop bombers have razed at least 30 military bases, knocked out 127 antiaircraft batteries, shattered 34 bridges. In their wake the planes left ablaze 17 destroyed truck convoys and an equal number of weapons-carrying trains, along with 20 radar stations, 33 naval craft and the entire Dong Hoi airbase. Yet even as the bomb line crumped closer to crowded Hanoi, there was no sign of Ho's flinching ... What makes kindly old "Uncle Ho" so hard-nosed? What is it that sends the men from Uncle (some 6,000 or more this year alone) southward as insurgents against an enemy that could crush Hanoi in an instant? More than anything, it is a sense of confidence in methods that have worked splendidly in the past. Ho, after all, has been riding a winning streak for 20 years ... He now believes that the same techniques will work against the U.S.—not only in South Viet Nam but in all of Southeast Asia. —ROBERT F. JONES

Soldiers of the U.S.
Army's 1st Infantry
Division in Lai Khe wait
for a helicopter squadron
to move out against Viet
Cong positions in 1965

*Photograph by
Dirck Halstead*

American POWs in Asia
December 7, 1970
Photo-illustration by Fred Burrell

After a meticulously planned rescue mission reached a POW camp but found no POWs, the plight of the prisoners and missing grew as a political issue in Washington.

The relatives of the missing and imprisoned have a particularly difficult life because of the nature of the Viet Nam War. Where, in another kind of conflict, their men would be heroes, now antiwar groups in their own land denounce the cause for which the men were fighting in language like that used by the enemy. Crank telephone calls interrupt whatever tranquillity they can find. President Nixon has pronounced himself pleased with their patience, but their patience is wearing thin. Increasingly, some of the wives complain that the U.S. Government is not doing enough. Some of them have been driven to espouse the offer put forward by the Viet Cong's Mme. Nguyen Thi Binh in Paris last September: that talks on releasing the prisoners would begin when the U.S. agreed to withdrawal within a set period. Says Mrs. Frankie Ford of Orange Park, Fla.: "If it is true that they will not be released until the U.S. gets out, then why don't they set a date and get out now? This war cannot be successful. Why should one more man die on the battlefield or in the prisons?" —KEITH R. JOHNSON

Nixon's China Odyssey
March 6, 1972

Setting up a strategic recalibration of the U.S.-Soviet contest, Nixon made his historic trip to one of America's most vitriolic enemies, the People's Republic of China.

The scene in Peking's Great Hall of the People last week certainly had to be one of history's great ironies. There, while a Chinese army band played "America, the Beautiful," a U.S. President merrily clinked mao-tai glasses with his Chinese hosts, long considered the true "baddies" of the Communist world. Nor was it just any American President either; it was a conservative Republican who has long had a reputation as being the perfect cold warrior. The Chinese people must have been deeply startled by the change in their own leaders' attitudes, but they, after all, live under a system not too distant from *1984*'s state-manipulated memory control. Subject to no such constraint, however, the American public could be excused if it found its neck wrenched and its equilibrium upset by the surprising spectacle of Nixon chumming it up with his former enemies and sitting patiently through a revolutionary ballet in Peking ... That the public seemed to have taken it all fairly calmly is due in large part to the fact that in their lifetime most Americans have lived through so many sudden reversals of policy, so many deviations from previously stated principle, so many changes in institutions, that they have come to regard such turnabouts as part of modern life. —EDWIN G. WARNER

Deng Xiaoping
January 1, 1979
Portrait by Richard Hess

The diminutive leader (his name was transliterated Teng Hsiao-p'ing until TIME *adopted the pinyin system) started his country on the road that has made it the U.S.'s biggest rival in the 21st century.*

The People's Republic of China, separated so long from the outer world by an instinctive xenophobia and an admixture of reclusive Maoism, in 1978 began its Great Leap Outward, or what Peking's propagandists call the New Long March. The Chinese, their primitive economy threadbare and their morale exhausted by the years of Mao Tse-tung's disastrous Cultural Revolution, hope to have arrived by the year 2000 at a state of relative modernity, and become a world economic and military power. They may not arrive, or arrive on time, but their setting off is an extraordinary spectacle of national ambition ... The motive force behind the campaign to get the world's oldest continuous civilization to the 21st century on schedule is not Mao's titular successor, Hua Kuo-feng, 57, but Vice Premier Teng Hsiao-p'ing ... Tough, abrasive, resilient, Teng, 74, has made more political comebacks than Richard Nixon. Twice, at Mao's behest, he was purged by his radical enemies, and his last rehabilitation was only 17 months ago. Teng commands a broad power base among the senior officers of the People's Liberation Army as well as wide support among China's bureaucrats, technocrats and the intelligentsia. The last two were precisely those elements of Chinese society that, like Teng, were the chief victims of the Cultural Revolution. —LANCE MORROW

The Soviet Invasion of Afghanistan
January 14, 1980
Illustration by Barron Storey

Moscow sent 50,000 troops into Afghanistan to keep Kabul on its side. The resulting quagmire sapped the Soviet empire of its strength and started a chain of events that led to the rise of al-Qaeda.

Fighting the Soviet military machine is a disorganized and leaderless army of insurgents known as *mujahidin.* They are believed to number 15,000 to 20,000 in summer and as many as 60,000 in winter. Says a U.S. expert: "Winter is the killing season, when there is nothing to do but go out and shoot." The tribes are hopelessly disunited and fight constantly among themselves. But for the most part they dislike central authority, they distrust foreigners—particularly Russians— and they have fought with rising fervor against the Kabul government ever since the Soviet-backed regime of President [Noor Mohammed] Taraki came to power in April 1978 ... The rebels were doing well until the Soviet takeover. They had virtually surrounded Kabul and controlled as many as 22 of the country's 28 provinces. Not even armored-car escorts could ensure safe passage for trucks on the highway between Kabul and Kandahar ... Now, at least for the moment, the insurgents are on the run ... [But] others talked as truculently as ever. Said Gul Amir, 36: "The Russians can't stay in Afghanistan. They are so alien that even the animals hate them." —BURTON PINES

DECEMBER 29, 1980 $1.50

TIME
Shaking Up Communism

OUTLOOK '81
More Recession Ahead

Poland's
Lech Walesa

Lech Walesa
December 29, 1980
Portrait by Leslie Cabarga

The leader of the labor revolt against Poland's communist leaders would begin the popular unraveling of Soviet rule throughout Central and Eastern Europe in the decade that followed.

Poland poses the gravest threat to the Soviet Union since it forcibly formed the East bloc after World War II. Indeed, events there have, in a sense, stripped the clothes right off the empire. Walesa and his colleagues in the Solidarity leadership know that they are, as it were, condemned to Communism; their basic goal is not to reject the system but to make it work better. Nonetheless, the workers' revolt shouts out Communism's ... failures and reminds the world that the glue of Soviet hegemony is force and intimidation ... Says Seweryn Bialer, head of Columbia University's Research Institute on International Change: "Previous challenges to Soviet control have come from above, from the leaders of satellite nations. The Polish challenge comes from below, from the workers, the only class of which the Soviet Union is afraid." —STEPHEN SMITH

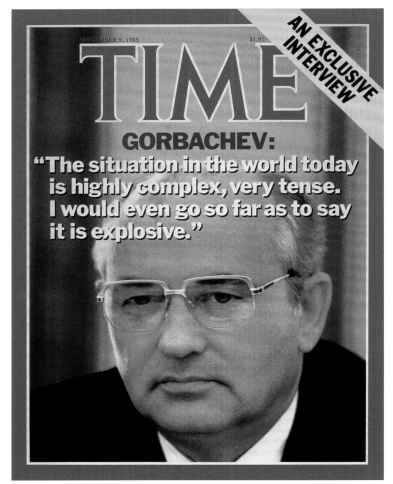

Mikhail Gorbachev
September 9, 1985
Photograph by Rudi Frey

The world was still trying to figure out the new Soviet leader when he gave TIME *a 2½-hour interview in Moscow. He would go on to try to reform the empire, only to see it fall apart in 1991.*

In assessing Gorbachev, Western Kremlinologists find points of resemblance to [Yuri] Andropov in his stress on economic reform, to [Joseph] Stalin in his insistence on discipline, to [Nikita] Khrushchev in his penchant for press-the-flesh politicking. But the dissimilarities between Gorbachev and his predecessors are greater still: he is a Soviet leader born long after the Bolshevik Revolution, with no adult memories of World War II, no involvement in Stalin's bloody purges, no strong ties to the Soviet military. Gorbachev is Gorbachev: an authoritarian with a common touch, a convinced Communist and believer in his country's social and economic system who is nonetheless outspoken in his insistence that the system can and must be made to work better—"a sort of Bolshevik Atari high-tech fan," in the pithy summary of Alexandre Adler, professor of Russian history at the University of Paris. He is a man with the intellect, political skill and force of personality that might have brought him to the top under any political system. —GEORGE J. CHURCH

Massacre in Beijing
June 12, 1989
Photograph by Mark Avery

With reporting from correspondents Sandra Burton and Jaime FlorCruz in Beijing, the magazine changed covers on a weekend to chronicle the Chinese government's hard-line response to dissent.

For seven weeks the world had marveled at the restraint demonstrated by both Beijing's rulers and the thousands of demonstrators for democracy who had occupied Tiananmen Square. The whole affair, in fact, had developed the aura of a surrealistic ritual, with both sides' forces stepping in circles as if they were performing some stately, stylized pavane. Violence, it seemed, was out of the question ... By Saturday afternoon, however, the mood changed. At 2 p.m. troops popped tear-gas shells and beat up people trying to stop them from moving into the center of Beijing. An hour later, behind the Great Hall of the People, helmeted soldiers began lashing out at students, bystanders and other citizens who, as if summoned by some irresistible call to the barricades, rushed to the district by the thousands. Soldiers stripped off their belts and used them to whip people; others beat anyone in their path with truncheons, bloodying heads as they tried to pry an opening through the mob. For 5½ hours the students held fast. Then the army inexplicably vanished. Within an hour, off Qianmen West Road on the southern end of the square, 1,200 more troops appeared. Once again they were surrounded by civilians; the soldiers again retreated. But those forays were only the prelude to death. —JESSE L. BIRNBAUM AND HOWARD CHUA-EOAN

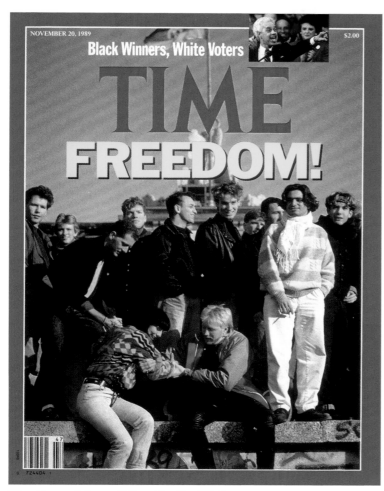

The Breaching of the Berlin Wall
November 20, 1989
Photograph by Chris Niedenthal

The structure that divided a city symbolically divided Europe and the world into ideological camps. Its fall symbolized the breakup of the Soviet bloc, a rebirth of liberty, the end of the Cold War.

For 28 years it had stood as the symbol of the division of Europe and the world, of Communist suppression, of the xenophobia of a regime that had to lock its people in lest they be tempted by another, freer life—the Berlin Wall, that hideous, 28-mile-long scar through the heart of a once proud European capital, not to mention the soul of a people. And then—*poof!*—it was gone. Not physically, at least yet, but gone as an effective barrier between East and West, opened in one unthinkable, stunning stroke to people it had kept apart for more than a generation. It was one of those rare times when the tectonic plates of history shift beneath men's feet, and nothing after is quite the same. What happened in Berlin last week was a combination of the fall of the Bastille and a New Year's Eve blowout, of revolution and celebration. At the stroke of midnight on Nov. 9, a date that not only Germans would remember, thousands who had gathered on both sides of the Wall let out a roar and started going through it, as well as up and over. West Berliners pulled East Berliners to the top of the barrier along which in years past many an East German had been shot while trying to escape; at times the Wall almost disappeared beneath waves of humanity. —GEORGE J. CHURCH

Boris Yeltsin
September 2, 1991
Photograph by Robert Wallis

A drunken coup against Gorbachev disintegrated under the heroic public protests led by Yeltsin. But change would prove elusive. Russia is now ruled by the autocratic Vladimir Putin.

They filled the air with old nightmares, throwbacks to a style of history that the world had been forgetting. The Soviet Union was seized by a sinister anachronism: its dying self. Men with faces the color of a sidewalk talked about a "state of emergency." They rolled in tanks and told stolid lies. The world imagined another totalitarian dusk, cold war again, and probably Soviet civil war as well. If Gorbachev was under arrest, who had possession of the nuclear codes? Three days: then the bats of history abruptly turned, flew back and vanished into the past. By act of will and absence of fear, the Russian people accomplished a kind of miracle, the reversal of a thousand years of autocracy ... Until last week the Russian character was judged to be politically passive, even receptive to brutal rule. At first the coup seemed to confirm the norm. The news administered a dark shock, followed immediately by a depressed sense of resignation: of course, of course, the Russians must revert to their essential selves, to their own history. Gorbachev and glasnost were the aberration; now we are back to fatal normality. "Every country has the government it deserves," Joseph de Maistre wrote in 1811. Now, after 74 years of communist dictatorship and, centuries before that, of czarist autocracy, the Russians may get a government they have earned—a democracy. —LANCE MORROW

Israelis and Palestinians: Whose Land?

Israel arose as the colonial empires of Europe devolved into new nations thrust into a world polarized by the Cold War between the U.S. and the Soviet Union. But the co-existence of the Jewish state and the Arabs with whom it shared what was once the British mandate of Palestine has defied resolution, longer-lived than the enmity of Moscow and Washington. Starting with a war that began on the very day Israel declared its independence in May 1948, it has lasted into the second decade of the 21st century, with missiles lobbed out of Gaza. In TIME's Aug. 16, 1948, cover story on Israel's founding Prime Minister, David Ben-Gurion, the magazine observed, "The Arabs, no less than the Jews, are victims of history. Four centuries of Turkish rule hurt them at least as badly as a decade of Naziism hurt the Jews. Now, in their morning of independence, the Arabs have suffered defeat at the hands of a small, despised people. It rankles ... Yet only in peace between Jews and Arabs is there much hope for either."

TIME marveled at Israel's military acumen (on the Six-Day War: "In a few astonishing hours of incredibly accurate bombing and strafing, Israel erased an expensive decade of Russian military aid to the Arab world") and admired many of the country's leaders (on Golda Meir: "The essence of the woman is conviction, without compromise, and expressed with all the subtlety of a Centurion tank"). But in Feb. 21, 1983, TIME reported that Defense Minister Ariel Sharon had discussions with Lebanese Phalangist leaders, urging them to avenge the assassination of their leader, resulting in the massacre of some 700 Palestinian refugees. After Sharon sued TIME for "blood libel," the trial revealed that the document at the heart of the allegation did not exist. U.S. libel law and its absence-of-malice clause led to a not-guilty verdict for TIME in 1985. But Sharon claimed a moral victory.

Despite the breakthrough between Israel's Menachem Begin and Egypt's Anwar Sadat in 1978, as well as the efforts of Yitzhak Rabin before his assassination in 1995, a lasting peace has been elusive. The Palestinians highlighted their plight by way of violent *intifadehs*, which proved counterproductive. They have, however, garnered some sympathy because of the expansion of Jewish settlements, which may augur a different tactic in the confrontation. Yasser Arafat, who never really lived down terrorist years, could not provide a sympathetic face for the Palestinian cause; but the unresolved future of his people and the security of Israel will continue to compel attention.

DAVID BEN-GURION | March 11, 1957

Portrait by Giro

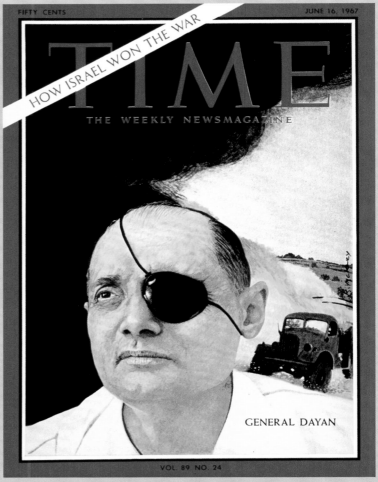

MOSHE DAYAN | June 16, 1967

Portrait by Robert Vickrey

GOLDA MEIR | September 19, 1969

Portrait by Boris Chaliapin

YASSER ARAFAT | November 11, 1974

Photograph by Claude Salhani

BEGIN AND SADAT | September 25, 1978

Portrait by Julian Allen

SHARON AND BEGIN | February 21, 1983

THE PALESTINIANS | July 23, 1990

Photograph by James Nachtwey

ISRAEL'S DILEMMA | January 19, 2009

Photo-illustration by Arthur Hochstein

Revolutionaries

Martin Luther King Jr. waving from the steps of the Lincoln Memorial on Aug. 28, 1963, at the culmination of the March on Washington

Photograph from AFP/Getty Images

THE 20TH CENTURY, AT LEAST ACCORDING TO TIME CO-FOUNDER Henry Luce, was the American century. The U.S. was the leviathan of the age, a political, economic and cultural juggernaut whose influence knew few bounds. In Luce's view, the acts and legacy of the world's looming hegemon were all imbued with a unique moral mandate: "the triumphal purpose of freedom," as he put it. But far from the U.S. as well—on occasion, in spite of it—freedoms were won by peoples long oppressed; new nations emerged from the dust of empires; new voices spoke loudly where once there

had been an overwhelming silence. On the eve of independence in 1947, India's first Prime Minister, Jawaharlal Nehru, heralded his country's arrival: "A moment comes, which comes but rarely in history, when we step out from the old to the new, when an age ends and when the soul of a nation, long suppressed, finds utterance."

Nehru's words were meant for Indians but echoed across continents. Before World War II, the globe was painted in broad strokes with the colors of European empires. Barely two decades later, it was a checkerboard of liberated states. While Americans fretted over the Cold War, decolonization—what one British Prime Minister conceded was the "wind of change"—had blown through Asia and Africa. National consciousness was no longer just the fancy of the West. Land once hoarded by imperial aristocracies was being radically redistributed to peasant farmers. Prophets of high modernism, architects like Louis Kahn and Le Corbusier, were drafted in to construct soaring edifices of power as new parliaments, monuments, cities rose from the earth. The emancipated Third World was stepping into a bold new future of its own making.

At the helm of this change were figures like Nehru, charismatic leaders who achieved heroic status in the global imagination of the age. Some, like China's Mao Zedong and Latin America's Che Guevara, did so via the barrel of a gun. Others, like Mohandas Gandhi, inspired through sheer moral courage. They endured hardships, imprisonment, deprivation. Theirs were the faces that launched a thousand rebellions. Their struggles and triumphs made them living metaphors—sometimes for epoch-defining ideologies, sometimes as the myths upon which nations were built.

These revolutionaries were hardly cut from the same cloth, but they all drew in some way from the utopianism of Marx—a philosophical tool to take apart imperialism and capitalism, the orthodoxies of the early 20th century. Nehru, Indonesia's Sukarno, Ghana's Kwame Nkrumah and Egypt's Gamal Abdel Nasser were all staunch socialists, suspicious of American enterprise and in favor of grand, galvanizing state projects. Even Nelson Mandela— the man who symbolized South Africa's struggle against the barbarism of apartheid—would be labeled a communist terrorist by white opponents. Burning with the memory of a shared oppression, a phantasmal solidarity linked peoples from the Caribbean to Africa to Asia.

But then the hope of the future faded into the grinding reality of the present. Revolutionary leaders turned into hectoring autocrats; old status quos gave way to new ones that, at times, were no less unjust, corrupt or hypocritical. Nehru's Third World moralism could not stave off wars with neighbors or lift the crushing poverty of his people. The bloated bureaucracies engendered by state socialism in both the developed and the developing worlds and the economic stagnation that came with it became an orthodoxy all of its own, leading to a new wave of politicians like the U.K.'s Margaret Thatcher intent on dismantling it—revolutions from the political right.

"You cannot fully appreciate the shape of the 20th century," said Tony Judt, the late great historian, "if you did not once share its illusions." He was thinking of European communists and Marxists, fellow travelers who couldn't reconcile their idealism with the abuses and horrors of the Soviet Union. They had been blinded by their passions, but the disenchantment that was to follow carried a special wisdom. The same can be said of the enduring legacies of decolonization.

In the U.S.—Luce's great haven of freedom—Martin Luther King Jr. found in India's experience the promise of liberation and the courage to pursue civil rights. Movements for racial equality, feminism and gay rights drew inspiration and borrowed from the language of uprisings elsewhere. Americans, like hundreds of millions around the world, came to realize that freedom has no single moment of triumph. Rather, it exists only through a relentless, constant questioning of power. The arc of history may bend toward justice, and it is human action that bends it.

TIME charted this grand sweep of history, at times on the wrong side of it. Its Cold War–era prejudices made the magazine unduly wary of great statesmen it considered too friendly with Moscow if only through sympathies with communism. Consistent throughout its coverage, though, was a sense of the tidal movements shaping the 20th century and the titans who crested its waves. But this age of heroes may be at an end. TIME's 2011 Person of the Year cover, the Protester, mapped a new phenomenon of global dissent, in which leaderless multitudes, knitted together by their ire and the Internet, paralyze cities and bring governments to heel. The revolution will be televised and blogged and tweeted, but the rebels are now masked, faceless. —ISHAAN THAROOR

FIFTEEN CENTS · AUGUST 24, 1942

TIME
THE WEEKLY NEWSMAGAZINE

INDIA'S NEHRU
When do the British go? When do the Japs come?
(Foreign News)

VOLUME XL · (REG. U. S. PAT. OFF.) · NUMBER 8

FIFTEEN CENTS · APRIL 22, 1946

TIME
THE WEEKLY NEWSMAGAZINE

MOHAMED ALI JINNAH
His Moslem tiger wants to eat the Hindu cow.

VOLUME XLVII · (REG. U. S. PAT. OFF.) · NUMBER 16

Jawaharlal Nehru
August 24, 1942
Portrait by Boris Chaliapin

He ruled for 17 years as the first Prime Minister of an independent India but could not quell violence. His daughter Indira Gandhi and grandson Rajiv Gandhi both led the country but were assassinated.

During a National Week demonstration in 1932 his mother was beaten and left unconscious on the side of the road near her home in Allahabad. She was dead now, and so were his father and his wife Kamala, all helped along to funeral pyres on the banks of the Ganges by their work in India's struggle for independence. There was cold fury in him at the Himalayan stupidity of Tory imperialists, and bitterness at the failure of the West he understood to meet the East, which at times still baffled him. Basically, said Nehru, the Indian crisis is the result of Europe's and America's concept of Asia. "What has astounded me," said Idealist Nehru, "is the total inability of the English-speaking peoples to think of the new world-situation in terms of realism—realism being more than military realism. It is political, psychological, economic realism ... Their concept of us is that of a mass people fallen low, a backward people who must be lifted out from the depths by good works." —FILLMORE CALHOUN

Mohamed Ali Jinnah
April 22, 1946
Portrait by Boris Chaliapin

Fearing that Muslims would be powerless in a majority-Hindu India, he founded Pakistan as a Muslim homeland. However, partition led only to massacres and, in the years to come, spasms of war.

At a crucial meeting in March 1940 Jinnah first publicly plumped for Pakistan. A hundred thousand followers thronged into the shade of a huge *pandal* (big tent) in Lahore, where the League was meeting, overflowed into the scorching heat outside, heard Jinnah proclaim over the loudspeaker ... "The only course open to us all is to allow the major nations [of India] to separate to their homelands." He warned that any democratic government in a unified India which gave Moslems a permanent minority "must lead to civil war and the raising of private armies." An enthusiastic woman follower tore off her veil, came from behind the purdah screen, mounted the speakers' platform. But Moslem revolutionary ardor was not ready to break with tradition; she was quietly escorted back to purdah by a uniformed guard.

When Gandhi led Congress into civil disobedience after the failure of the Cripps mission [to obtain his and Jinnah's cooperation in the war effort] in 1942, Jinnah ordered his Moslems to take no part, promised a "state of benevolent neutrality" that would not hamper the British in fighting the Japanese. —HERBERT LAING MERILLAT AND MAX WAYS

Sukarno

December 23, 1946
Portrait by Boris Chaliapin

After World War II, Dutch rule over the archipelago that would become Indonesia was effectively at an end. The charismatic Sukarno (we used to spell it Soekarno) knit together a diverse republic.

Few men in the postwar world evoke the fanatic devotion of millions as does this 45-year-old child of luck and revolution. He is tall for an Indonesian (5 ft. 8 in.) and, by native standards, superlatively handsome. His Malay is self-consciously choice; in fact, he is so insistent on advancing the native speech that he is called Indonesia's Webster (meaning Noah, not Daniel). He is quite an orator, too—TIME's Jakarta correspondent cabled the following picture of Soekarno addressing an audience of 5,000 women:

"Mostly he spoke extemporaneously (65 minutes). Occasionally he slipped on horn-rimmed spectacles, read a note. I have never seen an orator who held an audience in the palm of his hand so easily and confidently. Soekarno would speak slowly, then at machine-gun pace. Some times he shook a finger at the audience, again he stood arms akimbo and bit off his words." —ROBERT LUBAR

Eva Peron

July 14, 1947
Portrait by Boris Chaliapin

Rising from actress to Argentina's First Lady, Juan Peron's wife was so beloved by the working class she championed that they campaigned to have her named a saint after her death at the age of 33.

With messianic fervor she encouraged the public to call her "Evita," in a land where nicknames are restricted to the closest friends. While society ladies shuddered, huge, larger-than-life-sized pictures of the First Lady blossomed all over the country with the legend: "I prefer to be simply EVITA to being the wife of the President, if this EVITA is used to better conditions in the homes of my country." On the radio other feminists were silenced to make Evita's voice the louder …

Devoted and well aware of his wife's value as a press agent, Juancito gave her a free hand with her campaign for women's suffrage, her labor reforms and her peripatetic philanthropies. An undistinguished glassblower who had succeeded Peron as Secretary of Labor was moved aside to give Eva office space.

She still has no official title, but every day, after breakfast with her husband at 7, she shows up in her office, to work from 9 to noon receiving delegations of workers and trade unionists, hearing hard-luck stories and doling out advice and aid. A battery of secretaries is always on hand to take notes and handle a voluminous correspondence. —ROGER S. HEWLETT

Kwame Nkrumah
February 9, 1953
Portrait by Boris Chaliapin

In 1957, Ghana—once the Gold Coast—would transition to independence from Britain, and Nkrumah would be its first President. In 1966, however, he would be overthrown by the military.

Suddenly, like the Red Sea parting before the Israelites, the noisy crowd opened. Through a forest of waving palm branches, an open car bore a husky black man with fine-sculptured lips, melancholy eyes and a halo of frizzy black hair. The Right Honorable Kwame Nkrumah ... Bachelor of Divinity, Master of Arts, Doctor of Law and Prime Minister of the Gold Coast, waved a white handkerchief to his countrymen as they fought to touch the hem of his tunic. Then, as the band hit the groove, he jigged his broad shoulders in time to the whirling rhythm, and passed on, exalted. "You see," cried a delirious Gold Coaster ... "He is one of us. A man of the people. Now that you have seen, you must understand: we can govern ourselves" ... The "we" are 4,500,000 tribesmen ... scattered across a rectangular patch of jungle, swamp and bushland that juts into the westward bulge of Africa ... [They] have been chosen by Imperial Britain to pioneer its boldest experiment in African home rule. In 1951 the British gave the Gold Coast its first democratic constitution; last year they designated as Prime Minister [Nkrumah] a histrionic radical who had once openly flirted with Communism ... Today, in the Gold Coast cabinet, only three of eleven members are British civil servants, and in Nkrumah's words, they are cooperating in making themselves expendable. —ELDON GRIFFITHS

Thurgood Marshall
September 19, 1955
Portrait by James Chapin

A dozen years after persuading the U.S. Supreme Court to desegregate public schools, he would become the first African-American Justice in the nation's highest judicial body.

In 1943, a group of 100 N.A.A.C.P. leaders, mostly lawyers, met in Manhattan. Marshall recalls: "Like somebody at the meeting said, while it was true a lot of us might die without ever seeing the goal realized we were going to have to change directions if our children weren't going to die as black bastards too. So we decided to make segregation itself our target."

"Segregation itself" had long been a target of Negro spokesmen. But Thurgood Marshall is not primarily a Negro spokesman; he is a constitutional lawyer. The problem facing him and his colleagues was how to attack segregation itself on legal grounds. The weight of the precedents ran against them. Where would they find evidence to turn the balance?

The answer was peculiarly contemporary and peculiarly American. Just as U.S military staffs swim—and sometimes drown—in rivers of expert reports, just as U.S. business turns more and more to specialized organizers of facts, so Marshall & Co. mobilized a small army of psychologists, psychiatrists, sociologists and anthropologists to prove what every Negro among them believed to be obvious: that segregated education could not be "equal." —MAX WAYS

Black children in Kansas getting off a school bus the year before the Supreme Court's historic 1954 *Brown v. Board of Education* decision

Photograph by Carl Iwasaki

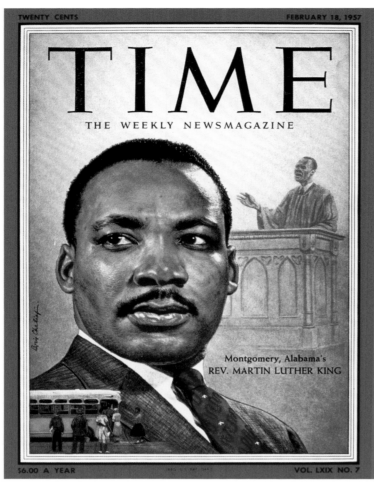

Martin Luther King Jr.
February 18, 1957
Portrait by Boris Chaliapin

Adopting the techniques of Mohandas Gandhi, he helped lead the U.S. out of segregation and would be awarded the Nobel Peace Prize in 1964, four years before he would be assassinated in Memphis.

Negro leaders look toward Montgomery, Ala., the cradle of the Confederacy, for advice and counsel on how to gain the desegregation that the U.S. Supreme Court has guaranteed them. The man whose word they seek is not a judge, or a lawyer, or a political strategist or a flaming orator. He is a scholarly, 28-year-old Negro Baptist minister, the Rev. Martin Luther King Jr., who in little more than a year has risen from nowhere to become one of the nation's remarkable leaders of men.

In Montgomery, Negroes are riding side by side with whites on integrated buses for the first time in history. They won this right by court order. But their presence is accepted, however reluctantly, by the majority of Montgomery's white citizens because of Martin King and the way he conducted a year-long boycott of the transit system. In terms of concrete victories, this makes King a poor second to the brigade of lawyers who won the big case before the Supreme Court in 1954, and who are now fighting their way from court to court, writ to writ, seeking to build the legal framework for desegregation. But King's leadership extends beyond any single battle. —CHAMP CLARK

Gamal Abdel Nasser
March 29, 1963
Portrait by Robert Vickrey

The army officer ousted and exiled King Farouk in 1952, then served as Egypt's President and the undisputed leader of the Arab world for 14 years.

His picture, with its Pepsodent smile, is found in every corner of the Middle East, from Iraqi bazaars to the huts of royalist Yemeni tribesmen who still cling to Nasser's picture even though they are fighting Nasser's troops.

What Nasser has working for him is the deep desire of all Arabs to be united in a single Arab nation, and their conviction—grudging or enthusiastic—that Nasser represents the best hope of achieving it. This dream of unity harks back to the golden age of the 7th century when, spurred by the messianic Moslem religion handed down by Mohammed the Prophet, Arab warriors burst from their desert peninsula and conquered everything in sight. In less than 150 years, the Arabs swept victoriously north to Asia Minor and the walls of Byzantine Constantinople, south over Persia and Afghanistan to the heart of India, east through Central Asia to the borders of China, west over Egypt and Africa to Spain and southern France. It was an incredible empire—larger than any carved out by Alexander the Great or Imperial Rome.

It was also an empire that fell swiftly apart.

—ROBERT MCLAUGHLIN

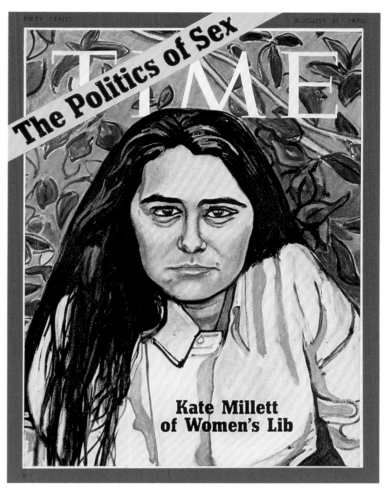

Cesar Chavez
July 4, 1969
Portrait by Manuel Gregorio Acosta

Out of San Jose, Calif., the labor leader organized migrant workers and turned eating grapes into a moral dilemma even as he faced political opposition from the American labor movement.

Edward and Ethel Kennedy, following the late Robert Kennedy's example, have embraced Cesar Chavez as a brother. The so-called Beautiful People, from Peter, Paul and Mary to the Ford sisters, Anne Uzielli and Charlotte Niarchos, are helping to raise funds for the strikers. That support is one of the few issues that find Chicago Mayor Richard Daley, iconoclastic Writer Gloria Steinem, and liberal Senators Jacob Javits and George McGovern in total agreement. Ralph Abernathy lends black help to what is becoming the Brown Power movement.

The fact that it is a movement has magnified *la huelga* far beyond its economic and geographic confines. At stake are not only the interests of 384,100 agricultural workers in California but potentially those of more than 4,000,000 in the U.S. Such workers have never won collective bargaining rights, partially because they have not been highly motivated to organize and partially because their often itinerant lives have made them difficult to weld into a group that would have the clout of an industrial union. By trying to organize the grape pickers, Chavez hopes to inspire militancy among all farm laborers —KEITH R. JOHNSON

Kate Millett
August 31, 1970
Portrait by Alice Neel

The feminist author and artist raised consciousness and roused society by publishing a book that claimed that the battle between the sexes was an uneven struggle for power.

Reading the book is like sitting with your testicles in a nutcracker," says George Stade, assistant professor of English at Columbia University. He should know; the book was Kate's Ph.D. thesis, and he was one of her advisers.

In a way, the book has made Millett the Mao Tse-tung of Women's Liberation. That is the sort of description she and her sisters despise, for the movement rejects the notion of leaders and heroines as creations of the media—and mimicry of the ways that men use to organize their world. Despite the fact that it is essentially a polemic suspended awkwardly in academic traction, *Sexual Politics* so far has sold more than 15,000 copies and is in its fourth printing.

In her book, Millett defines politics as the "power-structured relationships" by which one group—in this case the male elite—governs others. Patriarchy is thus limned as the institutional foe. Labeling it as the "most pervasive ideology of our culture," she argues that it provides our "fundamental concept of power." Women are helpless, in other words, because men control the basic mechanisms of society. —BOB MCCABE AND B.J. PHILLIPS

Margaret Thatcher

February 16, 1981
Portrait by David Suter

The first female Prime Minister of the U.K., she and her Tory revolution scaled back the country's welfare state, winning the love of conservatives and the unending enmity of social progressives.

Hard-edged and superconfident, Thatcher swept into office 21 months ago with a handsome 43-seat parliamentary majority from an electorate that had soured on the Labor government of James Callaghan and was fed up with Britain's intractable unions in the bitter winter of 1979. Labor's image as the only party capable of dealing with the powerful trade unions was sorely damaged when strikes and industrial strife spread across the country. Touting the "monetarist" theories of Milton Friedman, the conservative American economist, Thatcher won big with pledges to cut government spending, reduce income taxes, revitalize industry and create a new climate for business. With a survival-of-the-fittest philosophy, she warned that outdated, unprofitable industries would be allowed to die—but for the sake of new and vital ones. She promised Britons that she would get government off their backs and give them freedom to make their own choices. She called for a renewal of the British spirit she had known as a girl growing up over her father's grocery store in her Lincolnshire birthplace of Grantham. —MARGUERITE JOHNSON

Nelson Mandela

May 9, 1994
Portrait by Janet Woolley

Emerging from 28 years of incarceration in 1990, he peacefully negotiated the end of apartheid in South Africa with F.W. de Klerk, whom he would succeed as President of South Africa.

His style derives from a hard-won discipline. Oliver Tambo, his former law partner and the longtime leader of the A.N.C. in exile who died last year, once described the youthful Mandela as "passionate, emotional, sensitive, quickly stung to bitterness and retaliation by insult and patronage." Who can discern those characteristics in the controlled Nelson Mandela of today? He now prizes rationality, logic, compromise, and distrusts sentiment. Prison steeled him, and over the decades he came to see emotion not as an ally but as a demon to be shunned. How was the man who emerged from prison different from the one who went in? His reply: "I came out mature." It is not simply that he harbors little bitterness in his heart; he knows that bitterness will not move him an inch closer to his goal.

If there has been a consistent criticism of Mandela over the years, it is that he is too willing to see the good in people. If this is a flaw, it is one he accepts because it grows out of his great strength, his generosity of heart toward his enemies. He defends himself by noting that thinking too well of people sometimes makes them behave better than they otherwise would. He believes in the essential goodness of the human heart, even though he has spent a lifetime suffering the wounds of heartless authorities. —RICHARD STENGEL

NELSON MANDELA

TIME

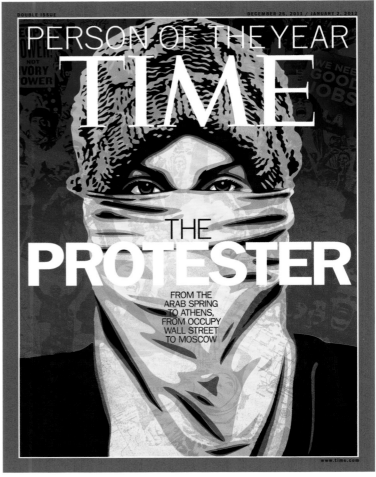

Julian Assange
December 13, 2010
Photo-illustration by D.W. Pine

After the Australian computer programmer founded WikiLeaks, he set off a global firestorm of controversy by releasing myriad private and classified government and corporate documents.

For governments have been trying to keep their intentions secret since the Greeks left a horse stuffed with soldiers outside the gates of Troy, and they have been plagued by leaks of information for about as long. Some information really should be secret, and some leaks really do have consequences: the Civil War battle of Antietam might not have gone the way it did had Confederate General Robert E. Lee's orders not been found wrapped around cigars by Union troops a few days before. But in the past few years, governments have designated so much information secret that you wonder whether they intend the time of day to be classified. The number of new secrets designated as such by the U.S. government has risen 75%, from 105,163 in 1996 to 183,224 in 2009, according to the U.S. Information Security Oversight Office. At the same time, the number of documents and other communications created using those secrets has skyrocketed nearly 10 times, from 5,685,462 in 1996 to 54,651,765 in 2009. —MASSIMO CALABRESI

The Protester
December 26, 2011
Illustration by Shepard Fairey

The anonymous face of massive street dissent shook the world as the Arab Spring roiled the Middle East and the Occupy movement took on the world's financial overlords.

It's remarkable how much the protest vanguards share. Everywhere they are disproportionately young, middle class and educated. Almost all the protests this year began as independent affairs, without much encouragement from or endorsement by existing political parties or opposition bigwigs. All over the world, the protesters of 2011 share a belief that their countries' political systems and economies have grown dysfunctional and corrupt—sham democracies rigged to favor the rich and powerful and prevent significant change. They are fervent small-*d* democrats. Two decades after the final failure and abandonment of communism, they believe they're experiencing the failure of hell-bent megascaled crony hypercapitalism and pine for some third way, a new social contract.

During the bubble years, perhaps, there was enough money trickling down to keep them happyish, but now the unending financial crisis and economic stagnation make them feel like suckers. This year, instead of plugging in the headphones, entering an Internet-induced fugue state and quietly giving in to hopelessness, they used the Internet to find one another and take to the streets to insist on fairness and (in the Arab world) freedom. —KURT ANDERSEN

Same-Sex Marriage
April 8, 2013
Photographs by Peter Hapak

About three months after this issue, the Supreme Court threw out a law that barred federal recognition of same-sex couples—joining the shift in popular opinion to supporting gay unions.

What's most striking about this seismic social shift—as rapid and unpredictable as any turn in public opinion on record—is that it happened with very little planning ... For decades, prominent gay-rights activists dismissed the right to marry as a quixotic, even dangerous, cause and gave no support to the men and women at the grassroots who launched the uphill movement.

Changes in law and politics, medicine and demographics, popular culture and ivory-tower scholarship all added momentum to produce widespread changes of heart ... But then another seemingly separate strand of history was woven in: the AIDS epidemic ... This deadly scourge offered a painful education in the advantages of marriage. AIDS patients and their partners discovered that they weren't covered by each other's medical insurance, weren't entitled to enter the doctors' offices and hospital rooms of their loved ones, weren't authorized to claim remains or plan funerals or inherit estates. Grieving survivors were barred from collecting Social Security and pension benefits. Marriage began to be seen as the portal to a wide array of privileges and protections. The bourgeois ideal of stable monogamy could be a lifesaver. —DAVID VON DREHLE

The Age Of Terror

During its assault on the Israeli Olympic team in Munich in 1972, a member of the Black September terrorist squad looks out from a balcony

Photograph by Kurt Strumpf

SEPTEMBER 11
2001

AS EARLY AS 1977, TIME REFERRED TO THE PHRASE "ONE MAN'S terrorist is another man's freedom fighter" as an "old political maxim." Terrorism has always been in the eye of the beholder, which has made covering it, let alone defining it, one of the most difficult and politically fraught challenges of the past 90 years. ¶There are few words in the English language so ubiquitous yet contentious, so imprecise yet universally undesirable. No one consents to being called a terrorist. Revolutionaries, anarchists and jihadists are happy to be called by by those names. But a terrorist will turn the dictionary definition—one who wields violence against civilians in pursuit of a political aim—back on the accuser, saying he or the government or the system is the real terrorist.

It wasn't always this way. The first terrorists, the Jacobins of the French Revolution, were proud of the word and the concept it embodied: reshaping society and human nature through the ruthless exercise of violence—a reign of terror—by the state. When Robespierre's excesses made *terrorist* a dirty word, terrorism devolved into the work of rebels and subversives, like those who assassinated Russia's Alexander II in 1881 and Austria's Archduke Franz Ferdinand in 1914, sparking World War I. TIME first used the word just 21 weeks after the magazine's founding, in July 1923, to refer to a violent imposition of state power, possibly by the troublesome National Socialist Adolf Hitler, who was a few months away from his failed Beer Hall Putsch and 10 years from elections that swept him and the Nazis to power.

After World War II, the word *terrorism* was applied once again to revolutionaries, primarily among Asian, African and Middle Eastern groups rebelling against colonialism. In locales as diverse as Cyprus, Kenya, Algeria, Vietnam and what would become Israel (where the Jewish-Zionist Stern Gang waged terrorist campaigns against British rule in the 1940s), independence groups started exercising extreme violence and intimidation against civilians as much to break the resolve of their colonial overlords as to intimidate rival indigenous groups. In 1957, for example, TIME said, "Algerian nationalists staged a wave of terrorism to prove that France was far from having the situation in hand."

By the 1960s and '70s, the word *terrorism* had become an irredeemably intolerable insult, yet notions of what terrorism was and who practiced it began to splinter and multiply. It was no longer the domain of freedom fighters whose grievances and goals were easy to understand; more radical, nihilistic and baffling organizations—often headquartered in countries of relative plenty—began to use kidnapping, assassinations and bomb plots to spectacular yet unclear and inconclusive ends. The Red Army in Japan, the Baader-Meinhof Gang in Germany, the Red Brigade in Italy and the Symbionese Liberation Army in the U.S. all figured out that modern technology and mass media could be exploited to bring disproportionate attention to their hopelessly muddled causes. Exploiting lax security that would take decades to tighten, most of these groups and many others like them made skyjacking their métier, commandeering planes at rates that seem incomprehensible today.

While this strain of terrorism has largely died off, a near contemporaneous one has come to dominate what many Westerners believe to be terrorism: the all-out strategy pursued by a disaffected, Muslim ideology in a clash of civilizations with the West. While Fatah and the Palestinian Liberation Organization employed similar tactics since the mid-1960s in their struggle against what they saw as Israeli occupation and oppression, the Palestinian group Black September's massacre of 11 members of the Israeli Olympic team at the 1972 Munich Games was a watershed—for the savagery of the attacks and for the group's disregard for its own safety. The trend only intensified. Groups such as Hamas and Hizballah became even more confrontational and lethal as religious extremism radicalized notions of confronting the enemy.

As the final quarter of the 20th century wore on and the last colonial powers drifted from the stage, America saw itself increasingly the target. Iranian revolutionaries overran the U.S. embassy in Tehran in 1979, Islamic Jihad bombed the U.S. Marine barracks in Beirut in 1983, and Hizballah hijacked TWA Flight 847 in 1985, the same year that members of the Palestinian Liberation Front commandeered the cruise ship *Achille Lauro*. In 1986, Libyan operatives bombed a Berlin disco frequented by U.S. troops.

These and other attacks throughout the 1990s dismayed Americans. Why didn't everyone believe they were as good and just and benevolent as Americans believed themselves to be? Still, nothing prepared them for how the Saudi Osama bin Laden and al-Qaeda would take the battle to the U.S. on Sept. 11, 2011. As TIME wrote in the issue that it produced two days after hijacked planes struck New York City and Washington, "If you want to humble an empire, it makes sense to maim its cathedrals. They are symbols of its faith, and when they crumple and burn, it tells us we are not so powerful and we can't be safe."

George W. Bush declared not just a war on al-Qaeda but a "global war on terror." In 2009, TIME described Bush's vision as "a global, generation-defining struggle against an enemy of vast military and ideological power that would transform whole chunks of the world." The direct and proximate effects of that broadly and badly circumscribed war, in money and the lives of Afghans, Iraqis and Americans, are impossible to estimate. —JIM FREDERICK

The Arab Guerrillas
September 28, 1970
Illustration from a poster by Ismail Shammout for the PLO

A 1970 showdown between King Hussein of Jordan and Yasser Arafat's PLO guerrillas ended in Hussein's favor, but the conflict marked the PLO's arrival as a regional force for decades to come.

Savage street battles raged in Amman between Hussein's army and the fedayeen ("men of sacrifice") of the Palestine guerrilla organizations ... Casualties were heavy. In the Six-Day War with Israel three years ago, Jordan suffered only 162 dead and wounded.

Last week, after three days of intensive fighting, reports put the casualties at more than 5,000 in a nation of 2,200,000 ... The outbursts proved what Arab leaders have increasingly feared as the fedayeen grew from a handful to an army of 25,000 full-time fighters in Jordan alone: the movement is a greater threat to established Arab governments than it is to Israel. The guerrillas were also proving once again that they must be reckoned with in any Middle East peace settlement ... Since 1968, Hussein's successive Cabinets and the eleven guerrilla organizations that make up the Palestine Liberation Organization (PLO) have rubbed each other like two jagged pieces of Jordanian limestone. The government resented the fact that the guerrillas had become so strong that they were practically the joint rulers of Jordan ... The guerrillas resented the fact that Hussein's government did not show sufficient regard for the Palestinians, who make up 65% of Jordan's population. —SPENCER DAVIDSON

In the Shadow of the Gunmen
January 10, 1972
Photograph by Sylvain Julian

In the early 1970s, terrorism flourished in Northern Ireland, where the Catholic, independence-minded IRA clashed frequently with the British army. All too often, innocents were caught in the crossfire.

Sections of Londonderry and Belfast are as desolated as London during the blitz, and the scarred faces of empty, bombed-out buildings are pockmarked from gunfire ... On the red brick walls surrounding vacant lots, the children of Belfast—perhaps the most tragic victims of the war—have scrawled afresh the old slogans of idealism and hatred: "Up the I.R.A." and "Informers Beware" in the Catholic sections, "No Popery Here" in the Protestant areas. If nothing else, the signs are additional proof of the old saying that Ireland is a land with too much religion and not enough Christianity ... On New Year's Eve, Belfast was rocked by eight explosions. Gunmen fired on a police precinct house, while soldiers had to break up a riot between Catholic and Protestant youths. Earlier in the week, a sniper in Londonderry killed a patrolling soldier. The trooper, 20-year-old Richard Ham, was the 43rd British soldier killed during 1971, and the 206th person since the major riots of 1969. As if to emphasize the sense of despair that pervades the province, the British command announced that children playing with toy guns run the risk of being shot. The reason for the statement was that children in Ulster these days sometimes carry real guns. —GEORGE DICKERSON

The Hearst Nightmare
April 29, 1974
Portrait by Marilyn Conover

The surreal saga of how newspaper heiress Patty Hearst went from Symbionese Liberation Army kidnapping victim to true-believing terrorist-organization member and bank robber electrified the nation.

Only three months ago, Patty Hearst was a quiet, comely heiress to a famed publishing fortune who spent much of her time preparing for her intended marriage to Steven Andrew Weed, 26, a graduate philosophy student. Kidnapped on Feb. 4 by the obscure revolutionary band that grandiosely calls itself an army but is more of a ragtag platoon, she seemed close to release two weeks ago, after her family started a free-food program for the Bay Area's needy and aged that the S.L.A. had demanded. Then she stunned her family and friends by announcing that she had renounced them, joined her abductors, and adopted the name Tania, after the German-Argentine mistress of Latin American Revolutionary Che Guevara. Whether through conversion or coercion, she materialized last week in the role of a foul-mouthed bank robber. In the bewilderment shared by all who have followed the case, her anguished father Randolph A. Hearst exclaimed: "It's terrible! Sixty days ago, she was a lovely child. Now there's a picture of her in a bank with a gun in her hand." It was still not known whether Patty had actually been won over to the band's vague philosophy, with its Maoist cant and its dedication to deadly terrorism. —FRANK B. MERRICK

Carnage in Lebanon
October 31, 1983
Photograph by Hussein Ammar

The attack on U.S. Marine peacekeepers in Lebanon was the worst disaster faced by the Pentagon since the end of the Vietnam War. And it was a foreign policy debacle for Washington.

Only the cooks were up and about in the reinforced-concrete Aviation Safety Building on the edge of the Beirut International Airport, used as headquarters by the Eighth Marine Battalion of the U.S. part of the peace-keeping force. Built around a courtyard, the headquarters contained a gymnasium, a reading room, the administrative offices and the communications center for the battalion. It was also sleeping quarters for some 200 Marines; most were still in their cots, enjoying the luxury of Sunday, the one day of the week when they were free from reveille. Suddenly a truck, laden with dynamite, on a fanatical suicide mission crashed into the building's lobby and exploded with such force that the structure collapsed in seconds, killing or wounding most of the Marines inside. By evening the toll, still incomplete as rescuers picked through the rubble, stood at 147 dead, 60 wounded. —WILLIAM E. SMITH

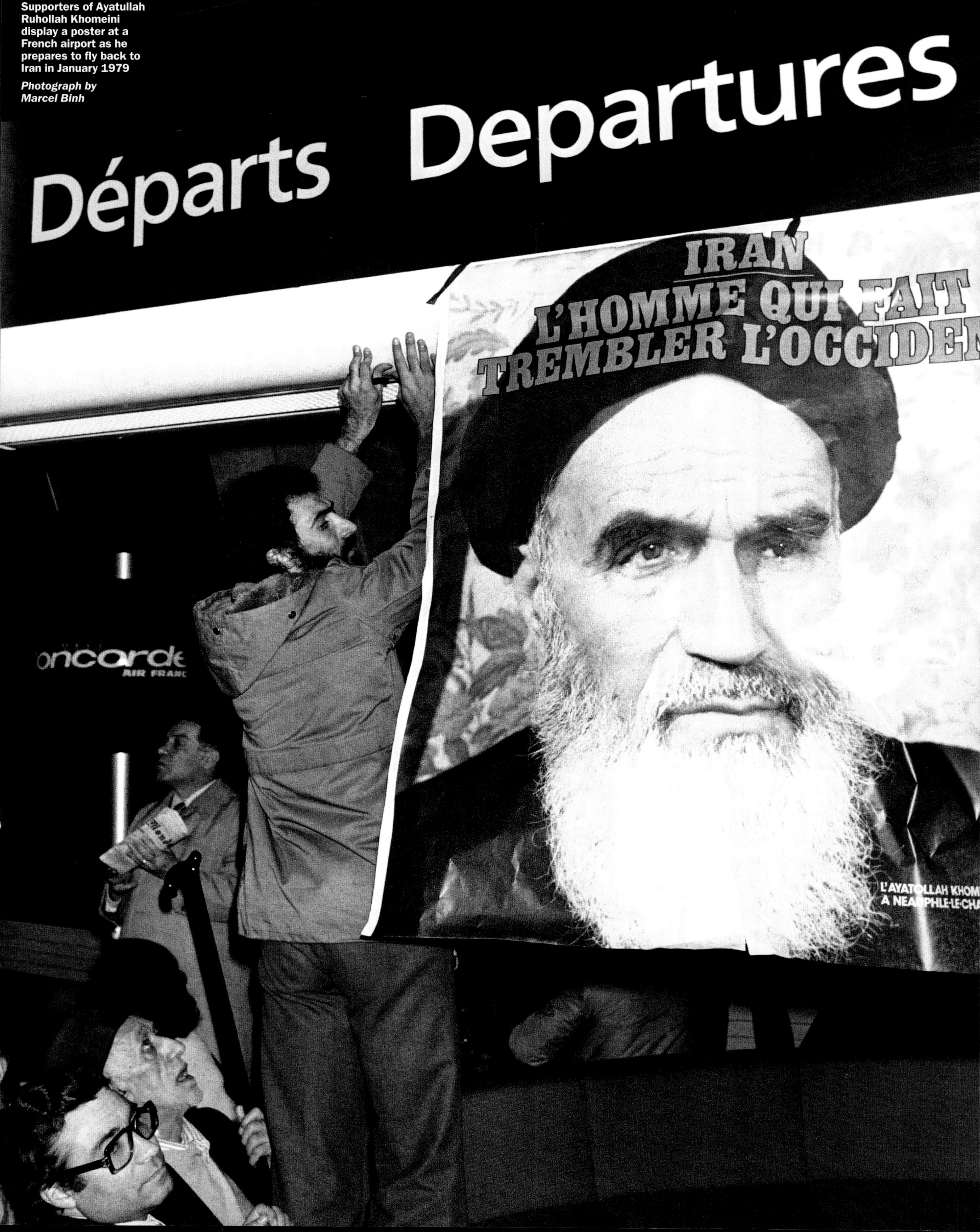

Départs Departures

IRAN
L'HOMME QUI FAIT
TREMBLER L'OCCIDEN

L'AYATOLLAH KHOM
A NEAUPHLE-LE-CHA

Hijacking
July 1, 1985
Illustration by Burt Silverman

Modern technology, mass media and lax airline security all collided with the hijacking of TWA Flight 847 by Lebanese extremists to produce an ongoing real-life TV drama.

It was like a nightmarish rerun of the Iranian hostage drama, with a surreal twist. Once again American hostages were paraded before the cameras by their terrorist captors. Only this time they were not blindfolded, as the American embassy officials had been in Tehran, or made to grovel by bug-eyed radicals shouting "Death to America!" Rather, the prisoners, some unshaven, all uneasy, but combed and neat, were graciously ushered out to meet the press. Acting as a kind of terrorist talk-show host was Ali Hamdan, a well-groomed representative of the Lebanese Amal, the mainstream Shi'ite faction that had in effect hijacked the hostages from their original hijackers, the two brutal gunmen who had seized TWA's Flight 847 ... The five hostages returned and pronounced themselves healthy and well cared for ... It was as if terrorism had been refined, spruced up, made almost civilized for TV. The effect was strangely serene, almost lulling, at least until [hostage Allyn] Conwell warned in his calm drawl, "If negotiations fail, we will be returned back to the original hijackers. Let me say, based on experience, that is something that I would find most unappealing." Lest reporters miss the point, a shadowy figure stalked in the background, hoisting an AK-47. —EVAN THOMAS

The Nuclear Black Market
August 29, 1994
Photo-illustration by Matt Mahurin

When Carlos the Jackal, Europe's most prolific and wily—yet overhyped—terrorist was finally brought to heel, TIME recapped his career and assessed new threats on the horizon.

The first symptoms of the nuclear plague are spreading into Europe ... The emergence of a black market for the essential material of mass destruction is a historic and nightmarish challenge for the world. It makes the threat of nuclear proliferation far more urgent and increases the number of characters who could do it themselves. "We've crossed a threshold. You smuggle small amounts of the stuff often enough, and you've got a bomb," says Leonard Spector, director of the nonproliferation project at Washington's Carnegie Endowment for International Peace. Such fears have a foundation: the world has seen terrorism continuously evolve to new heights of ingenuity and depravity. This week Carlos the Jackal is in jail in France, and North Korea is using the threat of nuclear weapons to try to extort billions from its neighbors. Their juxtaposition in the news, linking the worst of 1970s-style terrorism with the brazen threat of irresponsible nuclear ambitions, shouts a warning of a different sort of terror, still indefinable but extremely frightening. The combination of brutality and fanaticism with nuclear weapons could bring about disasters almost too chilling to contemplate. —BRUCE W. NELAN

Rescue workers survey the ruins of the Alfred P. Murrah Federal Building in Oklahoma City after the April 19, 1995, attack that killed 168 people.

Photograph by Paul K. Buck

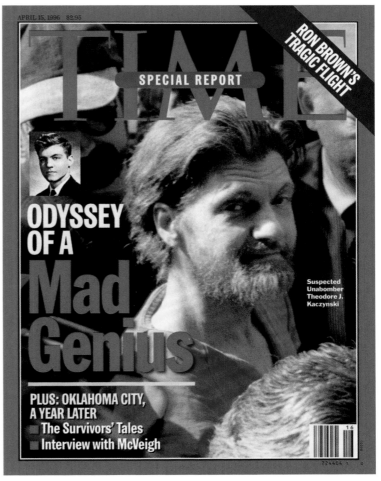

Oklahoma City Bombing

May 1, 1995

Photograph by Ralf-Finn Hestoft

Timothy McVeigh's bombing of an Oklahoma City federal building led TIME *to ask, "How many citizens feel so passionately that their government is the Great Satan that they would resort to such evil?"*

According to the complaint filed by the FBI on Friday night, McVeigh was known by a co-worker to hold "extreme right-wing views ... and was particularly agitated about the conduct of the Federal Government at Waco, Texas, in 1993"—so agitated, in fact, that he had visited the site. Indeed, as more details emerge, April 19— the date of last week's bombing and the anniversary of the apocalyptic fire at the Branch Davidian compound in Waco—has only gained in infamy, intricately bound as it is to the mythologies of homegrown zealots like McVeigh ... A sense of guilty introspection swept the country when the FBI released sketches of the suspects, distinctly Caucasian John Does 1 and 2. Immediately after the Oklahoma blast, some politicians and commentators had fingered Islamic terrorists as the most likely culprits, fueling anti-Muslim sentiment and triggering calls for tougher anti-immigration measures. The feds suggested that the Does, as McVeigh seems to bear out, were members of a right-wing citizen militia targeting government agencies housed in the Alfred P. Murrah Building. Although Oklahoma police authorities were schooled in the hate groups blooming like some deadly nightshade on the fringes of society, they had always had a hard time seeing these loose organizations as a danger. —ELIZABETH GLEICK

The Unabomber

April 15, 1996

Photograph by Michael Gallacher

With the arrest of Theodore Kaczynski a year after Timothy McVeigh, TIME *wondered why the U.S. seemed to spawn a particular kind of political criminal.*

American paranoias come in waves, and the past year or two have seen a surge in the dark dynamic: Waco and Ruby Ridge, then Oklahoma City, a commemoration of April 19, which has become a savage Guy Fawkes Day. Five days after Oklahoma City, the Unabomber struck in Sacramento, California, as if envious and eager to reclaim the attention. The paranoid screams self-importance; insignificance transforms itself into destructive power. The air filled with rhetoric about "angry white males," with middle-aged militiamen in weekend camouflage promising armed struggle against Washington. The National Rifle Association complained about the government's "jackbooted thugs." The assault-rifle fringe could hear black helicopters descending, as if to deliver Boutros Boutros-Ghali, dark men in blue helmets and World Government ... By last week it was clear the American psychology has changed, much for the better. Certain menacing uncertainties have resolved themselves. The man who seems to be the Unabomber was arrested—another example of the way in which a demon, hitherto concealed, may shrivel when brought into sunlight. The suspect's family turned him in because they recognized his writings—a killer betrayed by his own prose style. —LANCE MORROW

A U.S. flag was raised amid the ruins of the Twin Towers at the World Trade Center, destroyed by al-Qaeda on Sept. 11, 2001

Photograph by James Nachtwey

Mourning in America
September 24, 2001
Photograph by Doug Mills

Sept. 11 would drive much of U.S. foreign policy over the next decade, but in the week after the al-Qaeda attacks, America was still trying to make sense of what had happened.

Our enemies had turned the most familiar objects against us, turned shaving kits into holsters and airplanes into missiles and soccer coaches and newlyweds into involuntary suicide bombers. So while it was up to the President and his generals to plot the response, for the rest of us who are not soldiers and have no cruise missiles, we had candles, and we lit them on Friday night in an act of mourning, and an act of war ... If we falter, they win, even if they never plant another bomb. So after the early helplessness—What can I do? I've already given blood—people started to realize that what they could do was exactly, as precisely as possible, whatever they would have done if all this hadn't happened ... It will take us months, years, to understand what has been changed by this, and how. Irony is no longer safe for comics; comedy itself is in tears. Three decades of popular culture have turned into period pieces: *Working Girl* ... and *Sex and the City* and *The Sopranos* and every opening shot of the tip of the island that was designed to say, "We're in Manhattan right now." Now we will see those shots and know they came Before. —NANCY GIBBS

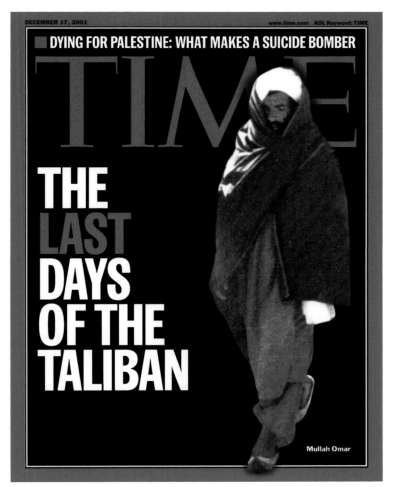

Manhunt
December 17, 2001

In a campaign that lasted just weeks, the U.S. and its allies overthrew the Taliban regime in Afghanistan, but Osama bin Laden remained elusive.

Last week the hush was shattered by the blasts of hundreds of American bombs, the rattle of Kalashnikovs and the roar of tanks and pickup trucks carrying about 1,000 anti-Taliban soldiers into the Tora Bora cave complex to deliver a final reckoning to Osama bin Laden ... But things did not proceed quite as planned. On Thursday, 60 fighters ventured past a front line near the village of Melawa and took up positions on a hill that offered a clear line of fire. Moments later al-Qaeda snipers protecting bin Laden began firing from a crest above. Six men were gravely wounded ...

For the Taliban, for Osama bin Laden and his dwindling legion of lieutenants, Tora Bora is the last sanctuary. The Taliban's barbaric and medieval rule unraveled for good last week as the regime's soldiers fled from Kandahar, their last stronghold. Some skulked back to their home villages with the idea of starting new lives. Others, like Mullah Mohammed Omar, the Taliban's supreme leader, went missing. As a fresh power struggle raged in Kandahar and a new Afghan government prepared to take over in Kabul, the black turbans and medieval strictures of Taliban rule began to seem like a bad dream. —ROMESH RATNESAR

A Nation on Edge
February 24, 2003
Photograph by Gregory Heisler

As the U.S. prepared for war against Iraq (even though its ties to 9/11 and al-Qaeda were nonexistent), Americans seemed to see terrorist threats everywhere.

On Sept. 11, a disaster brought us together, but anticipating the next one seems to be doing the reverse. All around the country, people see the same facts and run in opposite directions. You can find panic in a small Tennessee town and insouciance in midtown Manhattan, and vice versa. Some view taking precautions as a patriotic duty; others see it as complicity in a fearful campaign they want no part of. For some, the prospect of war with Iraq makes everything more frightening—why take action that might cause our enemies to multiply? For others, it seems only more necessary as the threat feels more real and the enemy more cunning. Some fear that the government is not doing enough to equip the police or seal the borders; others believe that it is doing too much, shredding civil liberty in pursuit of security. Some people are relieved that at least the intelligence agencies seem to be sharing some of what they know; others suspect that they are just trying to cover themselves because of how much they don't. —NANCY GIBBS

Shock and Awe
March 31, 2003
Photograph by Ramzi Haidar

The Bush Administration pushed the U.S. to war with Iraq on the basis of an argument that Saddam Hussein was pursuing weapons of mass destruction.

F--- Saddam. We're taking him out." Those were the words of President George W. Bush, who had poked his head into the office of National Security Adviser Condoleezza Rice. It was March 2002, and Rice was meeting with three U.S. Senators, discussing how to deal with Iraq through the United Nations, or perhaps in a coalition with America's Middle East allies. Bush wasn't interested. He waved his hand dismissively, recalls a participant, and neatly summed up his Iraq policy in that short phrase ... The U.S. has launched a war unlike any it has fought in the past. This one is being waged not to defend against an enemy that has attacked the U.S. or its interests but to pre-empt the possibility that one day it might do so. The war has turned much of the world against America ... The hope is that the Middle East, a cockpit of instability for decades, will eventually settle into habits of democracy, prosperity and peace. The risks are that Washington's rupture with some of its closest allies will deepen and that the war will become a cause for which a new generation of terrorists can be recruited. —ROMESH RATNESAR

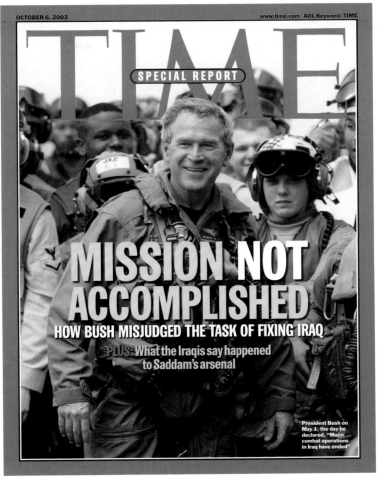

Saddam Hussein Ousted

April 21, 2003

Illustration by Roberto Prada

After only 21 days, U.S. and allied forces toppled Saddam's regime, but it was already becoming clear that winning the peace was going to be much harder than winning the war.

But the rebirth of a nation is messy and humbling, especially when it was brought about through battle. Many Iraqis were celebrating, but some were still shooting; some were pausing to rejoice on their way toward revenge. Baghdad was free for exactly one day before the first suicide bomber appeared; a few days later, 40 more bomb-stuffed vests were found in an elementary school. The Red Cross had to suspend operations after one worker was killed in cross fire, and there was little use rushing medicine into hospitals that had been stripped by looters to their last light bulb. Even as the other cities toppled—first Kirkuk, then Mosul—there were still people in Iraq who had nothing to do but fight and look for a chance to ambush a soldier with his guard down. From the comfort of their living rooms, Americans watched NBC broadcast a fire fight outside Baghdad so fierce that one wounded soldier was still firing from his stretcher, and the chaplain had to grab a rifle. Some of the biggest air strikes of the entire war came the night after Baghdad fell. —NANCY GIBBS

What Went Wrong?

October 6, 2003

Photograph by Brooks Kraft

Five months after the President declared victory, TIME looked at the mess Iraq had become and the Bush Administration's reluctant realization that the nation was in danger of failing utterly.

The reconstruction of Iraq has proved far more difficult than any official assumed it would be. Since May 1, 170 U.S. soldiers have died in Iraq, as sporadic guerrilla attacks have continued. Two potential leaders of the new Iraq— Ayatollah Mohammed Baqir al-Hakim and Akila al-Hashimi, a member of the U.S.-appointed Governing Council in Iraq— have been assassinated ... Over the long, hot Iraqi summer, frequent power cuts made life unbearable for millions, while the flow of oil, which the Administration had hoped would fund Iraq's reconstruction, was, on some days, less than half what it had been before the war. And despite five months of searching, the weapons of mass destruction (WMD), whose possession by Saddam Hussein had been the principal reason advanced by Bush for the war, are still nowhere to be found ... In the latest Gallup poll, Bush's approval ratings dropped to 50%, the lowest since right before Sept. 11, 2001. Some critics of the Administration's hard-liners pull no punches. "It reminds me of Vietnam," says retired Marine General Anthony Zinni, who headed the U.S. Central Command from 1997 to 2000. —MICHAEL ELLIOTT

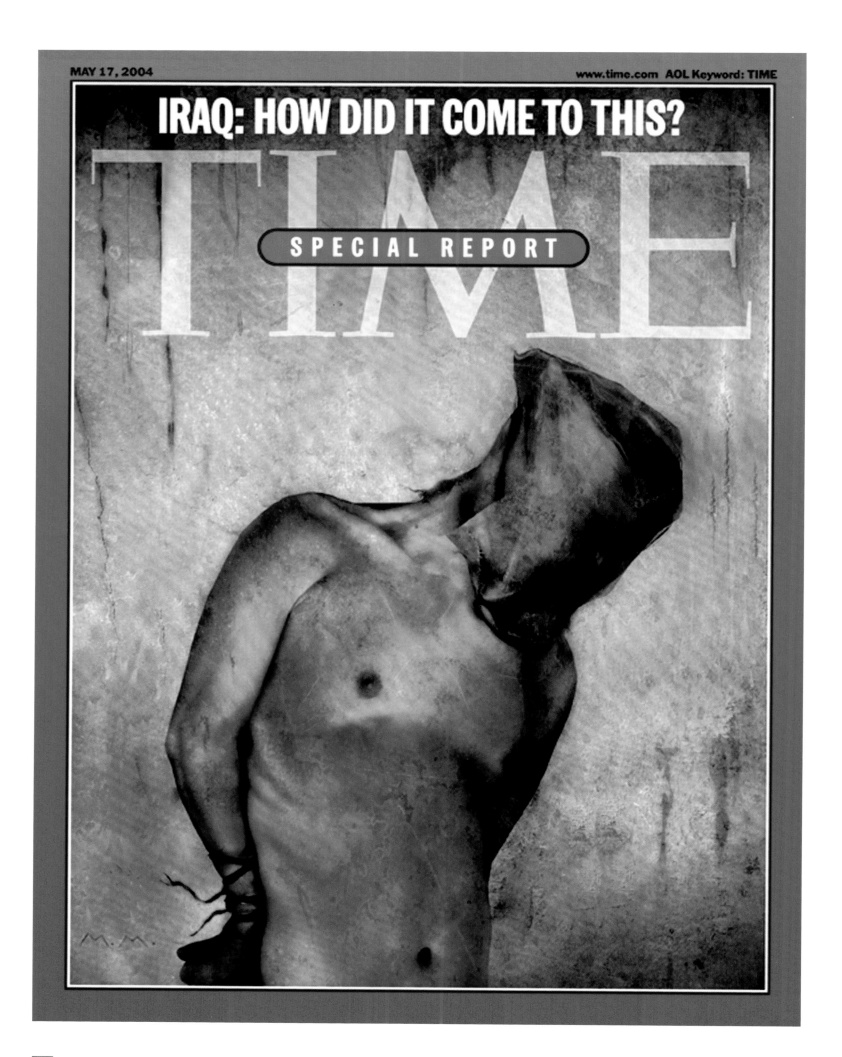

Guantánamo
June 20, 2005
Photograph by David Moore

To get Mohammed al-Qahtani—known as the 20th hijacker—to talk, the U.S. used a wide range of sometimes brutal tactics. A TIME report revealed how Gitmo interrogations really worked.

More than a year later, after al-Qahtani had been captured in Afghanistan and transferred to Gitmo's Camp X-Ray, his interrogation was going nowhere. So in late November 2002, according to an 84-page secret interrogation log obtained by TIME, al-Qahtani's questioners switched gears. They suggested to their captive that he had been spared by Allah in order to reveal the true meaning of the Koran and help bring down bin Laden. During a routine check of his medical condition, a sergeant approached al-Qahtani and whispered in his ear, "What is God telling you right now? Your 19 friends died in a fireball and you weren't with them. Was that God's choice? Is it God's will that you stay alive to tell us about his message?" At that point, the log states, al-Qahtani threw his head back and butted the sergeant in the eye. Two MPs wrestled al-Qahtani to the ground. The sergeant crouched down next to the thrashing terrorist, who tried to spit on him. The sergeant's response: "Go ahead and spit on me. It won't change anything. You're still here. I'm still talking to you and you won't leave until you've given God's message." —ADAM ZAGORIN AND MICHAEL DUFFY

The Abu Ghraib Scandal
May 17, 2004
Illustration by Matt Mahurin

News that the U.S. military was abusing Iraqi prisoners at the same notorious prison that Saddam Hussein had made a center of torture shocked the world.

Haider Sabbar Abed al-Abbadi kept his shame to himself until the world saw him stripped naked, his head in a hood, a nude fellow prisoner kneeling before him simulating oral sex. "That is me," he claims to a TIME reporter ... "I felt a mouth close around my penis. It was only when they took the bag off my head that I saw it was my friend ..." On that awful November night, four months after his arrest, he thought he and six other prisoners were being punished for a petty scuffle.

They were herded into Cellblock 1A. The guards cut off their clothes, and then the degrading demands began. Through it all, al-Abbadi knew the Americans were taking photos ... He says he is the hooded man in the picture in which a petite, dark-haired woman in camouflage pants and an Army T shirt gives a thumbs-up as she points to a prisoner's genitals. He says he was in the pileup of naked men ordered to lie on the backs of other detainees as a smiling soldier in glasses looks on. And al-Abbadi says he was told to masturbate, though he was too scared to do more than pretend, as a female soldier flaunted her bare breasts. —JOHANNA MCGEARY

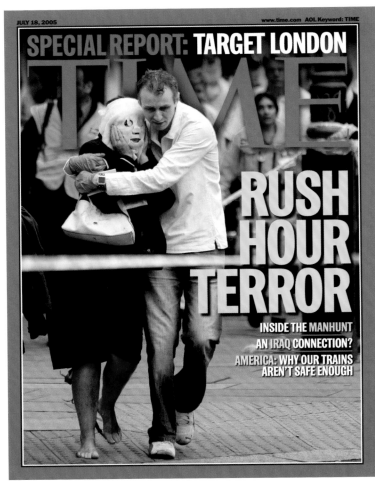

The London Attacks
July 18, 2005

An al-Qaeda plot struck right at the heart of London. It was a sobering reminder that after four years of war in Iraq and Afghanistan, the terrorist ring still possessed the ability to hit back.

As George Psaradakis, 49, drove a No. 30 double-decker red bus through the streets of London last Thursday, there were signs that something was wrong ... Thousands of commuters had left Underground train stations and were milling about the streets looking for alternative ways to get to work. Few of them had any idea of the scale of the devastation below: moments before, three bombs had gone off in the space of a minute on London's Underground railway. Psaradakis, whose bus was packed, had been forced to divert from the main roads into the leafy squares of Bloomsbury, home to the colleges of the University of London. At 9:47 he stopped his bus in Tavistock Square to get directions. Just then, Lou Stein, an American theater producer who has lived in London for 20 years, heard a tremendous thud from his apartment 100 yards away and ran outside ... The top of the bus was lifted off, like the top of a tin can that's just been ripped open. There was smoke everywhere ..." Psaradakis survived, but at least 13 others died in the blast. —MICHAEL ELLIOTT

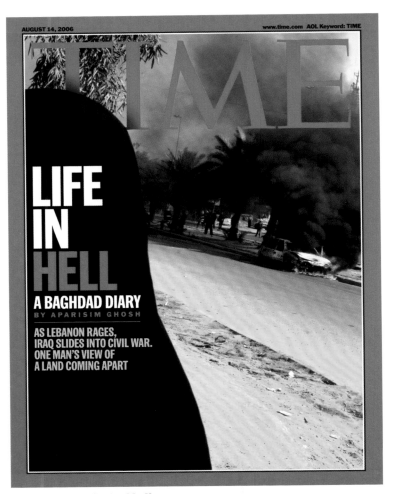

Baghdad: Life in Hell
August 14, 2006
Photograph by Franco Pagetti

In more than 20 trips to Baghdad, TIME's Bobby Ghosh navigated countless perils. In 2006, his personal story brought a unique immediacy to the ruined nation's dysfunction.

A knot begins to form in my stomach exactly at 8 a.m., when I step into the small Fokker F-28 jet that will take me and 50 other passengers from Amman, Jordan, to Baghdad. I know what lies ahead: an hour's uneventful flying over unchanging desert, followed by the world's scariest landing—a steep, corkscrewing plunge into what used to be Saddam Hussein International Airport. Then an eight-mile drive into the city along what's known as the Highway of Death. I've made this trip more than 20 times since Royal Jordanian's civilian flights started three years ago, and you'd expect it would get easier. But the knot takes hold in my stomach every time ... The only thing worse than the view from the window is being seated next to someone who hasn't taken the flight before ... In 2004, a retired American cop wouldn't stop screaming "Oh, God! Oh, God!" I finally had to slap him on the face— on instructions from the flight attendant. —BOBBY GHOSH

The Fort Hood Massacre
November 23, 2009

The Plight of Afghan Women
August 9, 2010
Photograph by Jodi Bieber

When Major Nidal Malik Hasan, a Muslim U.S. Army psychiatrist, shot and killed 13 people at Fort Hood, Texas, TIME reckoned with the likelihood that the military had a radical jihadist in its midst.

The image of 18-year old Aisha, disfigured by her husband's family, became an omen of what may befall Afghanistan's women if the Taliban return to power.

What a surprise it must have been when Major Nidal Malik Hasan woke up from his coma to find himself not in paradise but in Brooke Army Medical Center, deep in the heart of Texas, under security so tight that there were armed guards patrolling both the intensive-care unit and checkpoints at the nearest freeway off-ramp. This was not the finalé he had scripted when he gave away all his earthly goods—his desk lamp and air mattress, his frozen broccoli and spinach, his copies of the Koran. He had told his imam he was planning to visit his parents before deploying to Afghanistan. He did not mention that his parents had been dead for nearly 10 years ... And who denied him his martyrdom? That would be Kimberly Munley, the SWAT-team markswoman nicknamed Mighty Mouse, who with her partner ran toward the sound of gunshots at the Soldier Readiness Center, where men and women about to deploy gather for vaccinations and eye exams. It's practically been a motto stitched on their sleeves—"Better to fight the terrorists there than here"—except now they were at home, and there was one of their own, a U.S. officer, jumping up, shouting "God is great" in a language he could barely speak and then opening fire. —NANCY GIBBS

As the war in Afghanistan enters its ninth year, the need for an exit strategy weighs on the minds of U.S. policymakers. The publication of some 90,000 documents on the war by the freedom-of-information activists at WikiLeaks ... has intensified international debate. Though the documents mainly consist of low-level intelligence reports, taken together they reveal a war in which a shadowy insurgency shows determined resilience; where fighting that enemy often claims the lives of innocent civilians; and where supposed allies, like Pakistan's security services, are suspected of playing a deadly double game ... As frustrations mount over a war that even top U.S. commanders think is not susceptible to a purely military solution, demands intensify for a political way out of the quagmire. Such an outcome, it is assumed, would involve a reconciliation with the Taliban or, at the very least, some elements within its fold. But without safeguards, that would pose significant risks to the very women U.S. Secretary of State Hillary Clinton promised in May not to abandon. "We will stand with you always," she said to female members of Karzai's delegation in Washington. Afghan women are not convinced. They fear that in the quest for a quick peace, their progress may be sidelined. —ARYN BAKER

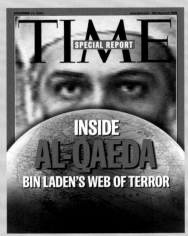

OCTOBER 1, 2001   NOVEMBER 12, 2001

NOVEMBER 26, 2001

On the Trail of Osama bin Laden

For Americans, one man became the face of terrorism after Sept. 11, 2001: Osama bin Laden. The son of a successful Saudi construction magnate, bin Laden founded a small, decentralized yet fanatical Islamic group called al-Qaeda in the waning days of the Soviet misadventure in Afghanistan. It pursued the establishment of a caliphate with a ruthlessness and zealotry never before seen. Dedicated to resisting Western dominance, bin Laden and al-Qaeda claimed to have been incensed over the stationing of U.S. troops on the holy ground of Saudi Arabia. Even before 9/11, al-Qaeda waged its war of terrorism, bombing U.S. embassies in Kenya and Tanzania in 1998 and the U.S.S. *Cole* in 2000 while it was docked in Yemen. Bin Laden had been on TIME's radar even earlier. In 1996, correspondent Scott Macleod interviewed him in Sudan, where the future mastermind of 9/11 waxed piously on the the *mujahedin* holy war against the Soviets in Afghanistan. "In our religion, there is a special place in the hereafter for those who participate in jihad," bin Laden said. "One day in Afghanistan was like 1,000 days of praying in an ordinary mosque."

After 9/11, America both pursued and feared bin Laden, recycling tales of his hiding out in a cave attached to a dialysis machine or plotting new attacks on the U.S. and its allies. Expecting U.S. intelligence to hunt him down in Afghanistan sooner rather than later, TIME asked illustrator Tim O'Brien to prepare an *X* cover—the same iconic treatment it gave in World War II to the fall of Hitler and Japan. But it would be nearly a decade after the attacks for the U.S. to track down bin Laden, in Abbottabad, Pakistan. As TIME reported in the issue with the cover that had waited years to run, "Bin Laden was shot in the head and in the chest. One of bin Laden's wives confirmed his identity even as a photograph of the dead man's face was relayed for examination by a facial-recognition program." On television on May 1, 2011, President Barack Obama declared, "We got him."

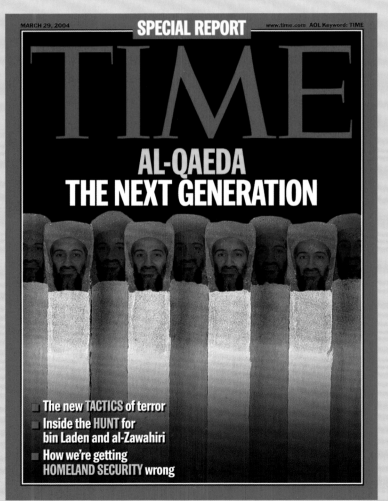

MARCH 29, 2004

OCTOBER 28, 2002

NOVEMBER 25, 2002

MAY 20, 2011

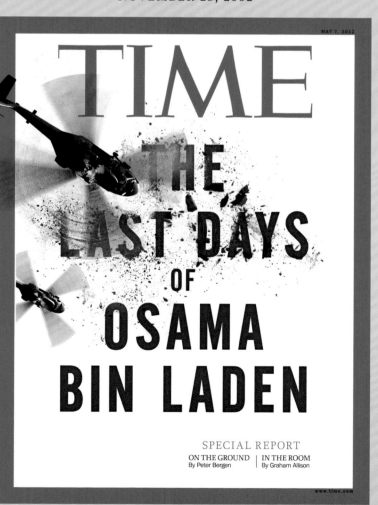

MAY 7, 2012

☐ Builders & Titans

In 1995, Microsoft chairman Bill Gates demonstrated the storage capacity of CD-ROMs by scaling hard copies of what one disc could hold

Photograph by Louie Psihoyos

TWENTY CENTS

MAY 15, 1950

TIME

THE WEEKLY NEWSMAGAZINE

ARTZYBASHEFF

WORLD & FRIEND
Love that piaster, that lira, that tickey, and that American way of life.

$6.00 A YEAR

(REG. U. S. PAT. OFF.)

VOL. LV NO. 20

I N JAPANESE, THE WORD *TAIKUN* MEANS "GREAT LORD," AND IT WAS used as an honorific for the shogun and men distinguished for military might as well as noble birth. In the U.S. in the 1920s, a vibrant and often ruthless mercantile class was winning power and influence through risky financial endeavors as well as inherited wealth. TIME's founders, Henry Luce and Briton Hadden, called them tycoons—one of several foreign words, like *pundit* (from Hindi) and *kudos* (from Greek) to which the magazine gave fresh currency. *Tycoon* soon became shorthand for a businessman at the height of

his powers. The second decade of U.S. industrialization, the era in which TIME was born, was full of tobacco tycoons, sugar tycoons and railway tycoons, all of whom appeared in the pages of the magazine. They were the personages in Luce's vision of a world shaped by the ambitions of extraordinary individuals, the men—and they have been almost exclusively men—whose names have become signposts in the story of American business: Henry Ford, John D. Rockefeller, the J.P. Morgans (father and son).

Businessmen weren't just getting rich; they were saving the world. The younger Morgan had become America's designated savior for Germany, which was about to default on the onerous debts inflicted on it as punishment for losing World War I. TIME—like the rest of the U.S.—was fascinated by how the tycoons made their money as well as by how they lived. Its first cover story on John D. Rockefeller, the richest man in the world, detailed the daily routine of a man who had been retired for three decades: it included walking about his estate singing to himself in "a rather pleasant baritone."

Then the Depression came, and the rich weren't the solution. Luce's vision was difficult to reconcile with Franklin D. Roosevelt's New Deal, which was repairing the social and economic fabric of the country through a series of reforms that involved mere bureaucrats—not tycoons—in the Works Progress Administration, the Farm Security Administration and the Social Security Administration. A 1937 story on the issuing of the first Social Security numbers pointedly said they were called accounts, "lest workers feel they are being numbered like convicts."

The world that emerged after the Depression and World War II provided TIME with a new canvas for depicting commerce and industry, a cosmos not of re-emerging tycoons but of titanic corporations. The postwar boom was created not only by men but also by corporations that embodied the American ideal as the country—all of it—sought to become richer. As consumer-oriented companies competed to reach the young, optimistic population, TIME emerged as a channel into the heart of the new mass market. The magazine became an emblem of the aspiring American middle class, embodying its sensibility and documenting how its tastes were having a global impact. In the cover story on Coca-Cola, TIME celebrated the soft-drink company's "peaceful near-conquest of the world." The story described Coke as

a different kind of American success story, built on salesmanship rather than the country's rich natural resources. "Where there is no desire for it, Coke creates desire. Its advertising, which garnishes the world from the edge of the Arctic to the Cape of Good Hope, has created more new appetites and thirsts in more people than an army of dancing girls bearing jugs of wine ..." It was a particularly American dream, built on aspiration and flim-flam, a desire for upward mobility combined with the potent hocus-pocus of salesmanship, design and, of course, technological progress. In Coke's case, "built on a little water, sugar and flavoring."

Coke was just one of the great American brands that came to dominate global business in the 1950s and '60s. TIME pulled back the curtain on personalities—the new tycoons—that built many of them: Harlow Curtice styling the 1955 Chevy into an icon of youth, Walt Disney creating a modern mythology from his mass-produced cartoon menagerie, Bowman Gray of R.J. Reynolds Tobacco defying mounting scientific evidence to celebrate the flavors of cigarette smoking with an audacious advertising campaign.

Eventually, however, the rest of the world began to catch up. Saudi Arabia would use its oil wealth to get its way politically and diplomatically. Japan Inc., led by Sony's Akio Morita, would stun the world with innovations and clever marketing of high-quality, portable electronics. Europe would emerge as a solid counterbalance to the weight of U.S. capital. And by the late 20th century, China began to lead a host of other countries into fierce competition for the top ranks in trade and industry.

America still produced its singularly colorful tycoons. Sam Walton turned a small-town Ozarks retailer into the world's biggest private employer (with 2 million employees), and Oprah Winfrey, born to a single mother, became the most powerful woman in the entertainment industry. The digital revolution built enormous fortunes and legends around Microsoft's Bill Gates and Apple's Steve Jobs. But the U.S. has been racked by the greed of the financial sector, which has contributed to cataclysmic cycles of boom and bust, as the pursuit of wealth—on all social levels—has taken priority over everything else. Even in the eyes of Warren Buffett, perhaps the most successful investor of the 20th century, that is not sustainable. "We can rise to any challenge," he said, "but not if people feel we're in a plutocracy." It is the world the tycoons have wrought. —JYOTI THOTTAM

Henry Ford
July 27, 1925
Portrait by S.J. Woolf

Almost 17 years after the Model T's intro-duction and just before his 62nd birthday, Ford was the subject of a TIME *cover.*

Mr. Ford does not like modern dances, thinks the old ones will come back, is preparing a book to show why. He has also written a pamphlet against cigarette smoking and a discourse on why English should be a universal language. He collects American antiques. He has built a golf course for his employees and plays on it. He has opinions on politics; opinions and a hand in business. Age (62) cannot wither his infinite variety. He is always riding in many vehicles … Aeronautics. "I experimented twelve years with my motor car before I was convinced that it represented a lasting and stable product for the public. I have now only started to experiment with the airplane. And let me tell you that the commercial airplane is as yet a considerable distance of being a success."

John D. Rockefeller
May 21, 1928
Portrait by S.J. Woolf

The founder of Standard Oil was the world's richest man. By the time this story ran, he had been in retirement for 31 years.

Arises at 7 a.m., takes needle shower, carefully chooses clothes from large wardrobe … Appears at breakfast table promptly at 8, sips orange juice and coffee, eats a fair amount of oatmeal, nibbles bits of toast, rolls, eggs, bacon; gives new dimes or nickels to servants and guests. He has distributed some 22,000 of these gleaming coins in the last two decades. To those he sees every day, he usually gives nickels; to others, dimes … After breakfast, he remains at the table, reads out loud from *Sunlit Days* (a poem and a prayer for each day of the year). Then a guest reads to him from *My Daily Meditation* by the late Rev. J. H. Jowett and from a modern version of the New Testament … He reads the New York *Times,* consults with his secretary, strolls about the estate whistling and singing to himself. His voice is a rather pleasant baritone … Golf follows, usually nine holes. His best score, made at Pocantico when he was 65, was a 39. His average is between 45 and 55.

J. Pierpont Morgan Jr.
February 25, 1929
Portrait by S.J. Woolf

Often compared with his father, who helped create General Electric, "Jack" Morgan consolidated a banking empire.

In the early primeval times of Big Business the Elder Morgan was simply the biggest, most voracious brontosaurus. In the present years of Titanic Business it is the Morgan hand in a velvet glove which directs a fiscal juggernaut capable of thundering over mere business brontosauri. Il Magnifico in all his purple pride never had to do with a loan of more than 200 million dollars; but austere, reserved, patrician "Mr. Morgan" quietly arranged the Anglo-French loan of a half-billion dollars in 1915. It is said that the Allies wanted to borrow a round billion at that time; but Mr. Morgan led the British fiscal representative, Lord Reading, into his sanctum, and thoughtfully observed: "Reading, I wouldn't ask a billion if I were you. I think you'd best limit the issue to half a billion."

William Paley
September 19, 1938
Photograph by Paul Dorsey

The network in question consisted of radio stations, not yet television, but Paley was laying the foundations for a media empire of tremendous longevity.

Ten years ago, when Congress Cigar Co.'s Son & Heir Bill Paley became CBS's 27-year-old president, it was a puny network. Although irreverent young employees stealthily called him Pale Billy (purely a trick of transposition, for he likes hot countries, bright sunlight, is usually healthily bronzed), in three months he tightened CBS's contracts with its affiliates, gathered 22 more stations into his network, refused to sell CBS to Paramount Publix Corp. for $1,500,000. Nine months later he sold Paramount Publix a half interest for $5,000,000, within three years bought the half interest back for $5,200,000 ... Youngest and oldest chief executive in the network business, he has come a long way from cigars. He now smokes cigarettes.

Abdul Aziz ibn Saud
March 5, 1945
Portrait by Ernest Hamlin Baker

The ruthless ruler of a young but religiously conservative nation, the King was also one of the canniest businessmen and used oil wealth to stabilize Saudi Arabia.

He is also fond of automobiles, telephones and radios, all of which he has put to good use in unifying the scattered tribes in the wastes of his domain. When Ibn Saud introduced the telephone, some of Saudi Arabia's more fanatical isolationists cried that it was a work of the devil. Replied Ibn Saud: "Of a certainty if it is the work of the devil, the holy words of the Koran will not pass over it." Holy words passed over the new line in Riyadh to Mecca; the objectors subsided. The money for these innovations comes largely from two sources: 1) the income derived from pilgrims to Islam's Holy City, Mecca (where Mohammed was born); 2) his revenues from a great oil concession granted twelve years ago to the principal U.S. agency in his country, the Arabian-American Oil Co. (owned fifty-fifty by Texas Co. and Standard Oil Co. of California). The company is just getting substantial production (57,000 bbl. daily) and should do very well with or without the projected U.S. oil line across Saudi Arabia to the Mediterranean. —JOHN BARKHAM AND MAX WAYS

George Merck
August 18, 1952
Portrait by Boris Chaliapin

The huge expansion of the pharmaceutical industry was the result of the years he presided over Merck & Co., originally founded as the U.S. arm of his German family's firm.

The arsenal from which these new weapons come is as far removed from the apothecary's pestle and mortar as penicillin is from a medicine man's snake-oil elixir. In Merck's four producing plants in the U.S. (Rahway, N.J., Danville, Pa., Elkton, Va., and South San Francisco), almost 2,000 chemical operators perform their mysteries in a weird, surrealistic jungle assembled by welders, riveters and pipe fitters. Rising from the floor, which may cover an acre or more, are the great boles of the chemical forest: row on row of cylindrical stills and vats. Around and among them is a secondary growth of filters and crystallization tanks, their clusters broken by the stumps of centrifuges. Dangling like lianas from the upper branches are hundreds or thousands of pipes, from an inch to a foot in diameter, marked (usually at eye level) by a cluster of iron flowers—the handwheels of the valves. Everywhere there are pipes and more pipes. Like many another modern industry, the manufacture of the purest and most delicately constructed drugs takes place in a pipefitter's wonderland. —GILBERT CANT

Harlow Curtice
November 1, 1954
Portrait by Boris Chaliapin

TIME *was on hand to watch the CEO of General Motors— nicknamed Red—go over a proposed design for a new Chevy prior to its $300 million launch.*

Red Curtice had followed the progress of the new Chevrolet from first sketches to drafting board to quarter-scale model to clay mockup with all the anxious looks a young father-to-be bestows upon his wife. Now he slowly circled the car, squinting at its lines and lightly touching its smooth surface. When his eye lighted on a horizontal crease in the molding of the trunk, he shook his head. "That's not good," said Curtice. "You'll see that it casts a shadow on the bottom half of the lid. That shadow makes the car look higher and narrower. What we want is a lower automobile that looks wider." At the side of the car, Curtice stopped again. Why should the belt line (i.e., the line formed by the bottom of the windows) be straight and unbroken? When a designer explained that only the two-door models would have a racy dip in the belt line, Curtice suggested: "Don't you think we might try it on a four-door type, too?" —OSBORN ELLIOTT

Walt Disney

December 27, 1954
Portrait by Boris Chaliapin

The man who created Mickey Mouse—and built the Magic Kingdom with the rodent—was both a dreamer (employing the likes of Salvador Dalí at one point) and a practical businessman.

Like most self-educated men, Disney pulled himself up from nowhere by grabbing the tail of a runaway idea and hanging on for dear life. Even now, in middle life (he is 54) he seems to most acquaintances a "cheerful monomaniac." He works at least 14 hours a day, never takes a vacation ("I get enough vacation from having a change of troubles") ... Lacking a formal education ... Walt has few formal habits of thought. He cannot bear to read a book ("I'd rather have people tell me things"). Yet his intellectual weakness only throws him back the more strongly on his principal strength: a deep, intuitive identification with the common impulses of common people. A friend explains that he is really "a sort of visionary handyman, who has built a whole industry out of daydreams. He has that rarest of qualities, the courage of his doodles." —BRADFORD DARRACH JR.

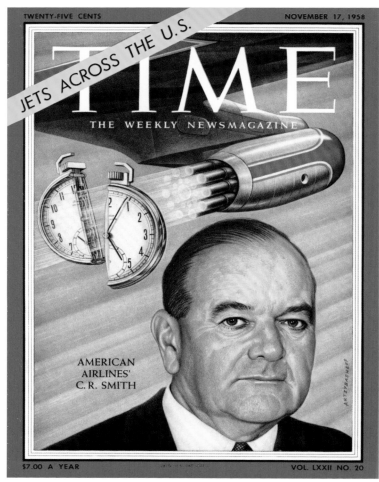

C.R. Smith
November 17, 1958
Portrait by Boris Artzybasheff

The CEO of American Airlines turned his company into the major player in the industry after breaking Pan Am's monopoly of international commercial aviation.

A big (6 ft. 1 in., 192 lbs.) gruff Texan, Smith has become a living legend in U.S. aviation. With the shrewd calculation of a gambler, the financial sagacity of a banker and the dedication of a monk, he has propelled American Airlines into first place in the industry—and in the process has done more than any other man to improve the service and standards of U.S. airlines ... Smith has some of the oddest working habits of any man in top industry. His typewriter is the most important piece of equipment American owns, and Smith pecks away at it for hours on end. He writes all his own speeches, many of American's institutional ads and stockholders' reports. Though he had the same secretary for 25 years (until she retired recently), he never let her write more than a handful of letters a year ... But the chief product of Smith's typewriter is his short, sharp memos, which rarely exceed a page. They cover everything from ideas on a new plane American is considering buying to complaints about an airliner's coffee, are dispatched in a steady stream to every corner of American's operations. —ED JAMIESON

The Telephone Man
February 23, 1959
Illustration by Boris Artzybasheff

To Americans, for decades telephones meant Ma Bell—the enormous corporation AT&T, which would be broken up by an antitrust decision in 1982.

For most Americans, the telephone is synonymous with the American Telephone & Telegraph Co., the colossus that embraces 20 regional telephone companies in a nationwide Bell System. So thoroughly has the telephone blanketed U.S. life that A. T. & T.'s stock is the world's most famous and most widely held, owned by so many people (1,619,397) that more than 15,000 are named Smith ... The biggest U.S. private enterprise, including its Bell System satellites, has $19,493,951,000 in assets (more than General Motors and Standard Oil Co.—N.J.—combined) and 725,000 employees, operates 54,684,342 telephones, more than 80% of the nation's total. The U.S. watches most of its TV shows over Bell's television coaxial-cable network, which reaches 610 stations in 403 cities, makes all its long-distance calls over 63 million miles of A. T. & T.'s long-distance channels, puts through 2,600,000 overseas calls a year via Bell cables to Britain, Hawaii, Alaska.

TWENTY-FIVE CENTS

APRIL 11, 1960

TIME

THE WEEKLY NEWSMAGAZINE

NUCLEAR TESTING
A Scientific & Political Primer

R. J. REYNOLDS'
BOWMAN GRAY

$7.00 A YEAR

(REG. U.S. PAT. OFF.)

VOL. LXXV NO. 15

Bowman Gray

April 11, 1960

Portrait by Boris Artzybasheff

The R.J. Reynolds Tobacco Co. had been run by Gray's father and uncle before him. At the time this story ran, the company was exulting in the apparent trend against filtered cigarettes.

Reynolds and Bowman Gray, 53, have been stressing taste all along because, says Gray, "people smoke for fun and the simple pleasure of it." Except for occasional flirtations with throat therapy, e.g., in its T-zone ads of the 1940s, the company has largely steered away from the health issue. When the cancer controversy started, it was Bowman Gray, then Reynolds' advertising chief, who concluded that the wisest course was to stick with the theme of taste instead of test tubes, to push flavor before filtration ... Gray—who began smoking when he was nine—is the man with the golden tongue ... Says he: "I do believe that if a cigarette appeals to me—I'm a pretty average fella—it might appeal to the population ..." Through his mouth and into his windpipe he rolled the smoke with all the sober concentration of a wine taster. —ED JAMIESON

U.S. Advertising Executives
October 12, 1962
Backdrop illustration by Richard Vickrey

The Mad Men *era was all too real. Indeed, the television series' office sets would be inspired by the decor of the Time & Life Building, which was built in 1959.*

Madison Avenue," the all-purpose handle for the advertising business, is a street named Desire that starts in Manhattan and wends into every household in the land. Americans are seeing more advertisements now—an average of 1,600 per person per day—and whether they are enjoying them less is a matter of argument. But the inescapable fact is that the pleas and promises of Madison Avenue dance before the eyes of the ordinary American whenever he reads, rides, watches television, strolls down the street or strikes a match. The $12 billion that U.S. business will spend on advertising this year exceeds the gross national products of Austria and Norway combined ... Behind this vast expenditure lies one truth that both critics and practitioners of advertising agree upon: advertising is an aggressively creative force that makes music at the cash registers by stimulating the public's desire to acquire goods. This is an overriding consideration for the nation's businessmen at a time when the U.S. is geared to produce more than it consumes and when nothing would help the economy more than a surge in consumer spending. —MARSHALL LOEB

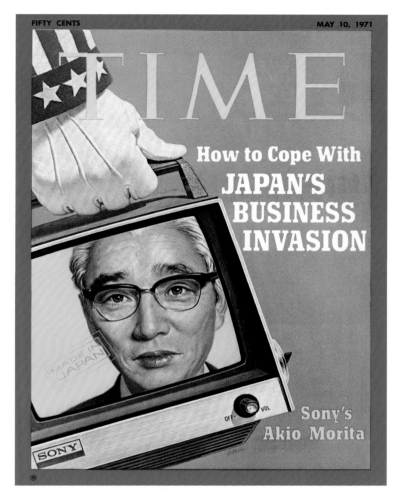

Akio Morita
May 10, 1971
Portrait by Birney Lettick

The age of high-quality, consumer electronics was the result of Morita's inspired work. In 1980, he would revolutionize portable electronics with the Walkman.

In 1953, a young businessman named Akio Morita made his first trip outside Japan to investigate export prospects for his struggling little electronics company. He was dismayed to find that in the sophisticated markets of the U.S. and Europe, the words *Made in Japan* were a mocking phrase for shoddiness. But in The Netherlands, he recalls, "I saw an agricultural country with many windmills and many bicycles, and yet it was producing goods of excellent quality and had worldwide sales power. I thought that maybe we Japanese could do it too ..." Indeed, they could. A month ago, Morita took off on his 94th or 95th transpacific trip (he has lost exact count). This time he came as the self-assured export chief and primary owner of Sony Corp., the firm that as much as any other has made Japanese goods synonymous with high quality as well as low price. —GEORGE CHURCH

Ray Kroc
September 17, 1973
Illustration by Robert Tallon

Kroc began by selling milkshake mixers to the McDonald brothers. But he saw how successful the burger franchises were and just had to buy up the company.

When I got there," says Kroc, "I saw more people waiting in line than I had ever seen at any drive-in. I said to myself: 'Son of a bitch, these guys have got something. How about if I open some of these places?'" Kroc talked the McDonalds into letting him franchise their outlets nationwide. Over the next five years he organized a chain of 228 McDonald's that even by 1960 were grossing $56 million a year ... he called the McDonalds in 1961 and asked them to name a price for selling out everything, including the name ... They did—and, says Kroc, "I dropped the phone, my teeth and everything else. They asked me what the noise was, and I told them it was me jumping out of the 20th floor of the LaSalle-Wacker Building. They wanted $2.7 million ..." Kroc borrowed the money from a group of college endowment funds at what was then an exorbitant price ... Says Kroc: "The $2.7 million ended up costing me $14 million. But I guess there was no way out. I needed the McDonald name and those golden arches. What are you going to do with a name like Kroc?" —DON MORRISON

Sam Walton
June 15, 1992
Photograph by Steven Pumphrey

The legendary founder of the retail giant, who died in April 1992, wrote a homespun memoir that was excerpted by TIME *shortly before its publication.*

A lot of folks ask me, Could a Wal-Mart type story still occur in this day and age? Of course it could happen again. Somewhere out there right now there's someone— probably hundreds of thousands of someones—with good enough ideas to take it all the way. So the next time some overeager, slightly eccentric shopkeeper opens up a business in your neck of the woods, before you write him off too quickly, remember those two old codgers who gave me 60 days to last in my dime store down in Fayetteville. Go check the new store out. See what they've got to offer, see how they treat you, and decide for yourself if you ever want to go back. Because this is what it's really all about. That shopkeeper's success is entirely up to you.

Bill Gates
June 5, 1995
Photograph by Gregory Heisler

While he was Microsoft's boss full time, Gates was one of the most formidable competitors in the world. He was not fond of this cover story.

Gates has amassed a net worth of more than $10 billion, making him either the richest or the second richest man in America, depending on the closing price of his 141 million shares. He was married last year on the Hawaiian island of Lanai; the wedding was attended by publisher Katharine Graham and fellow billionaire Warren Buffett. He is building a $40 million-plus home on suburban Seattle's Lake Washington, with video "walls" to display an ever changing collection of electronic art, a trampoline room with a 25-ft. vaulted ceiling where he can burn off steam, a 20-car underground garage and a trout stream. *The Road Ahead,* a book on which Gates is collaborating with Nathan Myhrvold, a Microsoft group V.P., and journalist Peter Rinearson ... received a $2.5 million advance from Penguin, a record for a book by a few computer geeks ... None of which gives anyone at the Microsoft "campus" in Redmond, Washington, an excuse to relax. One of the most remarkable traits of Microsoft's corporate personality—inherited directly from its restless chairman—is its inability to sit still. —PHILIP ELMER-DEWITT

Steve Case
September 22, 1997
Photo-illustration by James Porto

Case would merge AOL with Time Warner in 2000—a marriage that would sour soon after. Case would leave the company in 2003, and AOL would be spun off in 2009.

Only in the digital age can an outfit go from worst to first so quickly. In the past 24 months, AOL has dodged everything from a Bill Gates bull rush (his Microsoft Network spent millions to compete with AOL) to a tussle with the Internet, whose wide-open spaces threatened to make AOL's narrower "gated community" irrelevant. Case, 39, has been famously (if inadvertently) self-destructive, infuriating AOL members by offering too little capacity and too many headaches. Overeager users have crashed parts of the service twice in the past year by bombarding it with more calls than computers could handle. And as "America On Hold" angered customers, it perplexed Wall Street. Accountants demanded that AOL refigure its books, erasing every dollar of profit the company ever made. It faced potential lawsuits from the attorneys general of 36 states over billing practices. William Razzouk, a hotshot executive from FedEx, split after just five flabbergasted months as president of the service. The company endured, inevitably, a collapse of its too-rich stock price. Twice. —JOSHUA COOPER RAMO

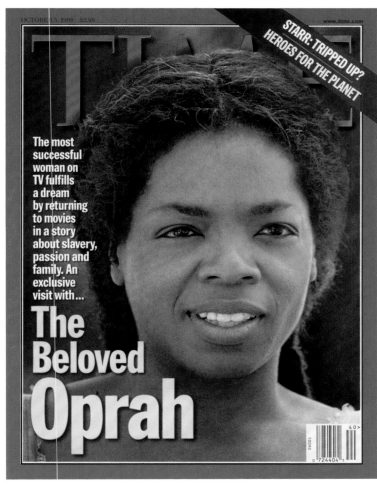

Oprah Winfrey
October 5, 1998
Photograph by Ken Regan

With an estimated net worth of $2.8 billion, Winfrey continues to be an enormous influence on television and entertainment. Her cable network, OWN, however, debuted in 2011 to tepid success.

Supermodels and Nobel prizewinners tend to travel in separate circles, but at a recent party held in honor of Oprah Winfrey in downtown Manhattan, both Toni Morrison and Cindy Crawford were in attendance. The gathering, held at a restaurant where it's difficult to get a reservation unless you call long in advance or are a recent recipient of an MTV Video Music Award, was a starry one. Mariah Carey. Barbara Walters. Maya Angelou. They were all there. Oprah worked the room, shining attention on each guest briefly but brightly, a passing Lexus with her high beams on. The occasion was a celebration of Oprah's star turn in the new film *Beloved* and of her appearance on the cover of *Vogue* magazine. She posed next to a huge blowup of the cover, bathed in camera light. The woman who once dragged a cart of fat into a TV studio to dramatize her battles with obesity, the nappy-headed girl who grew up poor in Kosciusko, Miss., had become a full-fledged movie star. —CHRISTOPHER JOHN FARLEY

Jeff Bezos
December 27, 1999
Photograph by Gregory Heisler

The founder of Amazon was TIME's Man of the Year for 1999. He has broadened the company's reach from books to consumer electronics to streaming video.

Jeffrey Preston Bezos had that same experience when he first peered into the maze of connected computers called the World Wide Web and realized that the future of retailing was glowing back at him. It's not that nobody else noticed—eBay's Pierre Omidyar also knew he was on to something. But Bezos' vision of the online retailing universe was so complete, his Amazon.com site so elegant and appealing, that it became from Day One the point of reference for anyone who had anything to sell online. And that, it turns out, is everyone ... There was a time when Bezos could say, "If I had a nickel for every time a potential investor told me this wouldn't work ..." and then lapse off into head shaking. Now he follows that line with a wild, giggly laugh. No wonder: as of last week, Bezos had 200 billion nickels. —JOSHUA QUITTNER

121

Larry Page, Eric Schmidt and Sergey Brin
February 20, 2006
Photograph by David Strick

The founding duo of Brin and Page became a triumvirate in 2001 with CEO Schmidt. Page replaced Schmidt as CEO in 2011.

Google owes much of its success to the brilliance of Brin and Page, but also to a series of fortunate events. It was Page who, at Stanford in 1996, initiated the academic project that eventually became Google's search engine. Brin, who had met Page at student orientation a year earlier, joined the project early on. Their breakthrough, simply put, was that when their search engine crawled the Web, it did more than just look for word matches; it also tallied and ranked a host of other critical factors like how websites link to one another. That delivered far better results than anything else. Brin and Page meant to name their creation Googol (the mathematical term for the number 1 followed by 100 zeroes), but someone misspelled the word so it stuck as Google. They raised money from prescient professors and venture capitalists, and moved off campus to turn Google into a business. Perhaps their biggest stroke of luck came early on when they tried to license their technology to other search engines, but no one met their price, and they built it up on their own. —ADI IGNATIUS

The Banking Crisis
September 29, 2008
Photo-illustration by Arthur Hochstein

Warren Buffett in 2003 called the derivatives beloved by the banking industry "weapons of financial mass destruction." He was right. But greed was the fuel.

Didn't the folks on Wall Street, who are nothing if not smart, know that someday the music would end? Sure. But they couldn't help behaving the way they did because of Wall Street's classic business model, which works like a dream for Wall Street employees (during good times) but can be a nightmare for the customers. Here's how it goes. You bet big with someone else's money. If you win, you get a huge bonus, based on the profits. If you lose, you lose someone else's money rather than your own, and you move on to the next job. If you're especially smart—like Lehman chief executive Dick Fuld—you take a lot of money off the table. During his tenure as CEO, Fuld made $490 million (before taxes) cashing in stock options and stock he received as compensation. A lot of employees, whose wealth was tied to the company's stock, were financially eviscerated when Lehman bombed. But Fuld is unlikely to show up applying for food stamps. —ANDY SERWER AND ALLAN SLOAN

JANUARY 23, 2012

Election 2012
When super PACs attack **by Michael Scherer**

Joe Klein Can Romney find a common touch?

Mark Halperin The power of Paulitics

George W. Bush grades No Child Left Behind

TIME

The Optimist

Why **Warren Buffett** is bullish on America

BY RANA FOROOHAR

www.time.com

Warren Buffett

January 23, 2012

Photograph by Mark Seliger

The Wizard of Omaha is one of the smartest and most reliable investors in history. He has taken to calling for the wealthy to take on more social and civic responsibility.

Buffett lives not on an isolated island of wealth but in Omaha, in a shingle-roofed five-bedroom house on an unpretentious street that looks as if it might belong to a successful dentist. He bought it for $31,500 in 1958. The corporation he runs, Berkshire Hathaway, owns 76 businesses—from a candy company to an electric utility—that throw off $1 billion a month in free cash, and he holds major stakes in many of the country's biggest blue-chip firms ... Yet aside from his indulgence in private air travel (he named his first jet the *Indefensible*), he estimates his personal yearly expenses to be no more than $150,000. The company canteen in his small office suite, where he has a habit of walking around turning off lights in empty rooms, features a beat-up wooden table, a faux-leather sectional couch and Formica countertops. —RANA FOROOHAR

The Relentless Vision (and Drive) Of Steve Jobs

Few people have altered how Americans imagine visionary businessmen the way Steve Jobs did. The world was transfixed by him, the products he introduced and, just as important, the way he sold them. TIME put him on the cover six times during his life, chronicling his saga at Apple—losing the company, reconquering it. When news of his death arrived as the Oct. 17, 2011, issue was going to press, we rushed to change the cover in tribute to him. As Walter Isaacson, a former managing editor of TIME and Jobs' biographer, summed up that week, "He revolutionized six industries: personal computers, animated movies, music, phones, tablet computing and digital publishing. You might even add a seventh: retailing, which Jobs did not quite revolutionize but did reimagine. Along the way, he produced not only transforming products but also, on his second try, a lasting company, endowed with his DNA, that is filled with creative designers and daredevil engineers who will carry forward his vision."

FEBRUARY 15, 1982 | *Portrait by Alan Magee*

JANUARY 14, 2002 | *Photographs by Michael O'Neill*

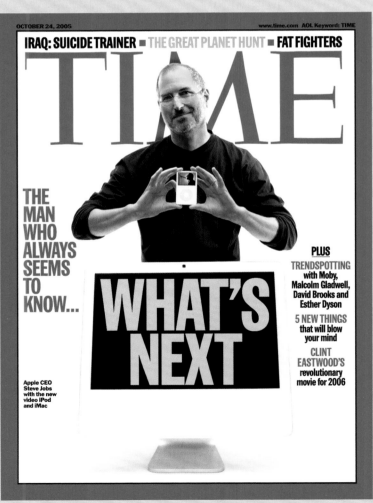

OCTOBER 24, 2005 | *Photograph by Art Streiber*

AUGUST 18, 1997 | *Photograph by Diana Walker*

OCTOBER 18, 1999 | *Photo-illustration by Arthur Hochstein*

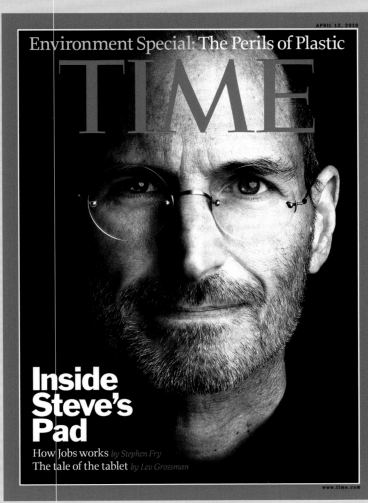

APRIL 12, 2010| *Photograph by Marco Grob*

OCTOBER 17, 2011 | *Photograph by Norman Seeff*

Sport

Muhammad Ali savors
victory over Sonny Liston
in 1965. The two
had engaged in trash
talking in the press for
weeks before the fight

*Photograph by
Neil Leifer*

TWENTY CENTS

SEPTEMBER 22, 1947

TIME

THE WEEKLY NEWSMAGAZINE

JACKIE ROBINSON

He and the boss took a chance.

(Sport)

$6.50 A YEAR

(REG. U. S. PAT. OFF)

VOL. L NO. 12

SPORT WENT INTO WORLD WAR I MOSTLY RURAL, AMATEUR and semi-pro and emerged urban, organized, capitalized and star-powered for the rest of the 20th century and beyond. Technology transformed it: fans who could not be at new arenas like Madison Square Garden and Yankee Stadium could still keep an eye or ear on the games. Daily newspapers published multiple editions, incorporating the finals of late horse races and even partial scores of afternoon ball games. While baseball debuted on the radio in 1921, it took more than a decade before every franchise

participated in the live broadcasts of games, so worried were owners that fans would stop attending in person if they could listen for free. The owners all finally converted when they saw advertising revenues from Gillette and Wheaties roll in. Athletes also cashed in; Babe Ruth endorsed Quaker puffed wheat, Barbasol shaving cream, Lee union suits, Remington shotguns, Louisville Slugger bats and his own line of cotton underwear, even though he never wore anything but silk underwear. Motion-picture cameras began capturing long jumps, batted balls, flying feet, albeit in brief snippets shown in newsreels, a useful medium that met the beginning of its end on May 17, 1939, at a Columbia-Princeton baseball game. That matchup was televised.

After World War II, technology continued to affect sport. Better air travel took baseball to the West Coast, and air-conditioning enabled Houston to build the Astrodome. Migration allowed burgs like Dallas and Atlanta to join the major leagues. Television changed everything. The national audience that was thrilled by the 1958 title game in which the Baltimore Colts beat the New York Giants in sudden-death overtime marked the beginning of a three-way love affair among football, fans and the new medium so deep that today the NFL draft alone has become a three-day television spectacle covered beginning to end by two networks. The national audience that caught the desperately exciting Game 6 of the 1975 World Series between the Boston Red Sox and the Cincinnati Reds led to a revival of the old pastime. The tiny TV audience that was expected to watch the 1979 Daytona 500 was swollen by fans housebound by a mammoth blizzard; they saw one of the most exciting races in history, featuring a last-lap crash and a fistfight, and NASCAR never looked back. Until television, the Olympics were a fringe event, exciting but full of odd sports played by people with long names. But once people could see Abebe Bikila and Jean-Claude Killy and Peggy Fleming and Olga Korbut, there was no ceiling. Now the Games are a global entertainment spectacle.

If sport were only spectacle, everything would be wrestling. But it is also a canvas, a metaphor, a key through which we understand the world. It is no accident that that ideologies of the 20th century were expressed in sport: the supermen of the "racially pure" Nazis, the powerful competitors that the Soviet system groomed from childhood and the meritocracy of the West, with its imperfectly

honored ideal of fair opportunity and clear standards. The son of an Italian immigrant fisherman can become Joe DiMaggio, at least if he can hit. A black college kid can humble an odious dictator, as long as he can outrun the Aryan supermen standing with him on the line. Nine times out of 10, the Soviet hockey machine will beat the college kids—ah, but if the 10th time is in the semifinals, the pros go home. When Jackie Robinson broke baseball's color barrier in 1947, many people attributed his success to strong moral habits and inner reserve, but as TIME reported in its cover story, Dodgers general manager Branch Rickey credited Robinson's athletic ability. "That's what I was betting on," Rickey told TIME. As the magazine described Robinson then, "He looks awkward, but isn't. He stops and starts as though turned off & on with a toggle switch. He seems to hit a baseball on the dead run. Once in motion, he wobbles along, elbows flying, hips swaying, shoulders rocking—creating the illusion that he will fly to pieces with each stride. But once he gains momentum, his shoulders come to order and his feet skim along like flying fish." More than six decades later, Rickey's wager keeps paying off: play the game to the best of your ability, and the rest will follow. In such victories, sport finds its proudly pounding heart.

TIME's founders knew that any publication that aspired to depict the "whirlpool of real life" had to include sports. They made it one of the magazine's six original editorial departments and in its first weeks and months produced cover stories on boxer Jack Dempsey, football star Red Grange and tennis champion Helen Wills. In the decades that followed, some duds have horned in. Spoofy tennis hustler Bobby Riggs made the cover for 1973's silly Battle of the Sexes but not the indomitable, influential Billie Jean King.

In the whirlpool of reality, sport is never played out in a single arena but in several, sometimes simultaneously. Wins and losses on playing fields may somehow end up in courtrooms, in legislative chambers, in stock markets, even on battlefields. The story of Jackie Robinson is inseparable from the civil rights movement. Any thorough understanding of Cold War politics has to include the judging of figure skating and the 1972 Olympics' USA-USSR gold-medal basketball game. As we have seen over and over, in the stories of Joe Louis and Max Schmeling, steroids and Lance Armstrong, Title IX and Mia Hamm, the final score may establish the winner, but it is only part of the tale. —JAMIE MALANOWSKI

JACKIE ROBINSON

SEPTEMBER 22, 1947 | *Portrait by Ernest Hamlin Baker*

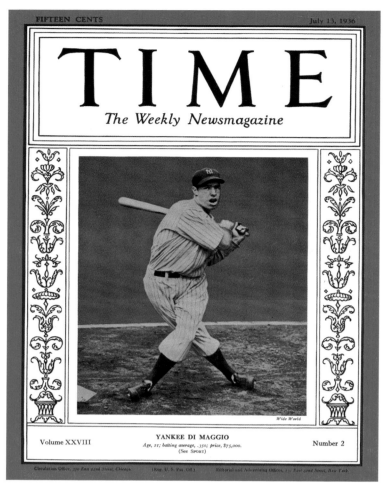

Joe DiMaggio
July 13, 1936

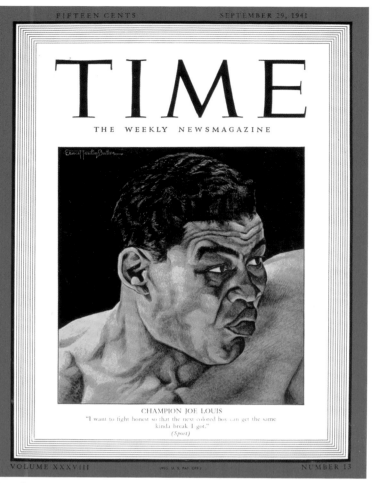

Joe Louis
September 29, 1941
Portrait by Ernest Hamlin Baker

"The American League's most sensational recruit since Ty Cobb" took only until the middle of his rookie season to achieve the first of his two covers for the magazine.

When New York sportswriters first encountered Di Maggio, they mistook for exaggerated evidences of self-assurance his promises to make good which, it became apparent even before he had time to fulfill them, were actually the entirely defensive protestations of a naturally diffident youth who had never before been more than 200 miles from home. Like many young brothers in large Italian families, young Di Maggio is characterized by a solemn, almost embarrassing humility which is exceedingly useful because it causes his elders and superiors to take paternal interest in him. When he was sold to the Yankees [from the San Francisco Seals of the Pacific Coast League], a celebration was arranged at which he was scheduled to talk into a microphone. The Seals' trainer, a onetime featherweight fighter named Bobby Johnson, prepared a speech and drilled it into him, but when the time came Di Maggio merely scuffed his feet, too frightened to open his mouth. He has since become an accomplished radio speaker … When anyone asks Di Maggio where he has been, he has a stock reply: "I've been meandering nonchalantly down the pike."

The first African American to make TIME's cover, "Black Moses" was profiled (in a rather patronizing way) before the 19th defense of his title, against erstwhile yoga student Lou Nova.

He is not only the idol of his race but one of the most respectable prizefighters of all time. From the sorry pass to which a series of second-raters had brought it (Sharkey, Camera, Baer, Braddock), he restored the world's championship to the gate and almost the vigor that it had in Dempsey's day.

He did other notable things: he took on all comers, fought 20 times in four years, was never accused of a fixed fight, an unfair punch, a disparaging comment … All this did not make Joe Louis a dramatic figure but it stored up treasure in Heaven and on earth for Joe Louis and his people. Joe makes no pretense of being a leader of his race. He knows his limitations. He is a good and honest fighter and a simple-minded young man. But intelligent Negroes are grateful to him for remaining his own natural self and thereby doing much to bring about better racial understanding in the U.S.—doing more, some of them say, than all the Negro race-leaders combined. —PEARL KROLL

Mickey Mantle

June 15, 1953
Portrait by Boris Chaliapin

In his third season, TIME wondered, "What does a pitcher throw to Mickey Mantle to get him out?" A decade of damage would pass before a dependable answer emerged.

White Sox Pitcher Billy Pierce, a lefthander, stared moodily down the 60-ft. stretch between the mound and home plate and faced a special problem. At the plate stood a corn-haired youngster just four years out of an Oklahoma high school, with NEW YORK spelled out in block letters on his flannel shirt, a big numeral 7 on his back. As the pitcher went into his windup, Mantle dug his spikes more firmly into the batter's box, hunching his fullback's body (5 ft. 11 in., 195 lbs.) into a deeper crouch. The pitch bulleted toward him at something like 80 m.p.h.—a fast ball, letter high, over the outside corner of the plate.

Mickey Mantle set a muscular chain reaction in motion. Starting in the ankles, rippling through knees, hips, torso, broad shoulders and 17-in. bull neck, he brought his bat around in a perfect arc to meet the ball with a sharp crack. High and deep it sailed. The White Sox centerfielder, playing deep, went a few steps back, then stood, face upturned, as the ball sailed over the fence for a 425-ft. home run. —DOUGLAS S. KENNEDY

Althea Gibson

August 26, 1957
Portrait by Boris Chaliapin

After collecting titles at the French Open and Wimbledon, Althea Gibson appeared in TIME at the start of the 1957 U.S. Open, where her groundbreaking success story continued.

After seven years of trying, Althea Gibson has yet to win the national singles title. As a Negro, she is still only a tolerated stranger in Forest Hills locker rooms ... But now none of that matters. For that Gibson girl has finally whipped the one opponent that could keep her down: her own self-doubt and defensive truculence. At 30, an age when most athletes have eased over to the far slope of their careers, Althea has begun the last, steep climb ... In Paris last year, she won the French championship, her first big-time title ... This year even Wimbledon succumbed, and Althea came home a queen, owner of tennis' brightest crown.

When Althea left for Wimbledon in May, only three close friends were at the airport to wish her luck. When she returned a winner, [the airport] was awash with people. Countless acquaintances suddenly ... crowded close to share her success. [New York City], which had offered Althea's parents a cramped railroad flat in which to raise their children, honored her with a ticker tape parade. And people breathlessly wanted to know how it had felt to shake hands with Queen Elizabeth at Wimbledon and what they had to say to each other. (The Queen: "It was a very enjoyable match, but you must have been very hot on the court." Althea: "I hope it wasn't as hot in the royal box." —RICHARD SEAMON

Jack Nicklaus
June 29, 1962
Portrait by Russell Hoban

For his very first professional victory, at the 1962 U.S. Open, Jack Nicklaus was rewarded with TIME's *cover. An astonishing 17 more championships in major tournaments were to follow.*

The youngest U.S. champion in 39 years, Nicklaus has not yet finished college (he has two quarters to go at Ohio State), but he won last week's Open with a rare blend of mature skill and courage, withstanding pressures fierce enough to unnerve the most seasoned competitor. In a tense, head-to-head play-off before a hostile gallery, Nicklaus beat the world's best-known golfer, Arnold Palmer, grimly refusing to yield to a classic Palmer surge, and winning finally by the comfortable margin of three strokes, 71 to 74. To get into the playoff, Nicklaus had to defeat 148 top-ranked pros and amateurs, including Defending Open Champion Gene Littler. To beat them, he put together rounds of 72, 70, 72, 69 for a 72-hole total of 283 that tied the competitive course record at Pennsylvania's Oakmont Country Club, one of the country's most exacting golf courses. When it was all over and he had beaten Palmer as well, Jack Nicklaus had stamped himself the No. 1 challenger for Palmer's uneasy crown—a confident, talented prodigy whose bold, intimidating game and precocious poise should keep him at the top for many years. —CHARLES PARMITER

Jim Brown
November 26, 1965
Portrait by Henry Koerner

TIME's *profile of Jimmy Brown showed that the great fullback's personality had much in common with his running style: sometimes subtle and complex but usually powerful and direct.*

There are several sides to Jimmy Brown. There is the dignified young executive, of whom the Browns' owner [Art] Modell keeps insisting: "He has no chip on his shoulder." There is the idol of adoring kids, who patiently signs autographs by the hour and tries to answer each of the 150 letters he gets a week. And there is the militant Negro who is the national chairman and chief benefactor ($12,000 worth) of an activist organization called the Negro Industrial and Economic Union, and says: "I am skeptical of white men, because even the best of them want me to be patient, to follow Martin Luther King's advice and turn the other cheek until God knows when."

Last year Brown was deluged by criticism when he spoke out on behalf of the Black Muslims ("The more commotion, the better")—although he does not share their separatist beliefs. Cleveland Sportscaster John Fitzgerald advised him on the air to pipe down and stick to football. Later, button-holing Brown in the Cleveland dressing room, he explained to him: "I've always admired you as a football player, Jim. I've never looked on you as a Negro." "That's ridiculous!" Brown snapped. "You have to look at me as a Negro. Look at me, man! I'm black!" —CHARLES PARMITER

**Tommie Smith and
John Carlos, who placed
first and third in the
200-m race, give the
black-power salute at
the 1968 Olympics**

*Photograph by
John Dominis*

MARCH 1, 1968

TIME

CHICAGO'S
BOBBY HULL
Fastest Shot
In the Fastest Game

Bobby Hull
March 1, 1968
Portrait by LeRoy Neiman

The Canadian, playing for the Chicago Blackhawks, was nicknamed the Golden Jet, distinguished for for his blistering speed and his superhard slap shot.

In the second period at Oakland last week, Bobby drew an awed gasp from the crowd with a blast that hit a defender's stick—and ricocheted all the way up to the 34th row of the stands. Not every opponent who crosses the path of a Hull missile gets off so lightly. Montreal Goalie Lorne (Gump) Worsley, who caught one in the face three years ago, firmly believes that the only reason he was not killed was that he was hit by the flat side rather than the edge ... Bobby is aware that he could permanently injure somebody, but he cannot permit himself to brood about it. "I'm certainly not out to maim anyone," he says, "but the goalies take their chances."

So does Hull. His front teeth sit out the game on a locker-room shelf, and his once handsome profile looks as if it had been rearranged in a demolition derby. His nose has been broken twice, and at last count 200 stitches have been taken to close all the various cuts and slices in his face. —CHARLES PARMITER

Joe Frazier and Muhammad Ali
March 8, 1971
Portrait by Jim Sharpe

After the ruling lords of boxing lifted their ban on Muhammad Ali, imposed after his conviction for draft evasion was reversed, the magazine previewed his much ballyhooed return to the sport to fight the reigning champ, Joe Frazier.

The Ali-Frazier match is the classic ring encounter: boxer against slugger. At 6 ft. 3 in. and 215 lbs., with the elusive speed of a middleweight and a basic hit-and-not-be-hit strategy, Ali may well be the most graceful big man in boxing history. Frazier, who will spot his rival 3¾ in. in height, a crucial 8½ in. in reach, and 10 or so lbs. in weight, is a swarming, wade-in, bullish brawler who willingly takes a punch or ten for the chance to score with his bludgeoning left hook.

The fight has become a classic in another way. Shrewd prefight publicity has turned the billing into Frazier the good citizen v. Ali the draft dodger, Frazier the white man's champ v. Ali the great black hope, Frazier the quiet loner v. Ali the irrepressible loudmouth, Frazier the simple Bible-reading Baptist v. Ali the slogan-spouting Black Muslim. Frazier, who is generally as impassive as a ring post, would have it otherwise, but he has no choice.

Ali, with his usual mix of con and conviction, plays up the disparities at every turn. "I'm not just fightin' one man," he preaches. "I'm fightin' a lot of men, showin' a lot of 'em here is one man they couldn't conquer. My mission is to bring freedom to 30 million black people. I'll win this fight because I've got a cause. Frazier has no cause. He's in it for the money alone." Caught in the crossfire, Frazier usually backs off. "I don't want to be no more than no more than what I am." he says. As a friend puts it, "Joe is just Joe." His feelings on the black movement? "I don't think he's ever thought about it." —RAY KENNEDY

FIFTY CENTS

MARCH 8, 1971

TIME

The $5,000,000 Fighters

Frazier Ali

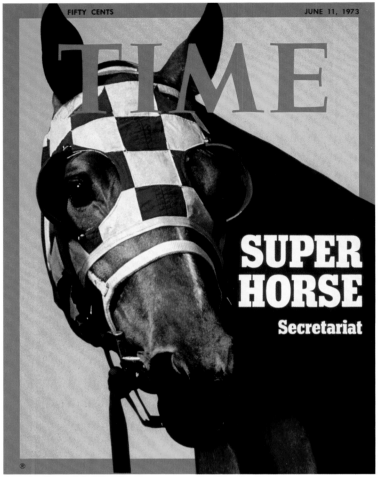

Boris Spassky and Bobby Fischer
July 31, 1972
Sculpture by Stanley Glaubach

Under global scrutiny, Boris Spassky, carrying the weight of the Soviet Union's vaunted chess superiority, faced temperamental American Bobby Fischer in the World Chess Championships.

In the third game [Fischer] seized the initiative on the eleventh move by swinging his knight to the edge of the board, a daring and unorthodox move for a piece that fights best in the center. Spassky pondered for a full 30 minutes, then, just as Fischer hoped he would, countered with a faulty line of attack. Before the game was adjourned for the day, Fischer scribbled his 41st move on a piece of paper, sealed it in an envelope and handed it to the referee. Afterward, he said, "I sealed a cruncher," and then went bowling. Spassky and his team of analysts, meanwhile, studied the position long and hard that night looking for a flaw in Fischer's assault. Next day, when Fischer was late in arriving, the referee opened his envelope and made the move: a bishop check on the king. It was indeed a cruncher, and Spassky, without bothering to reply, tipped over his king to signify his defeat. —RAY KENNEDY

Secretariat
June 11, 1973
Photograph by Ken Regan

TIME *caught up with the thoroughbred days before the Belmont Stakes after he set records in the Kentucky Derby and Preakness. The Triple Crown and immortality were imminent.*

At full speed, this huge and powerful combination of bone, muscle and glistening red chestnut coat covers just an inch short of 25 ft. in a single stride. He has finished first in 11 of 14 races. He has won $804,202 since last July 4—more than any other single competitor in any sport— and in 1972 as a mere two-year-old, he was named horse of the year. Now, having won both the Kentucky Derby and the Preakness this spring, Secretariat is an odds-on favorite to run away with the Belmont Stakes this Saturday and earn his right to the Triple Crown of American horse racing

Victory at Belmont would make Secretariat the first winner of the Triple Crown for three-year-olds since Citation turned the trick a quarter-century ago. He would be only the ninth horse in 91 years to accomplish the grand slam. The odds against any modern horse finishing first in all three races have grown longer every year ... Secretariat started out with about 25,000 contemporaries, all potential competitors. Further, the three major races, bunched within five weeks, present different problems in terms of length and race track surfaces. Yet, the chalk players have such confidence in Secretariat that a $2 bet will likely fetch no more than $2.10 or $2.20 if he wins at Belmont. —ERNEST HAVEMANN

$1.00   AUGUST 2, 1976

Inside: **MARS**

TIME

SHE'S PERFECT
But the Olympics
are in Trouble

Rumania's
Nadia Comaneci

Nadia Comaneci

August 2, 1976

Photograph by John G. Zimmerman

No gymnast in the modern Olympics had ever received a perfect score. But over five days in Montreal in 1976, Nadia Comaneci nailed it seven times.

There she stands, poised on the balance beam—a 4-in. strip of spruce, 16½ ft. long, 4 ft. above the padded flooring. The palms of her hands are coated with gymnasts' chalk that is as white as her uniform, as white as her face. She is an infinitely solemn wisp of a girl, 4 ft. 11 in. tall, a mere 86 lbs. ... Then, with no more strain than it would take to raise a hand to a friend, she is airborne: a backflip, landing on the sliver of a bar with a thunk so solid it reverberates; up, backward again, a second blind flip, and a landing. No 747 ever set itself down on a two-mile runway with more assurance or aplomb ... The 18,000 people in Montreal's Forum realize that they are witnessing an exhibition of individual achievement that is truly Olympian. The judges agree. Their verdict on Nadia Comaneci, 14, of Gheorghe Gheorghiu-Dej, Rumania: she is perfect. —TOM CALLAHAN

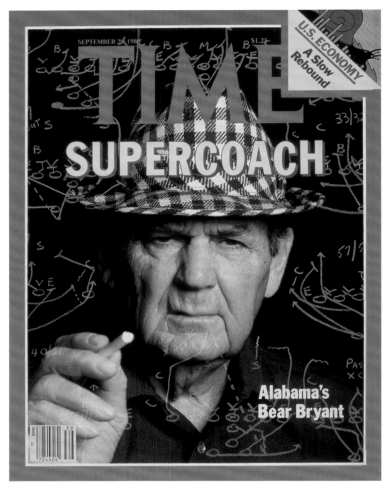

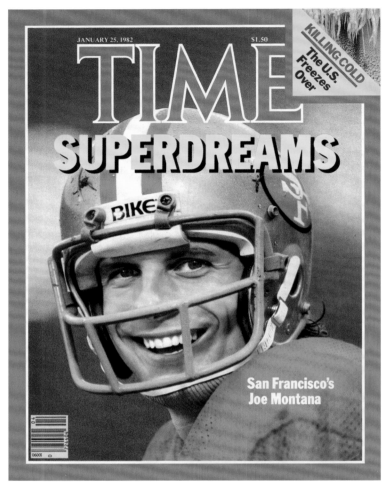

Bear Bryant
September 29, 1980
Photograph by Neil Leifer

*The magazine profiled Alabama's legendary football coach after
he had won two consecutive national titles. Famous as a fierce
disciplinarian, Bryant revealed that flexibility was the key to success.*

Bryant has earned the loyalty of young men as varied as
the burly veterans on the G.I. Bill, the obedient crew-cut
disciples of the Eisenhower era, the rebellious students
of the '60s and the cool careerists of the present generation.
Says he: "You can't treat them all equal, but you can treat
them fairly. That goes not just for how they're different as
individuals, but how they're different from other generations.
One player you have to shake up and get mad, but you'll break
another player if you treat him like that, so you try to gentle
him along, encourage him. The '60s were a rebellious period,
and you've got to realize that a player is going to feel that too.
Even the places you find good ballplayers can change. I used
to think I wanted strong old country boys like I used to be.
Now I think the best place to find players is around a Y.M.C.A.,
where they're playing lots of sports, getting smart and quick,
not just strong and dumb ..."

Alabama Trainer Jim Goosetree, who has watched Bryant
refine his approach in the past 22 years, puts it more precisely.
Says he: "There is a degree of fear motivation still present in his
personality. It's the fear of failing to live up to his expectations.
He has recognized that the values of young people are different
from what they were at one time; but in a fatherly way, he still
demands a degree of discipline that is high." —B.J. PHILLIPS

Joe Montana
January 25, 1982
Photograph by Andy Hayt

*Arguably the greatest quarterback in NFL history, Joe Montana
was in his first bloom of stardom after engineering a last-minute
victory in 1982's NFC title game.*

Most quarterbacks lose control right about here,"
says Coach Bill Walsh, "they're trying to think of
everything and they can't think." Their control begins
to waver; Montana's becomes focused.

Third and three, with 58 sec. on the clock. Unlike everyone else, the quarterback of the San Francisco 49ers sees the
live play in slow motion. He sees the receiver he will throw
the ball to, and he sees the linebacker he must loft the ball
over, and, on those fortunate occasions when he is not lying
on the ground by this time, he sees the ball in flight. Joe's
first target on this play, Freddie Solomon, was covered. Wide
Receiver Dwight Clark stationed himself at the back of the end
zone and then went sliding in the direction Joe was darting.
Under pressure and leaning the wrong way, Montana let go,
and Clark leaped for a ball aimed where he would get it or no
one could. The extra point was good, and when the Cowboys
tried to rally, they fumbled. By 28-27, the 49ers were going to
Super Bowl XVI. —TOM CALLAHAN

San Francisco's Dwight Clark completing "the catch," the legendary touchdown pass from Joe Montana to win the 1982 NFC championship

Photograph by Walter Iooss Jr.

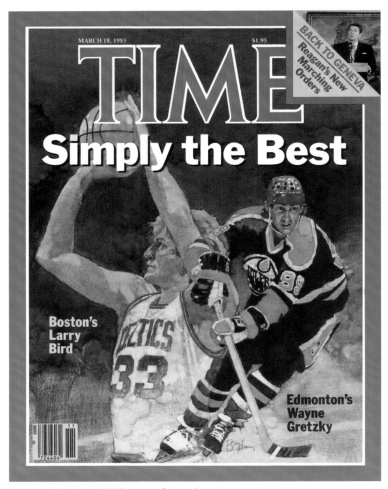

Larry Bird and Wayne Gretzky
March 18, 1985
Portraits by Bart Forbes

Basketball's Larry Bird and hockey's Wayne Gretzky had much in common: both were straw-haired farm boys; both were certified stars who were becoming all-time greats.

Gretzky and Bird are referred to as the best hockey and basketball players of all time. Both resist the idea ... [but neither] MVP denies his ability. "This game is all confidence," Bird says, "and, you know, sometimes it's scary. When I'm at my best, I can do just about anything I want, and no one can stop me. I feel like I'm in total control of everything." The signal for this is when, after shooting, he loops fully around and recoils down the court in triumph before the ball has even reached the basket. "I already know it's all net." His joy is regenerating. "I'll be tired ... but then the ball will go up, and all of a sudden I'm up too. It's wild." Gretzky, reaching that bracing elevation, can actually feel a shift in temperature. "When the play isn't so great, my hands are cold and my feet are freezing. But when it's really good, I can't get enough cold, it's so hot. And then I don't hear anything except the sound of the puck and the stick." —TOM CALLAHAN

Jackie Joyner-Kersee
September 19, 1988
Photograph by Gregory Heisler

Before being named the greatest female athlete of the 20th century, before capturing any Olympic gold, the fiercely focused heptathlete and long jumper already had the look of a champion.

The Olympics will be considered a success if the course of international sweetness and light runs and jumps and generally glides along as smoothly as Jackie Joyner-Kersee. A third of a second late [to win the gold] in 1984, she had to wait four full years for her time to come, to go flying leglong into Seoul like a streamer of confetti.

Dashing, racing, hurdling, hurtling, heaving cannon balls, slinging spears—long jumping on the side—Joyner-Kersee has at last reached the station her grandmother foretold 26 years ago in naming her after a First Lady of the U.S. Momentarily, Jacqueline means to be the First Lady of the world ...

As Daley Thompson has been the natural heir to Jim Thorpe, she would be the Seoul beneficiary of Babe Didrikson Zaharias. Joyner-Kersee and Thompson, the two-time Olympic decathlon champion, puffing for three, embody all the basic wonders of the Games and encompass almost every grade of emotion. One is just arriving at a place the other has been straining to maintain. She's the blur; he's the mist. —TOM CALLAHAN

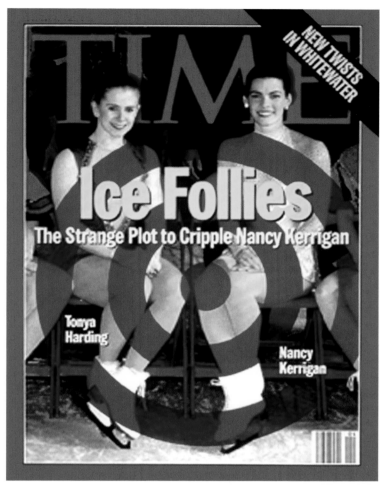

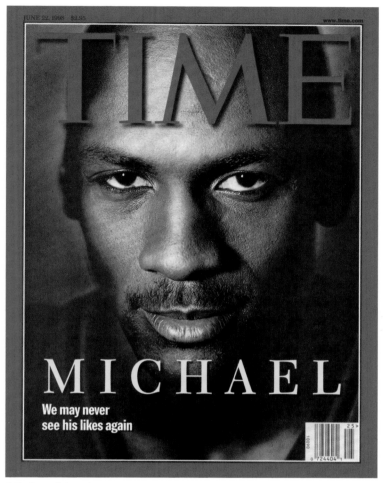

Tonya Harding and Nancy Kerrigan
January 24, 1994

Michael Jordan
June 22, 1998
Photograph by Walter Iooss Jr.

The allegation that a blue collar skater plotted to cripple her shimmering rival made for terrible sport but fabulous TV—a precursor of the reality show.

At the climax of Jordan's brilliant performance during the Bulls' run to their sixth championship—and of his career—the magazine examined the qualities that made him basketball's greatest player.

Tonya Harding is not—nor has she ever been—like most skaters. She is neither politic nor polished, sociable nor sophisticated. Instead, she is the bead of raw sweat in a field of dainty perspirers; the asthmatic who heaves uncontrollably while others pant prettily; the pool-playing, drag-racing, trash-talking bad girl of a sport that thrives on illusion and politesse. While rivals fairly float through their programs, she's the skater who best bullies gravity. She fights it off like a mugger, stroking the ice hard, pushing it away the same way she brushes off fans who pester her for autographs ...

She wants gold at the Olympics and the rewards of fame. "To be perfectly honest," she said last week, "what I'm really thinking about is dollar signs ..." But always the gossamer princesses seduced fortune and celebrity away, leaving her with only ire and ice. And one in particular kept crossing her path—until they both reached Detroit two weeks ago.

The Jan. 6 attack on skater Nancy Kerrigan was shocking and chilling enough. But when the rumblings began that Harding or her entourage might somehow be involved, a grimly familiar tale of random violence turned into something far more gothic ... Did the scrappy girl from the trailer parks, who has climbed so high and suffered so much, possibly plot to destroy her rival? —JILL SMOLOWE

What most fans saw was the balletlike quality of his drives to the basket, and what basketball professionals, coaches and scouts saw was the complete quality of his game, the almost perfect fundamentals he brought every night and the shrewd sense of each game's tempo, which made him almost a coach on the floor. When Jordan was at his prime, it was common among some professional basketball people to joke about the Carolina program and to zing Dean Smith for, it was presumed, suppressing the greatness of Jordan's game during his college years. But ... Smith and his assistants knew from the first time they saw Jordan that the great physical ability and the hunger for the game were a given, and so Smith set out in the three years he coached him to add all the other little things that became so critical to Jordan's greatness: the little moves on defense that came from repeating endless, boring drills; and the skills that allowed him to know when and how to pass off the double team or how to split it. The result was an almost perfect basketball player. —DAVID HALBERSTAM

The U.S. Women's Soccer Team

July 19, 1999
Photograph by Mark J. Terrill

For a glorious month, America was captivated by the exploits of its women's national soccer team. To mark their World Cup victory, TIME *chose an image of triumphant togetherness.*

It went to a penalty-kick shoot-out, which soccer players dread … the shoot-out is soccer's tie breaker: 12 yds. out, shooter against keeper, with the odds overwhelmingly against the keeper. That was true of the first four penalty kicks. On China's third shot, however, [Brianna] Scurry stepped forward, guessed left and threw herself in that direction, where she met Liu Ying's kick. "I just went totally on instinct," she said. "I knew if I could get one, it would be O.K." The crowd erupted and, after [Kristine] Lilly's left-footer beat Chinese goalie Gao [Hong], sensed something big was about to happen. China's next two shooters, Zhang Ouying and Sun [Wen], calmly found their marks, leaving it all up to [Brandi] Chastain, who had committed a huge gaffe against Germany in the quarterfinals when she scored in her own net. This time she found the right one, prompting the spontaneous strip. "Momentary insanity, nothing more, nothing less," she explained. "I wasn't thinking about anything. I thought, My God, this is the greatest moment of my life on a soccer field! I just lost my head." —BILL SAPORITO

Tiger Woods

August 14, 2000
Photograph by Herb Ritts

After an unparalleled run of victories to launch his career, Tiger Woods did something really dramatic to improve his game: he overhauled his swing.

Woods won six in a row in late '99 and early 2000 [with the new swing. Jack] Nicklaus never won more than seven Tour events in one year and never more than three in a row. With his victory in the British Open last month, Woods completed the career grand slam of pro golf's four major tournaments, a feat accomplished by only four other men: Gene Sarazen, Ben Hogan, Gary Player and Nicklaus. And Woods did it at age 24—two years younger than Nicklaus, whose career accomplishments Tiger had kept taped to the headboard of his bed, and in the crosshair of his ambition, since he was 10.

This year Woods has simply owned golf. He's already won six tournaments and earned $6 million in prize money, making him the all-time career money winner, with more than $17 million. Many weeks it seems, as Ernie Els, who finished second in the first three majors this year—and second four times this year to Woods alone—says, "The rest of us are playing one tournament, and there's Tiger, playing a different one." —DAN GOODGAME

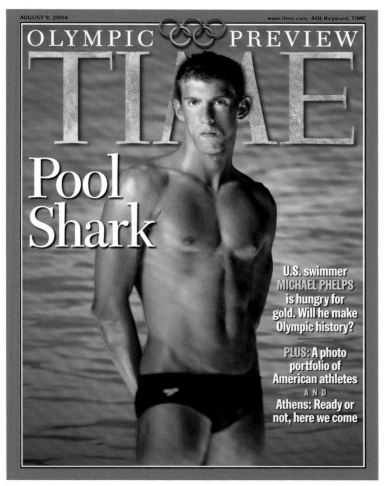

Venus Williams and Serena Williams
September 3, 2001

Michael Phelps
August 9, 2004
Photograph by Gregory Heisler

Correctly anticipating the upcoming U.S. Open women's finals, TIME profiled the dynamic Williams sisters, pondering what made them so controversial and so good.

Michael Phelps went to Athens in 2004 aiming to win an unprecedented eight gold medals. With six gold and two bronze, he fell short. Fortunately, four years later, Beijing beckoned.

Jealous people are always player-hating the Williams sisters, calling them arrogant or aloof or unfocused on tennis. Maybe it's sexism, the resentment of a dominant pro athlete's braggadocio, seen as unseemly in a woman. Maybe it's simple racism. Or maybe it's just that the Williams sisters, as good as they are, are kind of arrogant and aloof and unfocused on tennis. "People criticize me as being arrogant," Venus said last Monday during a tournament in New Haven, Conn., her toy Yorkshire popping out of her Kate Spade bag. "Maybe because I'm a little smarter than the others. Maybe it's because when they ask me a silly question, I refuse to answer it and make myself look foolish." There is a lot of silence at Williams sisters' press conferences ...

The Williams sisters draw most of the unfriendly fire because they are the kids in class who never let anyone see them study but show everyone their straight A's. They are huge women (Venus, 21, at 6 ft. 1 in.; Serena, 19, an even more muscled 5 ft. 10 in.) who learned the game at home in inner-city Compton, Calif., under an amateur coach, their father—not at the boot camp of coach Nick Bolletieri, where most promising kids are sent. They dominate through their athleticism. —JOEL STEIN

In a sport in which most athletes would be happy to qualify for one event, that he can try for eight medals is amazing ... "He is really redefining our expectations of swimming excellence," says Pablo Morales, a two-time Olympian. "He is blazing his own trail now, and there is probably a whole global army of young swimmers who are looking up to him."

His talent in the pool propelled Phelps to turn pro at age 16, before graduating from high school. He is an anomaly in the swimming world, a multimillionaire with endorsements ... [But] money isn't enough. Phelps wants to make swimming matter. He sees the attention that Americans lavish on their swimmers every four years evaporate between Games, and he desperately wants what Australian swimmer Ian Thorpe has— the prestige, the celebrity and, not least of all, the marketing clout ... Thorpe has called Phelps' attempt at a Spitzian haul of golds "ridiculous." Phelps' response: "He's saying he doesn't think it's possible for him to do that. I don't think I would say it's impossible." —ALICE PARK

Science & Medicine

Near Geneva, a scientist peers into the Compact Muon Solenoid of the Large Hadron Collider, where the Higgs boson was found

Photograph by Maximilien Brice

TWENTY CENTS

MARCH 29, 1954

TIME

THE WEEKLY NEWSMAGAZINE

ARTZYBASHEFF

POLIO FIGHTER SALK

Is this the year?

$6.00 A YEAR

VOL. LXIII NO. 13

THROUGH WAR AND PEACE, THE RISE AND FALL OF EMPIRES, seismic migrations from agrarian villages to thrumming cities and all the other epic transformations of the past 90 years, there has been one unbroken rhythm: the march of scientific progress. In fact, it has been less a steady drumbeat than a near constant acceleration. Propelled by the genius of Albert Einstein—TIME's Person of the Century—who published his general theory of relativity in 1915, the early decades of the 20th century produced a burst of insights into the fundamental questions facing humanity: What is the universe made of? How did it begin? When and how will it end?

Einstein's revelations that space and time stretch and curve and that mass and energy are two sides of one coin brought an end to the order and certainty of the Newtonian universe. In Einstein's wake came a range of even more startling ideas, many of which are now part of our general vocabulary: Erwin Schrödinger's 1926 equation for quantum mechanics (not to mention his cat!), Werner Heisenberg's 1927 uncertainty principle, Edwin Hubble's discoveries in 1924 and 1929 that there are galaxies beyond our Milky Way and they are flying ever farther apart, and Georges Lemaître's theory—now scientific dogma—that everything we know and everything that ever was began with the Big Bang.

In subsequent decades, Einstein's heirs, employing ever larger accelerators to smash atomic particles and ever more powerful telescopes to look further back in time, have discovered black holes and pulsars and hunted down the quirks and quarks of the standard model of particle physics right up through the 2012 discovery of the long-predicted Higgs boson. Along the way, they found evidence that much of the universe is made of mysterious dark matter and dark energy—the latter first proposed and then rejected by Einstein. The theoretical work also set the stage for practical efforts to harness the power of the atom, with decidedly mixed results: it brought us nuclear power and nuclear bombs.

If the theory of relativity shifted paradigms in physics, grasping the double-helix structure of DNA did the equivalent for the life sciences. "We have found the secret of life," boasted Francis Crick in a Cambridge pub in 1953 after he and James Watson made the discovery. It's hard to imagine any of today's work on neuroscience, genetics, cancer, HIV/AIDS and so many other biological fields without the fundamental understanding of how DNA is transcribed into RNA to produce the essential proteins of life.

From that moment, molecular biology seemed to move at warp speed, as TIME noted in its 1971 cover story on "The New Genetics." Breathless though it was, it could not anticipate that, just 50 years after Watson and Crick's eureka moment, the entire human genome—some 3 billion base pairs of A's and T's, C's and G's—would be transcribed: a book of life, a recipe for a human being!

While the benefits of the human genome project—personalized medicine, gene therapy, and other wonders—will more likely be realized in the next 90 years, other breakthroughs in biology and medicine came through more traditional methodologies. Old-fashioned crossbreeding of wheat cultivars in Mexico led to a great humanitarian triumph: the 1960s Green Revolution of high-yield, disease-resistant grains. For this achievement, which helped rescue the Indian subcontinent from famine, Norman Borlaug (who never graced a TIME cover) earned a 1970 Nobel Peace Prize and the epithet "the man who saved a billion lives."

And it was good old bench science and keen powers of observation that enabled Alexander Fleming to discover the antibiotic properties of penicillin, a moldy contaminant that was killing off the *Staphylococcus* colonies in his petri dishes. The world's first wonder drug saved thousands of troops from gangrene and death in World War II. It also laid the foundation of a new era of modern medicine, in which doctors were heroes. Among the most admired were Jonas Salk and Albert Sabin, who developed polio vaccines in the 1950s that proceeded to cut the worldwide number of cases from 500,000 in 1950 to about 200 in 2012.

Much of the medical magic of the postwar period was made possible by wondrous new machines that made inner anatomy visible: CT, PET, MRI and functional MRI. More recent decades brought the revolution in psychiatric drugs, leading TIME to ask in 1993, "Is Freud Dead?" They also brought the promise of stem-cell research, which may one day make organ transplants obsolete: better to grow a new liver than make do with someone else's.

While physicists, medical researchers and other scientists were among the biggest heroes of the past 90 years, their pedestals have acquired some tarnish. Even the greatest innovations have a dark side. With the nuclear age came a clear and ever present threat to human survival from stray bombs and power-plant meltdowns. With antibiotics came superstrains of multi-drug-resistant tuberculosis, malaria and other scourges. With new and improved seed crops came monoculture, rain-forest destruction, Big Agriculture and a pathway to today's obesity pandemic. And with those cleared rain forests and the expanding use of carbon-based fuels came the global threat of climate change.

Our early 20th-century enthusiasm for scientific progress has been tempered by popular movements—and TIME cover topics—like environmentalism and alternative medicine. We head into the next 90 years a little less starry-eyed but still hopeful about tomorrow's discoveries. —CLAUDIA WALLIS

DR. JONAS SALK
MARCH 29, 1954 | *Portrait by Boris Artzybasheff*

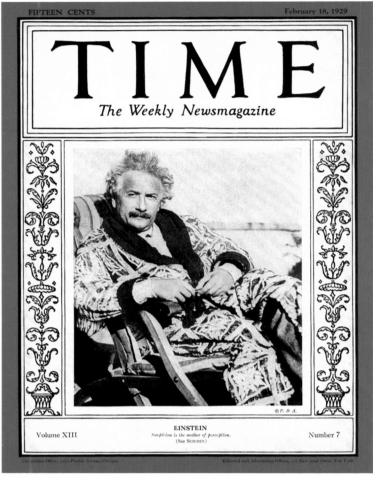

Sigmund Freud

October 27, 1924
Portrait by S. J. Woolf

The father of psychoanalysis was 68 and a towering—if controversial—figure when TIME *published the first of five covers featuring his image.*

It is difficult to analyse Freud's doctrine of psychoanalysis. Is it a science or a philosophy? As there can be no science with a philosophy, it is both. Freud says that injuries are caused to the body by the mind (neurosis); not the conscious mind, for no one is so foolish, but by the unconscious mind. The psychoanalyst's job is, therefore, to bring into the conscious mind those factors which are disturbing the unconscious mind and so cause them to disappear.

The study of the problems of the unconscious mind led Freud to dream interpretation, which was to become the principal method of psychoanalysis. It was the quickest route of reaching a patient's unconscious mind. Freud, in his *Interpretation of Dreams,* goes deeply into the whole subject and, as he almost always uses his own dreams as examples, the book is also an autobiography. In theory, psychoanalysis is the philosophy of the unconscious mind; in practice it is a means by which mental disorders can be cured.

Albert Einstein

February 18, 1929

A week after 24¢ copies of his "Coherent Field Theory" reached the U.S. and a month before his 50th birthday, TIME's *future Person of the Century made the first of six cover appearances.*

Einstein did not develop his conception of the world suddenly. He began by suspecting that nothing in the world was privileged, neither matter, nor motion, nor anything else. His suspicion led to the perception that there is one great physical law which describes everything.

First he inspected electrical and magnetic phenomena. Everyone knows, and had known, that they are intimately related. Electricity flowing through a wire coiled around a piece of iron makes that iron magnetic. As a piece of wire passes between the prongs of a horseshoe magnet, an electric current is generated. James Clerk Maxwell showed that the laws of electricity and of magnetism were very much alike. Albert Einstein, in 1905, showed that the forces were different aspects of the same mother force.

Maxwell said that two orphan boys resembled each other very much. Albert Einstein hunted around until he found that they were brothers, sons of the same electromagnetic mother.

Dr. Alexander Fleming

May 15, 1944
Portrait by Ernest Hamlin Baker

Scottish biologist Alexander Fleming discovered penicillin in 1928, but it wasn't until it was mass-produced during World War II that its miraculous, lifesaving powers were widely known and celebrated.

Last year penicillin patients were still rare enough to be frontpage news. First such case was two-year-old Patricia Malone of Jackson Heights, Queens. The New York *Journal-American,* which begged enough penicillin from Dr. Keefer to save her life from staphylococcic septicemia, last week won the Pulitzer Prize for the story. After that, the whole nation watched one "hopeless" case after another get well.

There were the three doctors in the California mountains last winter who saved a seven-year-old girl when gas gangrene had forced repeated amputations of her left arm up to the shoulder: "As a last resort, penicillin was given after all hope had been abandoned for a recovery, which came like a miracle." There was a doctor in Sioux Falls, S.D., who was astonished to save a man moribund with osteomyelitis and septicemia after sulfadiazine had failed: "This being the first case in which I have employed penicillin therapy, I feel that the results obtained, to say the least, were miraculous."

Doctors now know in general which diseases penicillin helps, have worked out a tentative schedule of dosage. —ANNA NORTH

Robert Oppenheimer

November 8, 1948
Portrait by Ernest Hamlin Baker

The first of two TIME covers on the father of the atomic bomb focused on his passionate postwar efforts to put the genie back in the bottle through nuclear regulation.

On July 16, 1945, all the long months at Los Alamos were put to the test in the New Mexico desert. Brigadier General Thomas F. Farrell was watching Oppenheimer when it happened: "He grew tenser as the last seconds ticked off. He scarcely breathed. He held on to a post to steady himself … When the announcer shouted 'Now!' and there came this tremendous burst of light, followed … by the deep-growling roar of the explosion, his face relaxed into an expression of tremendous relief." Oppenheimer recalls that two lines of the Bhagavad-Gita flashed through his mind: "I am become death, the shatterer of worlds."

Los Alamos and its aftermath left him with "a legacy of concern." Two years later Oppenheimer told his fellow physicists that their weapon had "dramatized so mercilessly the inhumanity and evil of modern war. In some sort of crude sense which no vulgarity, no humor, no overstatement can quite extinguish, the physicists have known sin; and this is a knowledge which they cannot lose." —ALLAN B. ECKER

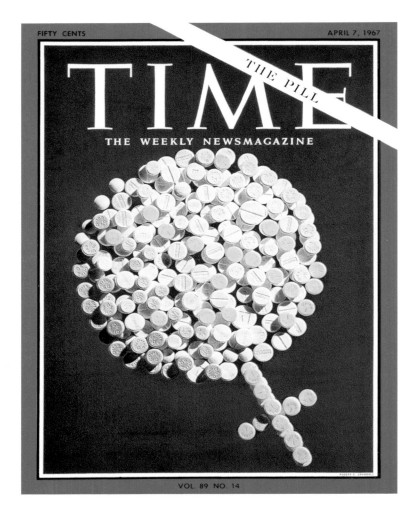

FIFTY CENTS   APRIL 7, 1967

TIME
THE PILL
THE WEEKLY NEWSMAGAZINE

VOL. 89 NO. 14

Contraception
April 7, 1967
Photograph by Robert S. Crandall

Seven years after the Pill was approved for prescription use in the U.S., TIME *hailed the way it had revolutionized "sex and family life" in America and would soon do so for millions abroad.*

The pill" is a miraculous tablet that contains as little as one thirty-thousandth of an ounce of chemical. It costs 11¢ to manufacture; a month's supply now sells for $2.00 retail. It is little more trouble to take on schedule than a daily vitamin. Yet in a mere [seven] years it has changed and liberated the sex and family life of a large and still growing segment of the U.S. population: eventually, it promises to do the same for much of the world.

"The pill," as oral contraceptives are now universally known, may well have as great an impact on the health of billions of people yet unborn as did the work of Pasteur in revealing the mechanism of infections, or of Lister in preventing them. For if the pill can defuse the population explosion, it will go far toward eliminating hunger, want and ignorance. So far, it has reached only a tiny fraction of the world's 700 million women of childbearing age, but its potential is clear from U.S. experience. Of the 39 million American women capable of motherhood, 7,000,000 have already taken the pills; some 5,700,000 are on them now. —GILBERT CANT

Dr. Christiaan Barnard
December 15, 1967
Portrait by Robert Vickrey

In Cape Town, South Africa, the world's first successful heart transplant captivated the imagination of humankind. It opened a new era of organ transplantation even as it raised ethical questions about defining life and death.

Dr. Christiaan Barnard moved into the first operating room and cut eight blood vessels to free Denise Darvall's heart; then he severed it from its ligament moorings. It was disconnected from the pump, and was carried to [Louis] Washkansky's room, where it was connected to a small-capacity heart-lung machine. There it lay, chilled and perfused with oxygenated blood, while Surgeon Barnard removed most—but not quite all— of Washkansky's heart ...

In painstaking sequence, Dr. Barnard stitched the donor heart in place. First the left-auricle, then the right. He joined the stub of Denise's aorta to Washkansky's, her pulmonary artery to his. Finally, the veins ...

Now, almost four hours after the first incision, history's first transplanted human heart was in place. But it had not been beating since Denise died. Would it work? Barnard stepped back and ordered electrodes placed on each side of the heart and the current (25 watt-seconds) applied. The heart leaped at the shock and began a swift beat. Dr. Barnard's heart leaped too. Through his mask, he exclaimed unprofessionally but pardonably, "Christ, it's going to work!" Work it did. —GILBERT CANT

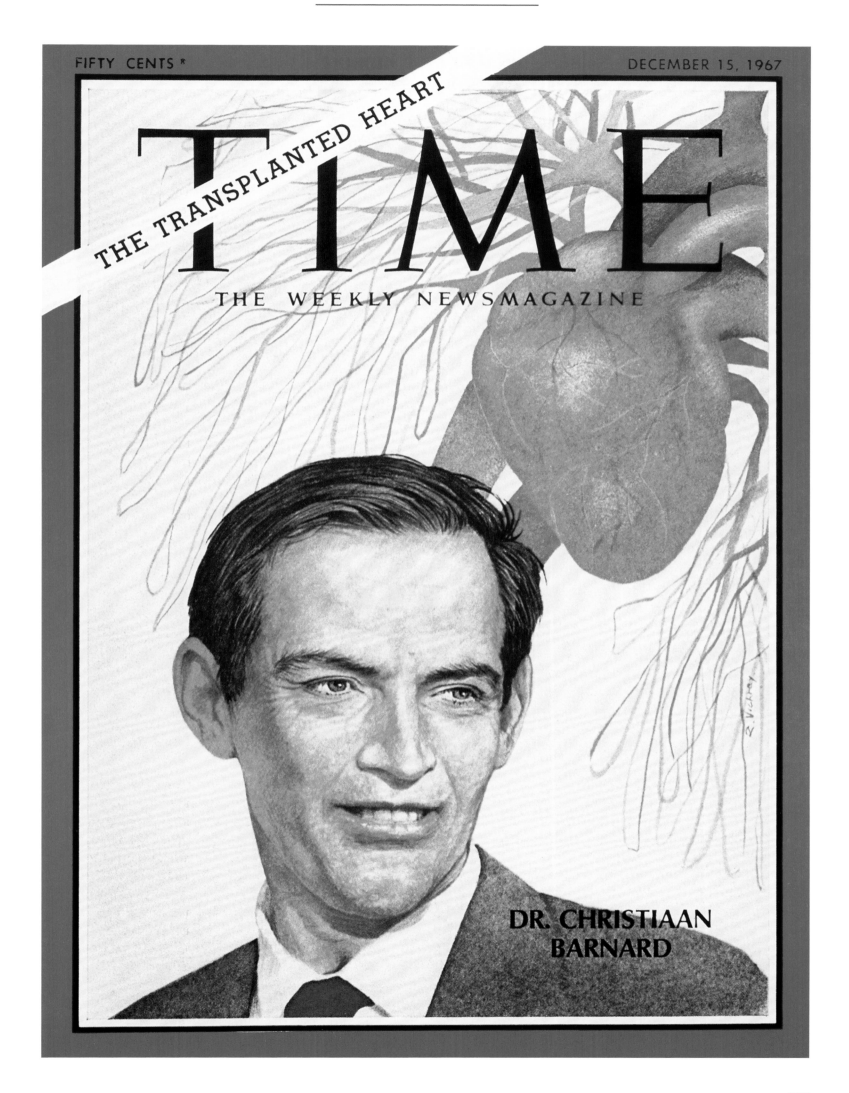

FIFTY CENTS ®

DECEMBER 15, 1967

THE TRANSPLANTED HEART

TIME

THE WEEKLY NEWSMAGAZINE

DR. CHRISTIAAN
BARNARD

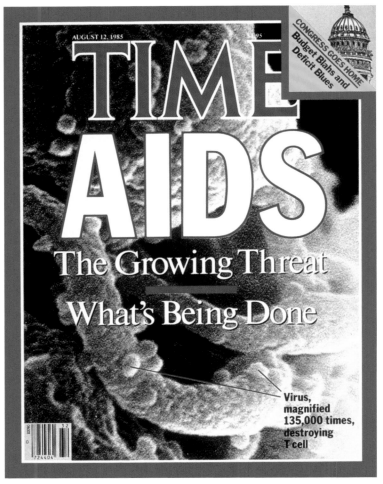

Richard Leakey
November 7, 1977
Photograph by Carl Fischer

A surge of early-hominid discoveries, many by Richard Leakey and including the remarkable Lucy, unearthed in 1974, led TIME to take a fresh look at the ascent of man.

The most exciting of the recent discoveries have come from East Africa and Richard Leakey ...
The result of these findings is a radical revision of long-held views of evolution. As recently as a decade ago, scientists talked about a direct, unbranching line of descent—*Australopithecus, Homo erectus,* modern man—one following the other in logical order. Now all that has changed. "We can no longer talk of a great chain of being in the 19th century sense, from which there is a missing link," says Phillip Tobias, 51, [Raymond] Dart's successor as professor of anatomy at the University of the Witwatersrand medical school in Johannesburg. "We should think rather of multiple strands forming a network of evolving populations, diverging and converging, some strands disappearing, others giving rise to further evolutionary development."

Anthropologists now believe that man's family tree ... goes back to a primate called *Dryopithecus,* a true ape that appeared some 20 million years ago. —PETER STOLER

AIDS
August 12, 1985
Photograph by Erskine Palmer

The revelation that screen star Rock Hudson was battling AIDS gave the burgeoning epidemic a public face, catapulting it out of the closet and onto the cover of TIME.

More than one normally understated scientist has termed AIDS "the disease of the century." Others have, in the tradition of divine justification, viewed it as God's revenge on sodomites and junkies. There have been far more pervasive epidemics, certainly. In 1918 and '19, Spanish flu killed more than 500,000 Americans and ultimately 20 million worldwide. A million Russians may have died of cholera in 1848 alone. But during these scourges there were always the possibility and hope that the fever would lift, strength would return, and life would go on. With AIDS, says Dr. Michael Gottlieb, the UCLA immunologist who is overseeing [Rock] Hudson's care, "the word *cure* is not yet in the vocabulary."

It is the virtual certainty of death from AIDS, once the syndrome has fully developed, that makes the disease so frightening, along with the uncertainty of nearly everything else about it ... In trying to understand AIDS, says Dr. William Haseltine, a leading investigator at Harvard's Dana-Farber Cancer Institute, "we have moved from being explorers in a canoe to explorers with a small sail on the vast sea of what we do not know." —CLAUDIA WALLIS

Global Warming

October 19, 1987

Photograph by Elle Schuster

Frightening new findings about a hole in Earth's ozone layer and mounting evidence for climate change prompted the first of eight cover stories on global warming, including 1989's Planet of the Year.

Atmospheric scientists have long known that there are broad historical cycles of global warming and cooling; most experts believe that the earth's surface gradually began warming after the last ice age peaked 18,000 years ago. But only recently has it dawned on scientists that these climatic cycles can be affected by man. Says Stephen Schneider, of the National Center for Atmospheric Research in Boulder: "Humans are altering the earth's surface and changing the atmosphere at such a rate that we have become a competitor with natural forces that maintain our climate. What is new is the potential irreversibility of the changes that are now taking place."

Indeed, if the ozone layer diminishes over populated areas—and there is some evidence that it has begun to do so, although nowhere as dramatically as in the Antarctic—the consequences could be dire ... Potentially more damaging than ozone depletion, and far harder to control, is the greenhouse effect, caused in large part by carbon dioxide (CO_2). —MICHAEL D. LEMONICK

Cloning

March 10, 1997

Photo-illustration by Arthur Hochstein

The successful cloning of a lamb, named Dolly, from an adult ewe's udder cell was a biological breakthrough that provoked worries about Frankensteinian science and human cloning.

Dolly, the clone, is an epochal—a cataclysmic—creature. Not because of the technology that produced it. Transferring nuclei has been done a hundred times. But because of the science. Dolly is living proof that an adult cell can revert to embryonic stage and produce a full new being. This was not supposed to happen.

It doesn't even happen in amphibians, those wondrously regenerative little creatures, some of which can regrow a cut-off limb or tail. Try to grow an organism from a frog cell, and what do you get? You get, to quote biologist Colin Stewart, "embryos rather ignominiously dying (croaking!) around the tadpole stage."

And what hath [Dr. Ian] Wilmut wrought? A fully formed, perfectly healthy mammal—a mammal!—born from a single adult cell. Not since God took Adam's rib and fashioned a helpmate for him has anything so fantastic occurred. —CHARLES KRAUTHAMMER

A scientist uses ultraviolet light to look at DNA-strand results at Washington University's human-genome lab in St. Louis

Photograph by Karen Kasmauski

J. Craig Venter and Francis Collins

July 3, 2000

Photograph by Gregory Heisler

The first great scientific achievement of the 2000s was mapping the human genome. TIME's cover story detailed the race between two rival teams and the potential they were unlocking.

After more than a decade of dreaming, planning and heroic number crunching, both groups [one led by Francis Collins and the other by J. Craig Venter] have deciphered essentially all the 3.1 billion biochemical "letters" of human DNA, the coded instructions for building and operating a fully functional human.

It's impossible to overstate the significance of this achievement. Armed with the genetic code, scientists can now start teasing out the secrets of human health and disease at the molecular level—secrets that will lead at the very least to a revolution in diagnosing and treating everything from Alzheimer's to heart disease to cancer, and more. In a matter of decades, the world of medicine will be utterly transformed, and history books will mark this week as the ceremonial start of the genomic era. —FREDERIC GOLDEN AND MICHAEL D. LEMONICK

Obesity

June 7, 2004

Photo-illustration by Arthur Hochstein

With two-thirds of U.S. adults overweight and 30% of kids overweight or at risk, obesity was fast becoming the leading threat to American health. The big fat problem earned a special issue.

It's natural to try to find something to blame—fast-food joints or food manufacturers or even ourselves for having too little willpower. But the ultimate reason for obesity may be rooted deep within our genes. Obedient to the inexorable laws of evolution, the human race adapted over millions of years to living in a world of scarcity, where it paid to eat every good-tasting thing in sight when you could find it.

Although our physiology has stayed pretty much the same for the past 50,000 years or so, we humans have utterly transformed our environment. Over the past century especially, technology has almost completely removed physical exercise from the day-to-day lives of most Americans. At the same time, it has filled supermarket shelves with cheap, mass-produced, good-tasting food that is packed with calories. And finally, technology has allowed advertisers to deliver constant, virtually irresistible messages that say "Eat this now" to everyone old enough to watch TV.

This artificial environment is most pervasive in the U.S. and other industrialized countries, and that's exactly where the fat crisis is most acute. —MICHAEL D. LEMONICK

ORVILLE WRIGHT | December 3, 1928

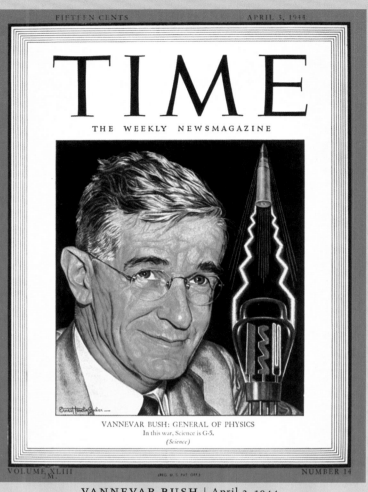

VANNEVAR BUSH | April 3, 1944
Portrait by Ernest Hamlin Baker

Technology: The Way America Works

War. Travel. Politics. Business. Entertainment. Even love. Every aspect of life has been transformed in the past 90 years by technological innovation. We've seen far-flung societies knit together by jet planes, fiber-optic cable, satellite links and, ultimately, the Internet—probably the most disruptive and democratizing innovation since Johannes Gutenberg's 15th century printing press.

The entire history of the programmable computer was written during this period, as hulking vacuum-tube machines gave way to sleeker models powered by transitors and tiny ones with silicon microchips at their heart—an evolution chronicled by TIME.

The military has also been a catalyst for new technology—as the magazine noted with a cover story on Vannevar Bush, who ran the Office of Scientific Research and Development, the Defense Department's innovation desk during World War II. DARPA (the Defense Advanced Research Projects Agency) was the Army brat that grew up to be the Internet. A more recent arrival is drone technology, which may ultimately find its best uses in peacetime.

COMPUTERS | February 20, 1978

Illustration by Alan Magee

NEW PRODUCTS | September 19, 1960

Illustration by Boris Artzybasheff

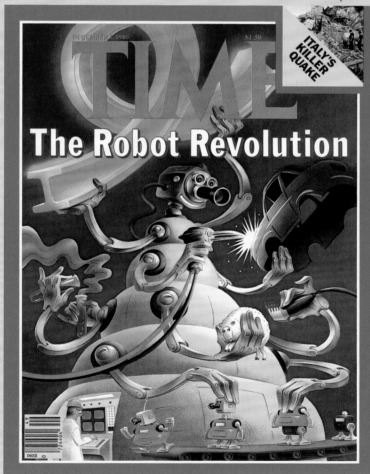

ROBOTS | December 8, 1980

Illustration by Robert Grossman

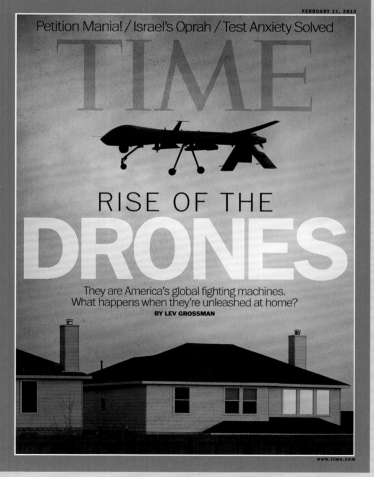

DRONES | February 11, 2013

Photo-illustration by Dan Winters

Bruce McCandless
floating in space with
a manned maneuvering
unit, a nitrogen-
propelled backpack,
on Feb. 12, 1984

*Photograph
from NASA*

□Space

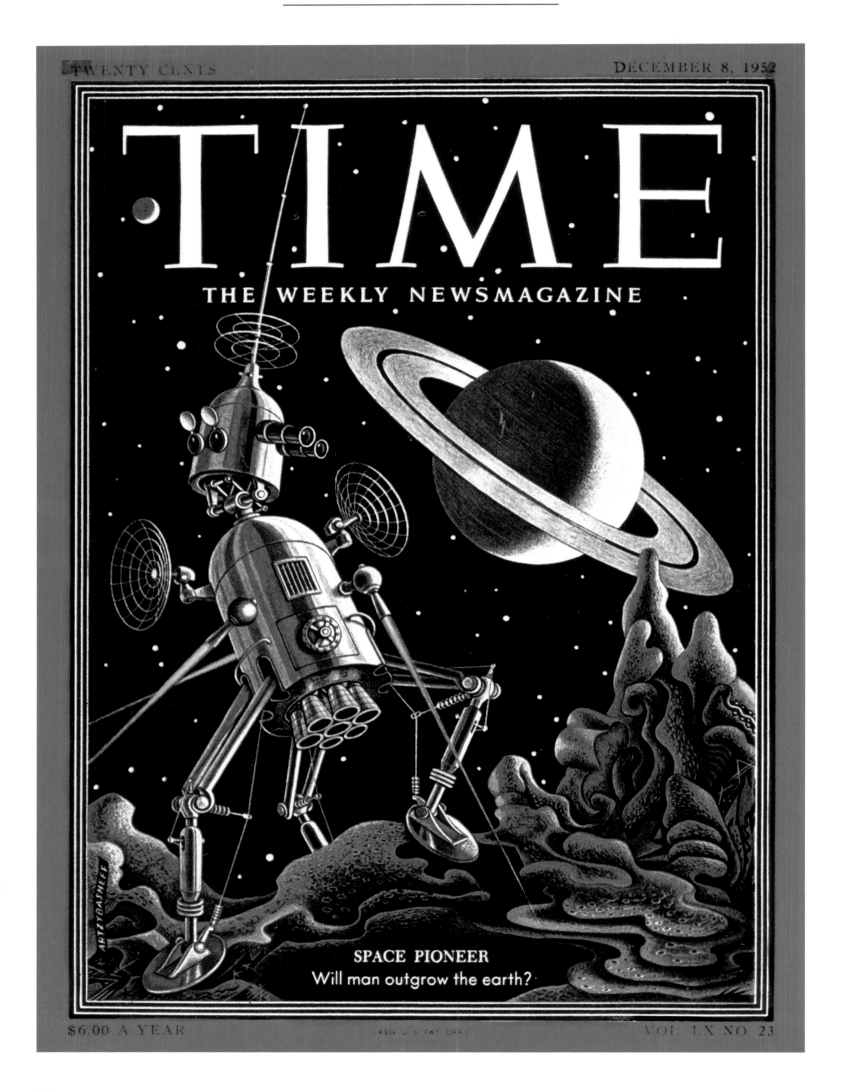

I**T'S BEEN A LONG TIME SINCE MOST OF US FELT THE NEED TO DRAW** a smiley face on the moon. Children do that all the time, but children like to see smiley faces everywhere—on dolls and balloons and lollipops and, yes, on pictures of the moon and the sun and the planets. Scary things—or at least strange things—become friendly when they have a happy face, so children's worlds are filled with them. Our entire species performs the same anthropomorphizing trick, often when we're not even trying. We see eyes and noses and teeth in the windows and headlights and grilles of our cars.

We look at the random swirls in a piece of marble, and a few errant markings sort themselves into a grin or a glower or a frown. Ages ago, we did the same thing with the lunar surface, with the mottled reflections of mountains and maria becoming what we call the man in the moon.

That humanizing impulse was quickly left behind after the U.S. and the U.S.S.R. lofted their Explorer and Sputnik satellites. Space was not, we quickly learned, a friendly and familiar place. It was a place of lethal energies and killing cold, of gravity fields that are crushingly evident and then suddenly absent, of pitiless physics that makes traveling through the void seem reasonable and achievable when you're working it all through on paper but is a whole different thing when you try it out for real.

And so the journey to space became not a grand sweep but a cautious creep, an incremental thing that both sides of the Cold War world reported with a mixture of pride and humility. TIME—reluctantly, surely—made Soviet leader Nikita Khrushchev its 1959 Man of the Year, featuring him on the cover with a comical Kremlin crown on his head and Sputnik balanced on his fingertips.

"Nikita has made the most of his shiny new rockets," TIME wrote. "He has exploited the Sputniks at home and abroad." We could try to make Khrushchev look the fool; we could describe his space machines as if they were toys; we could even infantilize him by referring to him by his first name only. But the man earned the cover, and we grudgingly let him have it.

It didn't get much better in 1961, when Yuri Gagarin—with his matinee-idol looks and his hammer-and-sickle heritage—became the first man in space, orbiting Earth aboard his Vostok 1 spacecraft. Gagarin, too, made TIME's cover, but this time the story was far more than merely political; it was epochal, and even the sulking Western press could not deny it.

"Hats were heaved aloft. Russians cheered, hugged each other, telephoned their friends," TIME wrote. "Vostok was not an unmanned satellite—impersonal, cold, emotionally empty. It had carried an ordinary man soaring across the face of the heavens, and mankind's imagination had soared with him."

That, really, was the nut of the matter. Rockets were great, satellites were great. But as soon as the machine carried a person—a diplomatic attaché representing the entire species—the game changed entirely.

It was for those high stakes that the exploration game was played—and mostly won—throughout the first half-century of the space age. TIME paid tribute to the men who flew the ships—Al Shepard and John Glenn, among the first Americans in space; Alexei Leonov, the chubby-faced, everyman cosmonaut who, 20 years before Mikhail Gorbachev, softened the image of the great Red Menace—and to the men who sent the explorers aloft: America's expat-German rocket designer Wernher von Braun, NASA's brilliant flight director Chris Kraft.

We paid tribute to the rhapsodic moments too. An ugly, convulsant 1968 ended with the sweet peace of a Christmas Eve broadcast by the Apollo 8 crewmen as they became the first human beings to orbit the moon, and astronauts Frank Borman, Jim Lovell and William Anders were named TIME's Men of the Year. Just seven months later, Neil Armstrong became the first person to walk on the moon, and with only grainy TV footage of the event available and the photographs that had been taken on the surface not yet having been carried to a darkroom, developed and distributed, TIME put an illustration of Armstrong on the cover and quoted Archibald MacLeish inside:

"O silver evasion in our farthest thought—
'the visiting moon' … 'the glimpses of the moon'
and we have touched you!"

There would be horror and sorrow and sadness to come. Seven men and women would die aboard the space shuttle *Challenger* in 1986; seven more would die aboard *Columbia* in 2003. And a spacecraft that probably never should have flown would be mothballed forever. Perhaps for lack of a new human mission, we came to love our robots too. The little Sojourner rover toddled across Mars in 1997, and the giant Curiosity rover followed in 2012, and we celebrated those accomplishments with at least some of the old Apollo joy—having grown up enough in the decades that had passed to realize that a robotic extension of human ingenuity is in some ways no less an emissary of the species than an actual man or woman.

We are, surely, still infants in the space game. Our most distant machines are only now leaving the solar system, and our astronauts have paddled no farther than the nearby moon. But we're coming of age slowly, slowly, in a universe that has nothing but time. It will be there waiting as we choose to edge farther and farther into its depths. —JEFFREY KLUGER

Wernher von Braun
February 17, 1958
Portrait by Boris Chaliapin

The U.S.S.R. stunned the world by launching its satellite Sputnik into space in 1957, but four months later, with the help of a rocket scientist trained in Germany, the U.S. orbited its own, Explorer I.

To some, Von Braun's transfer of loyalty from Nazi Germany to the U.S. seemed to come too fast, too easy. Von Braun's critics say he is more salesman than scientist; actually, he learned through the bitterest experience that his space dreams had to be sold ("I have to be a two-headed monster—scientist and public-relations man"). Others claim that the onetime boy wonder of rocketry has become too conservative, e.g., a West Coast rocketeer says that Von Braun is wary of unproved new ideas, no matter how promising, and that he "still takes the conventional view that we should go into space with chemical rockets, with overgrown missiles of conventional design." To this, Wernher von Braun pleads guilty. "The more you're in this business," he says, "the more conservative you get. I've been in it long enough to be very conservative, to want to improve what we've got rather than begin by building what we haven't." So long as the frontiers of space are broken, Wernher von Braun does not care how; he would happily ride a broomstick into the heavens. —CHAMP CLARK

U.S. vs. Russia
January 19, 1959
Illustration by Boris Artzybasheff

The Soviets fired another volley when its Lunik spacecraft left Earth's orbit. It overshot its intended target, the moon, but it threw another scare into the American public.

What is the motive for the push into space? This question gets many sharply conflicting answers. Some military strategists believe that a U.S. rocket base on the moon, which could never be destroyed by surprise attack, would provide the supreme deterrent to any earth aggressor. Most scientists do not agree. Nor do they think much of the idea of armed satellite bases. They see little reason to shoot from a satellite when a rocket shot from solid ground can hit any target on earth. But satellites may prove to have value as "eyes in the sky" over enemy territory. They can also serve as communication relays and act as aids for navigation.

But the rivalry with Russia is not a simple propaganda battle. Says one spaceman: "We could concentrate entirely on our military developments and let the Russians have space to themselves. Would we thus make ourselves impregnable? No, because the rest of the world simply would not believe that we were impregnable. It would look to Russia as the clear leader—and the battle would be lost before it was fought." —JONATHAN NORTON LEONARD

Yuri Gagarin
April 21, 1961
Portrait by Boris Chaliapin

For its next trick, Moscow sent a man into space. A Russian farm boy turned pilot orbited Earth for nearly two hours, turning mankind's fantasies of space travel into reality.

Standing atop the Lenin-Stalin tomb, the most sacred spot in Communist Moscow, Gagarin was greeted by the Presidium, the powerful ruling body of the Soviet Union. [Nikita] Khrushchev made a long speech comparing him to Columbus, naming him a Hero of the Soviet Union and awarding him the brand-new title of First Hero Cosmonaut. The new major, neat in his grey and blue uniform, spoke with admirable poise, the party line rolling easily off his tongue. He thanked the party, the government and Premier Khrushchev for trusting him, a simple Soviet pilot, with the first flight to outer space. "While in outer space," he said, "I was thinking about our party and about our homeland." Next day, the stories began to take on an added polish. Russian papers published reports that Gagarin had slept like a baby the night before his flight, that he had climbed into the Vostok as calmly as if he were taking off on a fishing trip. —JONATHAN NORTON LEONARD

Alan Shepard
May 12, 1961
Portrait by Boris Chaliapin

Upping the ante and seemingly sure of success, the U.S. invited the world to tune in on television to watch the first American astronaut shot into space, for a 15-minute ride around the globe.

In Europe and the U.S. most space spectators agreed with Leonard J. Carter, secretary of the British Interplanetary Society: "The Americans had the right way of doing it. Unlike the Russians, they allowed us all to take part in the fantastic adventure. I was pretty well right up there in the capsule with him." Even in the first flush of worldwide praise, U.S. spacemen did not deceive themselves. They still have a universe to conquer. The Russians are far in front of them, and even if Project Mercury puts a manned capsule into true orbit by the end of 1961 (a hopeful schedule that few scientists take seriously), there is always a chance that the Russians will make an even more spectacular shot.

But Shepard's flight was nevertheless a great U.S. gain, a shot in the arm for U.S. enthusiasts. U.S. spacemen, and the businessmen, engineers, Congressmen and assorted civilians who support them, are once again dreaming brave dreams. Daring and hopeful projects are making the rounds: there is confident talk of nuclear rockets that will penetrate far into space, giant, solid-propellant boosters to lift great weights off the earth and permit manned flights far beyond the known world. —JONATHAN NORTON LEONARD

At Cape Canaveral, Fla., spectators follow the launch of the Mercury spacecraft *Friendship 7*, manned by U.S. astronaut John Glenn

Photograph by Paul Slade

TWENTY-FIVE CENTS

MARCH 2, 1962

The Space Race Is GO

TIME

THE WEEKLY · NEWSMAGAZINE

SPACEMAN
GLENN

$7.50 A YEAR

(REG. U.S. PAT. OFF.)

VOL. LXXIX NO. 9

John Glenn

March 2, 1962

Portrait by Boris Artzybasheff

The world was transfixed as Glenn commanded the first U.S. manned orbital spaceflight. In four hours, 55 minutes and 23 seconds, he completed three rotations around Earth.

This is a new ocean," said President Kennedy, "and I believe that the U.S. must sail on it." The President, still tingling from a day of thrill and success, shared by the nation and the world, was paying tribute to Lieut. Colonel John Herschel Glenn, 40, the freshly commissioned admiral of that new ocean ... John Glenn accomplished through his flight in the heavens—which he laconically called a "successful outing" far more than a brief and exciting escape from man's earthbound environment ... By taking over the controls himself and proving that man can "fly" a capsule through space ... Glenn also struck a blow for man's genius and versatility, answering the critics who claim that instruments can do anything better in space than man. Said Glenn, "Now we can get rid of some of that automatic equipment and let man take over." —JIM ATWATER

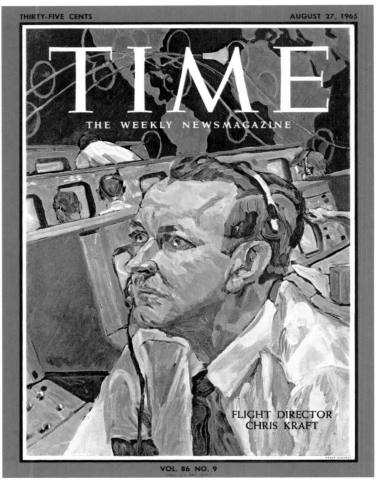

Aleksei Leonov
March 26, 1965

Chris Kraft
August 27, 1965
Portrait by Henry Koerner

Leonov was the first astronaut to walk in space. He wore an inflatable airlock suit that became very rigid as he made his way back to the capsule. Thinking on his feet, he bled some air out of the suit.

Thirty-six minutes after Gemini 5 launched, the oxygen-supply tank of the fuel system dropped to dangerously low levels, threatening to scuttle the mission. The flight would last the intended eight days.

Tied to a capsule by a 16-ft. tether, the first human satellite whirled through the vacuum of space at 18,000 m.p.h. For ten minutes Soviet Cosmonaut Aleksei Arkhipovich Leonov drifted and spun through dreamlike gyrations while he followed the spaceship *Voskhod II* in its swift, elliptical path around the distant earth. Then, as easily and efficiently as he had emerged from his ship, Leonov climbed back inside. After 15 more orbits, he and his comrade, Colonel Pavel Ivanovich Belyayev, began the long flight home …

Dim and probably purposely fuzzy shots showed the round white top of a helmet poking slowly out of a hatch. Then came the visored face of a man, followed by his shoulders and his arms. He seemed to push something away with his left hand before he moved his left arm back and forth as if to test its freedom. He reached for a hand rail, and quickly his entire body came clear of the hatch. Now it could be seen that he was dressed in a bulky pressure suit, with cylinders strapped on his back and a thick cable twisting behind him. The camera followed as Leonov tumbled and turned through casual somersaults while the curving edge of the distant, sunlit earth supplied a moving backdrop … Light streaming through a porthole showed the spacecraft to be revolving at about one revolution per minute. —JONATHAN NORTON LEONARD

An anxious quiet set in … Kraft faced his responsibility. Go? Or no go? Should he bring his ship down or reach for 18 revolutions? … The flight director called in his engineers, conferred with top NASA brass. Pride and prestige were involved; no manned U.S. spacecraft had ever failed to complete its planned mission. But Kraft, as ever, was the cool and deliberate flight engineer. He used every available moment to weigh every contingency. He ran a check of the spacecraft. All the key systems … were normal and running perfectly … By this time Kraft and his experts were satisfied that the oxygen pressure had stabilized at 71 lbs. … Said Kraft later: "We decided we were in reasonably good shape—that we had the minimum power we needed, and that there was a chance the problem might straighten itself out …"

The decision was a matter of hardheaded determination. With the guts to gamble after carefully considering the odds, Kraft and his ground controllers kept Gemini 5 up in the air, and they kept its chances of success very much alive. Their measured confidence in themselves, their machines and their spacemen was a testament to the considerable achievements of the space age—it was a reminder of how much man has learned about the arcane art of operating in the cold reaches beyond his own atmosphere. —JOHN NOBLE WILFORD

FIFTY CENTS •

DECEMBER 6, 1968

TIME

RACE FOR THE MOON

Race for the Moon

December 6, 1968

Illustration by Robert Grossman

Apollo 8—launched Dec. 21, 1968, on a Saturn V rocket, strong enough to propel a spaceship to the moon— was the first manned mission to a lunar orbit, eclipsing Soviet plans to send a man to the moon first.

The V-2 rocket and its designers eventually helped launch both the U.S. and the Russian missile programs, as well as the moon race that was to follow. Even today's liquid-fuel rockets are simply highly evolved descendants of that original V2 ... By 1961, when President Kennedy proclaimed a national goal of landing men on the moon before the end of the decade, the Soviets had already used huge rockets to blast far ahead of the U.S. In September 1959, only two years after they successfully orbited Sputnik 1, the Soviets hit the moon with Luna 2. That was 21 years before the U.S. matched the feat with Ranger 4 ... Not until more than six years later did Lunar Orbiter 1 televise similar shots to the U.S. In the middle '60s, however, a vitalized U.S. space program all but wiped out the Soviet lead in the moon race. —LEON JAROFF

At the end of the
turbulent terrestrial
year 1968, the crew of
Apollo 8, in lunar orbit,
sent back the peaceful
image known as *Earthrise*

*Photograph
from NASA*

FIFTY CENTS

JULY 25, 1969

TIME

MAN
ON THE
MOON

REG U S PAT OFF

Man on the Moon

July 25, 1969
Illustration by Louis Glanzman

"That's one small step for man, one giant leap for mankind." Neil Armstrong's iconic words spoken from the moon—a triumph of science and technology.

The tension was obvious in the voices of both the crew and the controller. Just 160 ft. from the surface ... only 114 seconds of fuel remained. [Neil] Armstrong and [Edwin] Aldrin had 40 seconds to decide if they could land within the next 20 seconds. If they could not, they would have to abort ... "Houston," Armstrong called. "Tranquillity Base here. The *Eagle* has landed ..." It was a wild, incredible moment. There were cheers, tears and frantic applause at Mission Control in Houston "You got a lot of guys around here about to turn blue," the NASA communicator radioed to *Eagle.* "We're breathing again." A little later, Houston added: "There's lots of smiling faces in this room, and all over the world." "There are two of them up here," responded *Eagle.* "And don't forget the one up here," [Michael] Collins piped in from the orbiting *Columbia.* —LEON JAROFF

James Lovell, Fred Haise and John Swigert
April 27, 1970

"Houston, we've had a problem here." The saga of Apollo 13 began. Two oxygen tanks failed, and for the next 10 days the world held its breath as it witnessed the marvel that was Mission Control.

For four days a fractured world inured to mass suffering and casual death had found common cause in the struggle to save three lives. The magic and mystery of space exploration, the realization that James Lovell, Fred Haise and John Swigert were not simply three Americans on a scientific mission but also humanity's envoys to the future, had served to bind men and nations in a rare moment of unity. Perhaps the largest audience in history watched the return, participating through TV's intimacy in every moment of the final, fiery descent. Journey's end was safe and all according to script, in sharp contrast to the crisis of mid-voyage, which had been full of unprecedented danger and breathtaking improvisation. —LAURENCE BARRETT

Space Spectacular
July 21, 1975
Illustration by Birney Lettick

The Apollo-Soyuz space project was the first joint space mission involving the U.S. and the Soviet Union. It tested docking systems and techniques that might be needed for space rescue.

At 8:02 a.m. E.D.T. on Saturday, after 44 hours of orbital togetherness, the ships will separate. They will link up once again briefly in a test of the Soviet docking mechanism. About three hours later, the spacemen will bid each other a final *do svedanya* and goodbye.

Traveling in a slightly lower orbit and at a higher speed, Soyuz will gradually pull away from Apollo. Some 38 hours later, it will fire its braking rocket and enter an arcing course back to earth. At 6:51 a.m. E.D.T. next Monday, Soyuz is scheduled to land under its single giant parachute east of the Kazakhstan launch site. The Americans will remain in orbit another three days before their Pacific splashdown on July 24, performing a variety of different chores—some aimed at understanding more about the earth. —FREDERIC GOLDEN

Saturn
November 24, 1980
Image by Jet Propulsion Laboratory

Voyager 1 took stunning images of the planet called the gem of the solar system, revealing that Saturn's rings are much more intricate than ever imagined.

As more pictures came in, Saturn's many-splendored rings began looking more and more like grooves in a celestial gold record. Even the Cassini division, a dark area first noticed three centuries ago and once thought to be the only gap in an otherwise solid surface, suddenly showed rings within it. At least two other rings were spotted slightly off center, like wobbly wheels on an old car, a curious and as yet inexplicable quirk. To complicate matters, near the outer edge of Saturn's phonograph disc, the ring shows sinewy strands of material that look as if they had been twisted into braiding. Equally perplexing, spokes seem to form in some regions of the rings as the material whirls out from the planet's shadow. Such aggregations of particles—apparently very tiny ones, judging from the way they reflect sunlight—should be quickly ripped apart, like a spoonful of sugar being stirred in a cup of coffee. Yet somehow the spokes survive for hours at a time, almost as if they were intentionally setting out to destroy scientific theories about the rings. Says University of Arizona Astronomer Bradford Smith, chief of Voyager's photo-interpretation team: "Those spokes are giving us nightmares!" —FREDERIC GOLDEN

The Space Shuttle
April 27, 1981
Photograph by Neil Leifer

The space shuttle was the most sophisticated craft ever built. It ushered in a new era of space travel, building enthusiasm in a nation that had grown weary of space travel and cost.

The real "show stopper," of course, might have been the landing. But it was breathtakingly "nominal," NASA lingo for "perfect." Crossing the coast below Big Sur at Mach 7, seven times the speed of sound, or about 5,100 m.p.h., [pilot Bob] Crippen crowed: "What a way to come to California!" [Commander John] Young lost his cool only after he had artfully landed *Columbia* right on the runway's center line. Eager to make an exit, he urged Houston to get the reception crews to speed up their "sniffing" chores—ridding the ship of noxious gases with exhausts and fans. When he was finally allowed to emerge, 63 min. after touchdown, he bounded down the stairs, checked out the tiles and landing gear, then jubilantly jabbed the air with his fists. It was probably Young's most uncontrolled move of the entire flight.

Curiously, Young's and Crippen's heartbeat patterns reversed on takeoff and landing. Both are normally in the 60s. At launch Young's rose only to 85 beats a minute, while Crippen's soared to 135. Returning, Young's pulse rate zipped up to 130 as he flew the craft in. Crippen's stayed around 85. To be sure, Young's racing pulse slowed down soon after landing—and the nation's is likely to do the same. —FREDERIC GOLDEN

Space Shuttle *Challenger*
February 10, 1986
Photograph by Bruce Weaver

It was one of NASA's darkest days. A faulty O ring in one of two solid rocket boosters burned a hole in the external fuel tank. Christa McAuliffe, America's first civilian in space, and six other astronauts perished.

R oger, go with throttle up," [commander Dick] Scobee confirmed. The message came at 70 seconds into *Challenger*'s flight. NASA's long-range television cameras had been following *Challenger*'s shiny white rocket plume, recording the graceful roll that had awed the spectators. But then the cameras caught an ominously unfamiliar sight, imperceptible to those below ... NASA analysts [later] said that an orange glow had first flickered just past the center of the orbiter ... Milliseconds later, the fire had flared out and danced upward. Suddenly, there was only a fireball. Piercing shades of orange and yellow and red burst out of a billowing white cloud, engulfing the disintegrating spacecraft ... The configuration resembled a giant monster in the sky, its two claws reaching frantically forward. —ED MAGNUSON

Life Beyond Planet Earth

February 5, 1996

Digital montage by Seth Shostack

New planets have been discovered. And some may contain water in liquid form, presenting the possibility of life as we know it. How many worlds are similar to ours?

Everyone wants to be the next to find a distant world. The scientists are eagerly awaiting the results from the Infrared Space Observatory (ISO), a newly orbiting European satellite that can detect the faint heat from distant planets. They're looking forward to the 1997 installation of a new infrared camera on the Hubble Space Telescope, which could take a picture of at least one of the newly discovered worlds.

Most promising of all, they're buoyed by a newly unveiled NASA initiative, known as the Origins project, that will build a generation of space telescopes to search for new worlds. Says NASA administrator Daniel Goldin: "We are restructuring the agency to focus on our customer, the American people." And the public excitement about this field, he says, "is beyond belief." —MICHAEL D. LEMONICK

Pathfinder on Mars

July 14, 1997

Photograph by Jet Propulsion Laboratory

The Mars Pathfinder mission delivered a lander and a robotic rover to the planet to conduct experiments and analyses, transmitting almost 17,000 images to Earth.

When Pathfinder was closer than seven miles above the Martian hardscrabble and two minutes from landing, a 40-ft. parachute opened. Less than 1,000 ft. up, a swaddling of shock-absorbing airbags inflated. Immediately after that, a cluster of retrorockets fired for a quick 2-sec. burst, applying a final brake. The almost comically balloonlike ship then struck the surface at about 22 m.p.h., bounced as high as 50 ft. and finally came to rest somewhere in the 4.6 billion-year-old dust …

It was just after 4 p.m. when the images began to appear on mission control monitors. They were, by any measure, astounding: scrub plains without the scrub, prairie land without the prairie grass. The eye, schooled to scout such familiar terrain for equally familiar landmarks, scanned briefly for cactus until common sense reminded the viewer that there would be none. "The little engine that could," said [chief engineer Rob] Manning after the first clutch of pictures appeared, "did." Added [flight systems manager Brian] Muirhead: "We've scored a major home run here." —JEFFREY KLUGER

Space Shuttle *Columbia*
February 10, 2003
Photograph by Dr. Scott Lieberman

The tragedy of Columbia *began on its launch, when a piece of foam broke off the external fuel tank and struck insulating tiles on the left wing's front edge. That doomed the crew upon re-entry.*

So the reunions were ready, the celebrations waiting at the Kennedy Space Center, where *Columbia* was due to land. In Spokane, Wash., neighbors of [commander Michael] Anderson's parents thought maybe they were having a party Saturday morning, a day to celebrate their son's second space adventure, but then it was the pastor coming and a neighbor with groceries because the truth was on TV.

The countdown clock in Florida had started counting back up, when the landing time had passed and the shuttle had not arrived. People watching in eastern Texas heard a crushing rumble outside, the dogs whined, and horses started, and a poisonous rain of broken shuttle pieces fell onto backyards and roadsides and parking lots, through the roof of a dentist's office, bits of machinery in Nacogdoches ... "There are no survivors," the President said, but by then we had been watching the endless video of what looked like the shooting stars of August, knowing that those bright white puffs of star were made of metal and rubber and men and women. —NANCY GIBBS

Curiosity Rover
August 20, 2012
Photo-illustration by Joe Zeff

NASA's Curiosity pushed space exploration into the 21st century. The massive, sophisticated rover's mission: to find out whether the Red Planet has the ingredients to harbor life.

Curiosity's landing site is a formation known as Gale Crater, 96 miles (155 km) wide. Located in the southern Martian hemisphere, it is thought to be up to 3.8 billion years old—well within Mars' likely wet period and thus once a large lake ... Channels that appear to have been carved by water run down both the crater walls and the mountain base, and an alluvial fan—the radiating channels that define earthly deltas—is stamped into the soil near the prime landing site. All this is irresistible to geologists searching for the basic conditions for life ...

The impulse to sentimentalize Curiosity—to treat it almost like a human astronaut—is hard to resist. "The rover is getting ready to wake up for its first day in a new place," said mission manager Jennifer Trosper at an early postlanding news conference. Describing what the science team's work schedule will be like, [mission systems manager Mike] Watkins says, "The rover's day ends on Mars around 3 or 4 p.m. The rover tells us what she did today, and that ... lets us plan her day tomorrow." —JEFFREY KLUGER

NGC 6302 spreads
insect-like 4,000
light-years away in the
constellation Scorpio,
as seen in 2009 by the
Hubble Space Telescope

*Photograph
from NASA*

Artists & Entertainers

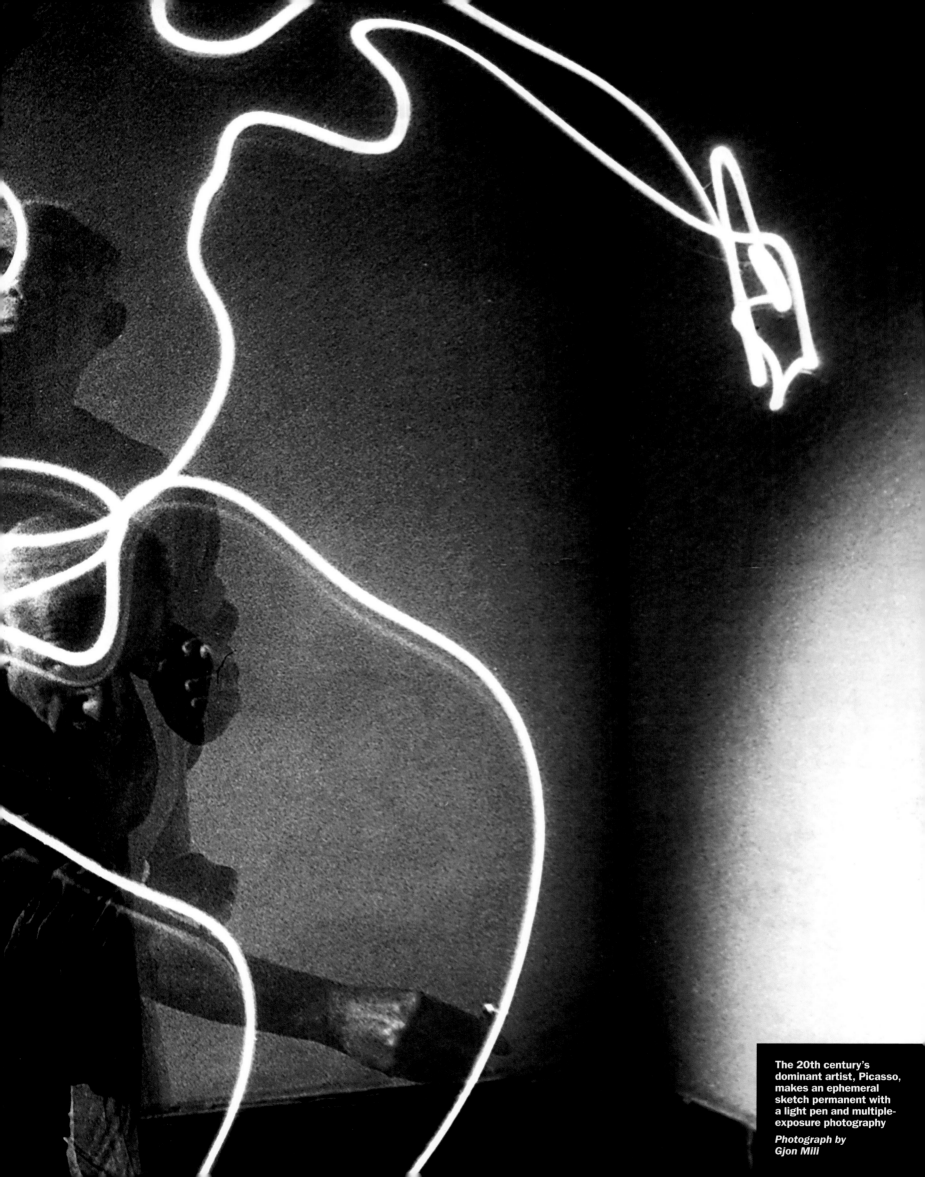

The 20th century's dominant artist, Picasso, makes an ephemeral sketch permanent with a light pen and multiple-exposure photography

Photograph by Gjon Mili

TWENTY CENTS

NOVEMBER 8, 1954

TIME

THE WEEKLY NEWSMAGAZINE

JAZZMAN DAVE BRUBECK
The joints are really flipping.

$6.00 A YEAR

(REG. U.S. PAT. OFF.)

VOL. LXIV NO. 19

A 1925 TIME COVER STORY ON GEORGE GERSHWIN OPENED ON a scene of the young "famed jazzbo," recently returned from Europe, packing a suitcase for the weekend. Newspapers littered his cluttered, tiny Manhattan apartment, one of them noting that Gershwin, in the midst of composing a concerto for the New York Symphony Orchestra, was next going to write the score for a musical comedy. The lead paragraph set a tone of happy chaos, as the musician paused to take a phone call, then "tossed a last striped shirt into his bag." This was the Jazz Age moment

that TIME was born into: a period of changing styles and shifting boundaries throughout the culture when high art and pop art were being jumbled together into the same suitcase. Gershwin—whose jazz symphony *Rhapsody in Blue* debuted the previous year—would become one of America's greatest classical composers and one of its greatest pop songwriters. He was one symbol of an era in art that was at once ambitious and democratic, that had its head in the clouds and its feet in a Lower East Side gutter.

Gershwin's high and low sensibilities were not separate but informed each other, much as they informed other art of the time. The year of that TIME cover, F. Scott Fitzgerald's *The Great Gatsby* mashed up literary fiction and flapper culture. Modern artists like Pablo Picasso were marrying the earthy and the abstract. Frank Lloyd Wright, named "the greatest architect of the 20th century" by TIME in 1938, made his legacy not only through massive edifices like the Guggenheim Museum but also with practical public buildings, homes like his masterpiece Fallingwater and populist projects like his affordable, well-made Usonian houses.

But it wasn't simply a case of high and low art meeting in the middle; often, the same work would push in both directions. In a way, TIME itself was an example of the kind of culture shift it was chronicling. Its mission was to bring the great stories and ideas of the time to people smartly, accessibly, en masse. And the very idea of mass, national (and even global) media was changing how culture was made, consumed and talked about. New kinds of celebrities emerged after World War II, made popular not only by the movies but also radio and TV; just as TIME compacted the world for an audience of millions, so were millions experiencing the same art and entertainment simultaneously.

There was Frank Sinatra, a people's singer and movie star, whom a 1955 cover story remembers as a "kid from Hoboken" who as a boy once turned on some street punks who made fun of his Little Lord Fauntleroy suit by chasing them down the street with a broken bottle. There was Marilyn Monroe, who emerged like a warm-up act for the sexual revolution that would come a decade later, offering, in TIME's words, "the tease without the squeeze, attraction without satisfaction, frisk without risk." When TV became popular in the 1950s, it was the largest communal stage the world had ever known, with *I Love Lucy* comedy out of a just-outside-of-ordinary marriage and Ed Sullivan playing middlebrow tastemaker.

In some ways, that midcentury period of mass media would be the high point of pop-culture unity, when TV shows, on a handful of networks, would regularly have audiences of 50 million people or more, when the Beatles (gracing TIME's cover in *Sgt. Pepper* 1967) could be both music's most popular performers and its most acclaimed experimentalists. The movies began to capture the ferment of the larger culture— sexual adventure, Vietnam-era cynicism and philosophical questing (in everything from *2001: A Space Odyssey* to the existential comedies of Woody Allen).

But in the latter part of the 20th century and into the 21st, the mass audience started to fragment, for reasons both cultural and technological. Radio and pop music subdivided into ever more formats. Movies like *Jaws* and *Star Wars* divided the cinema between blockbusters and critical hits. Television audiences—the most mass of mass culture—began to disperse among multiple cable and network choices. The mainstream became a delta; the *demos* became various demographics.

And along with that, TIME's cultural mission shifted; with fewer universally anointed icons, the TIME cover instead found and identified those artists and entertainers who managed to cut through the culture's divisions and find the universal. Sometimes it found them early in their careers: few biographies of Bruce Springsteen, for instance, will ignore the week in 1975 when he landed on the covers of both TIME and *Newsweek* on the same day, prefiguring a long reign as the Boss of rock 'n' roll. Sometimes it profiled the handful of true giants who still conquer both critically and commercially—the John Updikes and Toni Morrisons, the Steven Spielbergs and Michael Jacksons. (Jackson was captured visually by fellow pop-art colossus Andy Warhol, who did his cover in 1984.)

Ninety years after its launch, TIME covers a very different creative world than it did when it profiled Gershwin. Yet its mission and that of the popular arts are still much the same. To connect entertainment to what matters in the rest of our lives. To ask what it is that makes an artwork linger with us after the credits roll or we close the book cover (or turn off the e-reader). To listen to all the jumbled notes that make up a diverse, vibrant culture— high, low and in between—and find the points where they resolve together into a rhapsody. —JAMES PONIEWOZIK

DAVE BRUBEK
NOVEMBER 8, 1954 | *Portrait by Boris Artzybasheff*

George Gershwin
July 20, 1925

Drawing on classical training, the blues and jazz, this master of American music composed for symphony orchestras, Al Jolson and Broadway, notably the score of Porgy and Bess.

He plugged songs on tin-pan pianos—those renegade instruments that stay up late, every night, in the back rooms of cafés, in the smoky corners of third-string nightclubs, till their keys are yellow, and their tone is as hard as peroxided hair. Gershwin's fingers found a curious music in them. He made it hump along with a twang and a shuffle, hunch its shoulders and lick its lips. Diners applauded. "What's the name of that tune, honey?" asked a lady of Gershwin one night. "No name," said Gershwin. "It has no name." The ditty in question, afterward entitled "I Was So Young, and You Were So Beautiful," became Gershwin's first hit. Within a few years, he had written "Swanee," "I'll Build a Stairway to Paradise," "Yankee Doodle Blues," "The Nashville Nightingale," "Do It Again," "I Won't Say I Will," "Somebody Loves Me," "Lady, Be Good," "Fascinating Rhythm." Last year, he composed his famed *Rhapsody in Blue,* a jazz concerto constructed after Liszt. It took him three weeks to write it. He played it through twice with Conductor Paul Whiteman's celebrated jazz band. It was acclaimed in Carnegie Hall by a huge audience, hailed by daring critics as "the finest piece of music ever written in the U.S."

Frank Lloyd Wright
January 17, 1938
Photograph by Valentino Sarra

Hailed in the late 1990s by his profession as America's greatest architect, Wright's aim was to design structures that were in harmony with mankind and nature.

Wright's desert camp of canvas and boxwood, built by his apprentices in 1929, stands as one of his most brilliant pieces of geometrical design. Still ignored by conventional architects, never invited to take part in the Chicago World's Fair, whose blatant "modernism" was an unconscious tribute to his pioneer work, Wright nevertheless found clients who allowed his designs to materialize ... One quality these new buildings have in common is the clarity with which their basic problems have been grasped and solved. In Racine, Wis., Contractor Ben Wiltscheck is now finishing a business building for S.C. Johnson & Son, which is unlike any other in the world. A few miles from Racine, President Herbert Johnson has let Wright build him a house which lies along the prairie in four slim wings. A huge chimney with fireplaces on four sides is in the focal living room. At Bear Run, Pa., Wright has just finished his most beautiful job, "Fallingwater," a house cantilevered over a waterfall for Edgar Kaufmann of Pittsburgh.

LOUIS ARMSTRONG
When you got to ask what it is, you never get to know.
(Music)

ELIZABETH TAYLOR
Cinema sapphires from common clay.

Louis Armstrong
February 21, 1949
Portrait by Boris Artzybasheff

With his gravelly voice and jazz improvisations, he was the first black performer embraced by white audiences in the U.S. His 1964 "Hello, Dolly!" would knock the Beatles off the top of the charts.

Louis says: "Jazz and I grew up side by side when we were poor." The wonder is that both jazz and Louis emerged from streets of brutal poverty and professional vice—jazz to become an exciting art, Louis to be hailed almost without dissent as its greatest creator-practitioner. A generation of quibbling, cult-minded, critical cognoscenti has called New Orleans jazz many things, from "a rich and frequently dissonant polyphony" to "this dynamism [that] interprets life at its maximum intensity." But Louis grins wickedly and says: "Man, when you got to ask what is it, you'll never get to know." In his boyhood New Orleans, jazz was simply a story told in strongly rhythmic song, pumped out "from the heart" with a nervous, exciting beat. To Trumpeter Louis, jazz is still storytelling: "I like to tell them things that come naturally." —MAX GISSEN

Elizabeth Taylor
August 22, 1949
Portrait by Boris Chaliapin

She was 18 when she appeared on the cover. In the next six decades she would be married eight times (twice to Richard Burton), win the Oscar twice and become an AIDS activist.

For three years of "awkward age" she had only minor roles, went to the studio school, rode horses, and played with her turtles, fish, mice, rabbits, cats, dogs, ducks and chipmunks. She wrote a little story about one of the chipmunks, called "Nibbles and Me," which was published under her name but shows the tooth marks of some careful editorial nibbling. Then one day a Metro photographer walked up to Elizabeth and said: "I thought you'd like to know that the boys have voted you the most beautiful woman they have ever photographed." "Mother!" gasped Elizabeth, "did you hear what he said? He called me a woman!" Biologically, she was—and biology is good enough for Hollywood any time. Elizabeth soon got her first screen kiss in *Julia Misbehaves* and returned it charmingly; her fan mail climbed. Some Annapolis midshipmen were suddenly moved to vote her "The Girl We'd Abandon Ship For." Some Harvard boys added: "The Girl We'll Never Lampoon." As Elizabeth ripened, M-G-M ripened her roles. In *Conspirator,* not yet released, Robert Taylor (no kin) made love to Elizabeth so fiercely (said Hedda Hopper) that one of her vertebrae was dislocated. —HENRY BRADFORD DARRACH JR.

Lucille Ball

May 26, 1952
Photograph by John Engstead

Her pioneering television sitcom I Love Lucy *turned her into an American icon faster than anyone could say Vitameatavegamin. And reruns and downloads have made her immortal.*

Like its competitors, *Lucy* holds a somewhat grotesque mirror up to middle-class life, and finds its humor in exaggerating the commonplace incidents of marriage, business and the home. Lucille's Cuba-born husband, Desi Arnaz, is cast as the vain, easily flattered leader of an obscure rumba band. Lucille plays his ambitious wife, bubbling with elaborate and mostly ineffectual schemes to advance his career. But what televiewers see on their screens is the sort of cheerful rowdiness that has been rare in the U.S. since the days of the silent movies' Keystone Comedies. Lucille submits enthusiastically to being hit with pies; she falls over furniture, gets locked in home freezers, is chased by knife-wielding fanatics. Tricked out as a ballerina or a Hindu maharanee or a toothless hillbilly, she takes her assorted lumps and pratfalls with unflagging zest and good humor. Her mobile, rubbery face reflects a limitless variety of emotions, from maniacal pleasure to sepulchral gloom. Even on a flickering, pallid TV screen, her wide-set saucer eyes beam with the massed candlepower of a lighthouse on a dark night. —CARTER HARMAN

George Balanchine

January 25, 1954
Portrait by Boris Chaliapin

Born in St. Petersburg, he fled to the West soon after the revolution, bringing with him a strict ballet training and an insistence on spare elegance that transformed American dance.

Though it is sometimes called "American" ballet, it pays almost no attention to "Americana." The repertory leans heavily (about 60%) on the choreographic work of Balanchine himself. A typical program might contain his *Symphony in C,* set to Bizet and danced in simple costumes against a plain blue backdrop; his showy *Pas de Trois* (music from Minkus' *Don Quixote*) as a sop to oldtimers who like to watch three top soloists show off their grace and strength; his grotesque fantasy of insect life, *Metamorphoses* (music by Hindemith) and perhaps one of popular Choreographer Jerome Robbins' impudent romps such as *Pied Piper* (music by Copland). Balanchine style dispenses with elaborate sets. It concentrates on the rhythmic movement of trained bodies against plain backgrounds—whether the dancers are outfitted in feathers and fluffy skirts or simply in black bathing suits. "When you get older," says George Balanchine, who is 50 this week, "you eliminate things. You want to see things pure and clear." New York's ballet company is remarkable in still another way: it is not simply a showcase for a few rare stars. —CARTER HARMAN

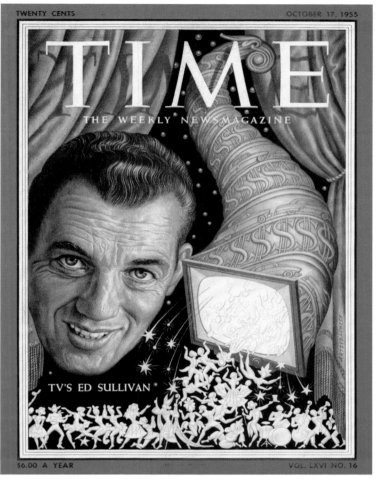

Frank Sinatra

August 29, 1955

Portrait by Aaron Bohrod

Ol' Blue Eyes beguiled generations with his cool, from his days as a teen idol to the leader of that emblematic swinging '60s bad-boy gang of pals known as the Rat Pack.

Francis Albert Sinatra, long grown out of his Little Lord Fauntleroy suit, is one of the most charming children in everyman's neighborhood; yet it is well to remember the jagged weapon. The one he carries nowadays is of the mind, and called ambition, but it takes an ever more exciting edge. With charm and sharp edges and a snake-slick gift of song, he has dazzled and slashed and coiled his way through a career unparalleled in extravagance by any other entertainer of his generation. And last week, still four months shy of 40, he was well away on a second career that promises to be if anything more brilliant than the first. "Frank Sinatra," says an agent who wishes he had Frank's account, "is just about the hottest item in show business today." Sinatra, who in *Who's Who* lists himself as "baritone" by occupation, has offers of more work than he could do in 20 years, and seems pleasantly certain to pay income tax for 1955 on something close to $1,000,000. —HENRY BRADFORD DARRACH JR.

Ed Sullivan

October 17, 1955

Portrait by Boris Artzybasheff

Bland and without any discernible talent, he was nonetheless the great impresario of new talent on his "really big show," bringing Elvis, the Beatles and the Rolling Stones to America's living rooms.

Sullivan started on TV in 1948. Where Milton Berle and Arthur Godfrey had their time of glory and then fell back exhausted, Ed has thrived and grown stronger in the heat of conflict. The battleground of TV is strewn with entertainers who could not quite stay the course—Red Buttons, Wally Cox, George Jessel, Ed Wynn, Ray Bolger, Bing Crosby. Sullivan is the first to admit that any one of these entertainers makes his own talents seem dim indeed. On camera, Ed has been likened to a cigar-store Indian, the Cardiff Giant and a stone-faced monument just off the boat from Easter Island. He moves like a sleepwalker; his smile is that of a man sucking a lemon; his speech is frequently lost in a thicket of syntax: his eyes pop from their sockets or sink so deep in their bags that they seem to be peering up at the camera from the bottom of twin wells. Yet, instead of frightening children, Ed Sullivan charms the whole family. —ROBERT MCLAUGHLIN

TWENTY CENTS

MAY 14, 1956

TIME

THE ~~WEEKLY NEWS~~MAGAZINE

MARILYN MONROE

$6.00 A YEAR

(REG. U.S. PAT. OFF.)

VOL. LXVII NO. 20

Marilyn Monroe
May 14, 1956
Portrait by Boris Chaliapin

Generations remain under her spell, fascinated by her tempestuous life and mysterious death.
She was emblematic of both the little girl lost and the femme fatale.

A friend got her the big break: a chance to play the shyster's house pet in John Huston's *The Asphalt Jungle* ... She was an instant sensation. Letters came in by the sackful. All asked the same question: "Who's that blonde?" Fox grabbed her back for $500 a week, raised her to $750 ... She was on her way to the top—when suddenly the bottom fell out. A columnist printed the news that the girl on the nude calendar was Marilyn, and the scandal broke full about her ears. She was terrified, but she decided to tell the truth: "I needed the money." The press was delighted— especially when, in reply to ... a newshen ("You mean you didn't have anything on?"), Marilyn delivered ... a famous Monroeism: "Oh yes, I had the radio on." —HENRY BRADFORD DARRACH JR.

Duke Ellington

August 20, 1956
Portrait by Peter Hurd

He ruled Harlem's Cotton Club in the 1920s, but a midcentury appearance at the Newport Jazz Festival sealed his fame.

At 57, Edward Kennedy Ellington, jazzman, composer, and beyond question one of America's topflight musicians, is a magic name to two generations of Americans. His "Mood Indigo," "Sophisticated Lady," "Solitude," and countless other dreamy tunes have become as familiar as any other songs since Stephen Foster. As jazz composer he is beyond categorizing—there is hardly a musician in the field who has not been influenced by the Ellington style. His style contains the succinctness of concert music and the excitement of jazz. His revival comes at a time when most bandleaders who thrived in the golden '30s are partly or completely out of business, and few have risen to replace them. The big news was something that the whole jazz world had long hoped to hear: the Ellington band was once again the most exciting thing in the business, Ellington himself had emerged from a long period of quiescence and was once again bursting with ideas and inspiration. —CARTER HARMAN

Leonard Bernstein

February 4, 1957
Portrait by Henry Koerner

He was everywhere, leading the New York Philharmonic, introducing kids to classical music on TV, wowing Broadway.

Everybody still keeps telling him that he is doing too much, that he will have to choose between careers. Since nobody wants him for a competitor, the composers tell him he ought to be a full-time conductor, and the conductors tell him he ought to be a full-time composer. But he replies that he cannot choose between his loves, that he must remain an artistic polygamist. Says he: "I don't want to give in and settle for some specialty. I don't want to spend the rest of my life, as Toscanini did, studying and restudying, say, 50 pieces of music. It would bore me to death. I want to conduct. I want to play the piano. I want to write music for Broadway and Hollywood. I want to write symphonic music. I want to keep on trying to be, in the full sense of that wonderful word, a musician. I also want to teach. I want to write books and poetry. And I think I can and still do justice to them all." —HENRY A. GRUNWALD AND HENRY BRADFORD DARRACH JR.

Jackie Gleason

December 29, 1961
Portrait by Russell Hoban

Like the clown Pagliaccio, he hinted at tragic depths and aimed for a career as a serious actor. But TV wanted Ralph Kramden.

His talent, in fact, is so elastic that he could probably make a living in any form of show business except midget-auto racing. From his start in vaudeville as a boy in Brooklyn, he developed his galloping wit in a string of tough nightclubs before becoming the Jack of all television. Now, as a serious actor and no longer merely a situation comedian, he is surrounded by competing actors schooled in the Method, but he holds his own with unquiet confidence, bellowing, as he always has: "I'm the world's greatest." Entering his new career with appetite akimbo, he has already completed another film, *Gigot,* for which he wrote the story himself, and in Manhattan last week he was at work on still another, *Requiem for a Heavyweight.* Gleason does his new job with remarkable ease. He memorizes at first sight. While Method actors search their souls and "live" their roles, Gleason riffles through a script and is ready to go. —JOHN MCPHEE

THIRTY CENTS

JANUARY 10, 1964

TIME

R. BUCKMINSTER FULLER

Artzybasheff

VOL. 83 NO. 2
(REG. U.S. PAT. OFF.)

Buckminster Fuller

January 10, 1964
Portrait by Boris Artzybasheff

The cover artist said portraying Fuller, the architect of the geodesic dome, as his own invention was "a simple, wonderful challenge … breaking up his head like that and still have it come out a likeness!"

Bucky produced his dome by cutting a hollow sphere in half. Unlike classic domes, Fuller's depends on no heavy vaults or flying buttresses to support it. It is self-sufficient as a butterfly's wing, and as strong as an eggshell. Fuller calls it a geodesic dome because the vertexes of the curved squares and tetrahedrons that form its structure mark the arcs of great circles that are known in geometry as "geodesies." The geodesic dome, then, is really a kind of benchmark of the universe, what 17th century Mystic Jakob Böhme might call "a signature of God." It crops up all over in nature—in viruses, testicles, the cornea of the eye. And for the time being at least, Bucky Fuller has this signature of God sewed up tight in U.S. patent No. 2,682,235, issued in June 1954. It is almost like having a patent on Archimedes' principle. —DOUGLAS AUCHINCLOSS

Thelonious Monk
February 28, 1964
Portrait by Boris Chaliapin

The creator of the bebop movement was idiosyncratic and playful, a prime mover of modern jazz's dissonant sound.

In the mid-'40s, when Monk's reputation at last took hold in the jazz underground, his name and his mystic utterances ("It's always night or we wouldn't need light") made him seem the ideal Dharma Bum to an audience of hipsters: anyone who wears a Chinese coolie hat and has a name like that must be cool ... Now Monk has arrived at the summit of serious recognition he deserved all along, and his name is spoken with the quiet reverence that jazz itself has come to demand. His music is discussed in composition courses at Juilliard, sophisticates find in it affinities with Webern, and French Critic Andre Hodeir hails him as the first jazzman to have "a feeling for specifically modern esthetic values." The complexity jazz has lately acquired has always been present in Monk's music, and there is hardly a jazz musician playing who is not in some way indebted to him. —BARRY FARRELL

Barbra Streisand
April 10, 1964
Portrait by Henry Koerner

Once she became a star, she never let go of the spotlight, proving herself a force behind the camera as well as in front of it.

This nose is a shrine. It starts at the summit of her hive-piled hair and ends where a trombone hits the D below middle C. The face it divides is long and sad, and the look in repose is the essence of hound. She is about as pretty, in short, as Fanny Brice; but as she sings number after number and grows in the mind, she touches the heart with her awkwardness, her lunging humor, and a bravery that is all the more winning because she seems so vulnerable. People start to nudge one another and say, "This girl is beautiful." The show she dominates *[Funny Girl]* has a big New York sound, full of brass and sentiment, something that could have been written by Horatio Algerstein for the *Ladies Home Journal.* A poor Jewish girl with limitless fight and no visible assets claws, clowns and sings her way to the top of show biz. She marries a beautiful cardboard man and realizes her most soaring dreams of love, only to lose him because she is more successful than he. —JOHN MCPHEE

Johnny Carson
May 19, 1967
Sculpture by Frank Lerner

The king of late-night television for 30 years, he succeeded by making his guests look good and dipping into vaudeville.

Carson's bag is unpredictability, not only in his offhand humor but in his visual performance. He is General Eclectic himself, a master of a thousand takes. He's got a Jack Paar smile, a Jack Benny stare, a Stan Laurel fluster. If a joke dies, he waits a second, and then yawns a fine Ed Sullivan "Ho-o-okay ..." A sudden thought— either his or a guest's—will launch him into an imitation of Jonathan Winters imitating an old granny. He can spread his eyes wide open into a wow. Semi-emancipated puritan that he is (he was reared a Methodist), he can, when a guest goes off-color, freeze his face into a blank that shows nothing but eyes and innocence. He is performer and critic, rapping out a whole percussion section of effects to suit a funny line—a wince that clacks like a rim shot, a wagging paradiddle indicating consternation, a flam of the head that says go, baby, go. Frequently, he uses an expression that disassociates him from the proceedings: a visual sigh suggesting that this dame is boring the life out of him, too; or a shake of the head, wondering where the devil this geek got all that garbage. —RICHARD BURGHEIM

The Beatles

September 22, 1067
Portrait by Gerald Scarfe

With their album Sgt. Pepper's Lonely Hearts Club Band, *the Fab Four from Liverpool had moved far beyond their mop-top pop period, taking rock into a whole new conceptual realm.*

Rich and secure enough to go on repeating themselves—or to do nothing at all—they have exercised a compulsion for growth, change and experimentation. Messengers from beyond rock 'n' roll, they are creating the most original, expressive and musically interesting sounds being heard in pop music. They are leading an evolution in which the best of current post-rock sounds are becoming something that pop music has never been before: an art form. "Serious musicians" are listening to them and marking their work as a historic departure in the progress of music—any music. Ned Rorem, composer of some of the best of today's art songs, says: "They are colleagues of mine, speaking the same language with different accents." —CHRISTOPHER PORTERFIELD

Bob Hope
December 22, 1967
Sculpture by Marisol

The comedian made light of his gifts as an actor, but he was a master entertainer—and tireless. Starting as a stage act, he moved on to movies and the medium that made him ubiquitous, television.

Bob Hope comes onstage with the cocky glide of a golfer who has just knocked off three birdies for a 68 and nailed Arnold Palmer to the clubhouse door. The crooked grin spreads wide, the clear brown eyes stay cool, and the audience roars its welcome; they can hardly wait for Hope to sock it to them. And so he does. Five, six gags a minute. Pertinent, impertinent, leering, perishing. And sometimes plopping, but only for an instant. When he misses, the famous scooped snoot shoots defiantly skyward, the prognathous jaw drops in mock anguish, or he goes into a stop-action freeze. Sometimes he just repeats the line until the audience gets it. They don't have to laugh of course—but if they don't, it's almost treason. Probably nobody recalls the sprightly Hope ebullience and the Hope-engendered laughs so well as two generations of U.S. military men. For twelve Christmases straight, Hope has spent the holidays with the troops—in Alaska and Korea, in the Azores and North Africa, in Guadalcanal and London and Viet Nam. —RICHARD BURGHEIM

Woody Allen
July 3, 1972
Photograph by Frank Cowan

Through fiction, screenwriting, directing and starring in his own films, he turned being a nebbish into an art form and the Woody Allen film into a genre of its own.

Peering dolefully at the world through weed-colored glasses, Woody Allen looks like a one-man illustration of the blind leading the halt. Nonetheless, at 36, he has become one of America's funniest writers and certainly its most unfettered comedian. He is also among its most amply rewarded artists. He has produced three bestselling record albums, and written two Broadway hits. Six movies using the Allen talent have grossed more than $35 million. The *New Yorker* publishes his prose. His last movie, *Play It Again, Sam,* is doing brisk business in neighborhood theaters across the U.S., while he is feverishly finishing his latest film, soon to be released, *Everything You Always Wanted to Know About Sex (But Were Afraid to Ask).* The relationship to Dr. David Reuben's bestseller is tenuous, and the movie will probably deserve an R rating (for Rabelaisian). In it, Gene Wilder plays a doctor madly in love with a sheep; and Allen plays, among other wonders, a sperm cell, a libidinous failure named Victor Shakapopolis, a spider, and a court jester caught by a king in the arms of a queen. —STEFAN KANFER

Marlon Brando
January 22, 1973
Portrait by Bob Peak

The near pornographic Last Tango in Paris *introduced Brando to a new generation. But critics would soon hail his performance in* The Godfather *as the best of his varied career.*

What little is known of his true nature comes from a handful of his friends and associates. By their testimony, he is intelligent, warm, charming, compassionate, humorous and unpretentious, as well as undisciplined, boorish, gloomy, supercilious, cruel and downright bent. About the only thing everybody can agree on is that he is a prankster. He delights in disguising his voice in his frequent phone calls to friends, assuming such identities as a job applicant, a woman, or a doctor reporting a comically grotesque diagnosis of some third party. He is also devastatingly adept at mimicry, something he does not only for laughs. "Actors have to observe," he says. "They have to know how much spit you've got in your mouth and where the weight of your elbows is. I could sit all day in the Optimo Cigar Store telephone booth and just watch the people pass by." In the other moods, though, his thoughts drift off—to one of his pet projects, perhaps, or to the South Seas. "Being in Tetiaroa gives me a sense of the one-to-one ratio of things," he says. "You have the coconut in the tree, the fish in the water, and if you want something to eat, you somehow have to get it." Brando still seems to need, as a friend once said, "to find something in life, something in himself, that is permanently true, and he needs to lay down his life for it." —CHRISTOPHER PORTERFIELD

Bruce Springsteen
October 27, 1975
Portrait by Whitesides

Seeing Elvis on The Ed Sullivan Show *inspired the Jersey boy to take up the guitar. And in rock 'n' roll's prophetic way, Presley the King prepared the way for Springsteen the Boss.*

He has been called the "last innocent in rock," which is at best partly true, but that is how he appears to audiences who are exhausted and on fire at the end of a concert. Springsteen is not a golden California boy or a glitter queen from Britain. Dressed usually in leather jacket and shredded undershirt, he is a glorified gutter rat from a dying New Jersey resort town who walks with an easy swagger that is part residual stage presence, part boardwalk braggadocio. He nurtures the look of a lowlife romantic even though he does not smoke, scarcely drinks and disdains every kind of drug. In all other ways, however, he is the dead-on image of a rock musician: street smart but sentimental, a little enigmatic, articulate mostly through his music. For 26 years Springsteen has known nothing but poverty and debt until, just in the past few weeks, the rock dream came true for him. ("Man, when I was nine I couldn't imagine anyone not wanting to be Elvis Presley.") But he is neither sentimental nor superficial. His music is primal, directly in touch with all the impulses of wild humor and glancing melancholy, street tragedy and punk anarchy that have made rock the distinctive voice of a generation. —JAY COCKS

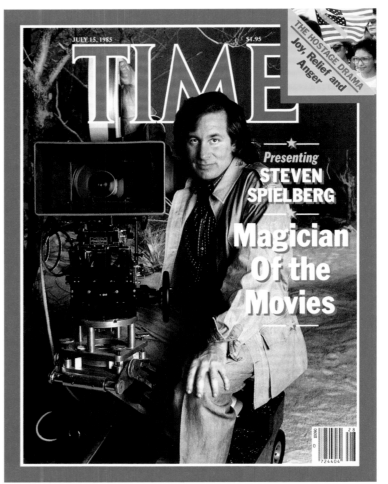

Meryl Streep

September 7, 1981

Photograph by Francesco Scavullo

*Nothing holds back the finest actress of her generation—
not accents or age or whether she's playing a Polish immigrant or
the Prime Minister of Britain.*

A viewer finds himself watching Meryl Streep much more closely than he is accustomed to watching actresses. More seems to be going on. It is not simply that she manages to make her face an astonishingly clear reflection of her character's complexities. It is not merely that this pale face, with its small, amused eyes and its nose long and curved as a flensing knife (when she kissed Alan Alda injudiciously in *[The Seduction of Joe] Tynan,* this precarious nose displaced the flesh of his cheek up toward his eyeball), is poised fascinatingly between beauty and harshness. What makes the viewer sit forward in his seat is that Streep is so thoroughly a creature of change. Her expression is shadowed by a dizzying mutability. There is no doubt that in an instant this woman could take flight toward any state of emotion or mind. In *The French Lieutenant's Woman,* a film in which the sanity of her 19th century character is in grave doubt, what Streep manages to convey when she is not speaking is extraordinary. She is pleased with the performance. "I luff effrythink I do, darlink," she says, giving a brief Zsa Zsa Gabor imitation. —JOHN SKOW

Steven Spielberg

July 15, 1985

Photograph by David Hume Kennedy

The director of E.T. *and the* Indiana Jones *movies was
turning toward more serious films like* The Color Purple *and,
later,* Schindler's List *and* Saving Private Ryan.

H e hardly needs to be told that fables about know-nothing adults and feel-it-all children are not the only tales worth spinning; that adults must face such plot twists as pain, exultation and emotional compromise; that there is drama to be found in the grown-up compulsions of power and, dare we say it, sex. Sure, Spielberg knows there is life after high school. "But after *E.T.,*" he says, "people expected a certain kind of film from me, a certain amount of screams and cheers and laughs and thrills. And I was caving in to that. I knew I could give it to them, but I realize it made me a little arrogant about my own style. It was all too easy. The whole titillation I've always felt about the unknown—of seeing that tree outside my bedroom window and shutting the drapes till morning—was taken away from me. And I got scared. I don't want to see where I'm going." —RICHARD CORLISS

Vladimir Horowitz

May 5, 1986

Portrait by R.B. Kitaj

With the Cold War thawing, the octogenarian pianist, who was born in czarist Russia, toured then-Soviet Russia for a series of concerts. The recordings topped music charts for more than a year.

The secret of Horowitz's appeal is twofold. His phenomenal technique, regarded by piano connoisseurs as the most dazzling since Franz Liszt set the standard of virtuosity in the mid-19th century, gets the listeners into the tent. Horowitz could always do anything he wanted at the keyboard, whether pounding out octaves or rippling off scales in thirds. But mere technique is not enough. Just as Luciano Pavarotti's high notes, in the tenor's prime ... were backed up by a gorgeous liquid and a supple sense of phrasing, so Horowitz's pianism offers many subtleties: the absolute independence of each finger, which makes it sound as though he were playing with three hands, and a rainbow tonal palette that realizes Liszt's ideal of turning the piano into an 88-key orchestra, with every instrument from the flute to the double bass represented. —MICHAEL WALSH

U2

April 27, 1987
Photograph by Neal Preston

Exploring American blues, gospel, country and folk, the Irish band makes cutting-edge music and, with lead singer Bono, uses the high profile to charge their brand of social activism.

The band's commitment, to its audience and its music, sanctions and encourages the kind of social concern that in the Reagan '80s became unfashionable, even antique. The album that *The Joshua Tree* displaced from the top of the chart is a revisionist rap record by the Beastie Boys, three well-born white teens copping street attitude but assuming social postures that teeter between preening smugness and snide irresponsibility. After arriving in Arizona, U2 discovered that Governor Evan Mecham had canceled the state's observance of Martin Luther King Jr.'s birthday. U2 considered canceling the concerts but did something better: made a contribution to the Mecham Watchdog Committee and played "Pride (In the Name of Love)"—a tribute to King— with a joyful vengeance. But it is not just that U2 is on the side of the angels. It has given a new charter and a fresh voice to conscience. "A sense of humor is something I value," Bono says, "but we don't play rock 'n' roll with a wink." Without sermonizing, they have become a rallying point for a new and youthful idealism. —JAY COCKS

Wynton Marsalis

October 22, 1990
Photograph by Ted Thai

By bringing jazz to Lincoln Center, the accomplished trumpeter gave the quintessential American genre pride of place with opera, ballet and classical music.

His glasses give him a scholarly look, partially offset by the sweat pants, T shirt and basketball shoes he favors when not onstage. He speaks softly, occasionally offering an impish smile or raising his eyebrows to make a point. He sips hot tea as he talks. Like most of today's young players, he stays away from alcohol, cigarettes and drugs. Marsalis sees jazz as a metaphor for democracy. "In terms of illuminating the meaning of America," he says, "jazz is the primary art form, especially New Orleans jazz. Because when it's played properly, it shows you how the individual can negotiate the greatest amount of personal freedom and put it humbly at the service of a group conception." He points to Ellington as the jazzman who best embodied the "mythology of this country" in his music. Over and over, Marsalis' conversation returns to a key concern: education. His antidote for what he considers the cultural mediocrity that reigns in America today is to promote jazz-education programs throughout the U.S. "I know this music can work," he says. "To play it, you have to have the belief in quality. And the belief in practice, the belief in study, belief in your history, belief in the people that you came out of. It is a statement of heroism against denigration." —THOMAS A. SANCTON

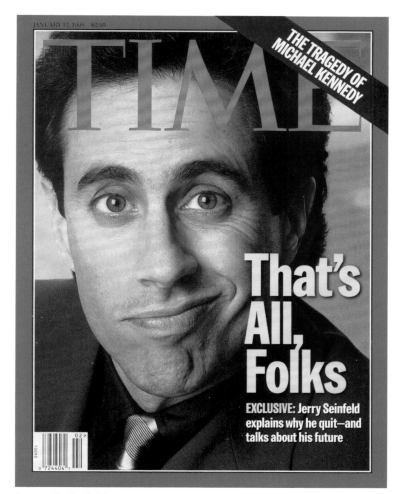

Jerry Seinfeld
January 12, 1998
Photograph by Firooz Zahedi

A co-creator of his namesake television show, Seinfeld reigned over the comedic landscape of the '90s with a show about best friends who interrelated with the finesse of bumper cars.

As Seinfeld is the first to admit, it's been an impressive and improbable run for a show he has famously said is about nothing, which, of course, is charmingly disingenuous. Because if *Seinfeld*—arguably television's first genuine comedy of manners since *Leave It to Beaver*—is about nothing, then so are the works of Jane Austen and Noel Coward. If *Seinfeld* seems trivial, it is only because manners have so devolved over the course of our century. Like the rest of us, the show's overly analytic foursome must pick their way through an increasingly chaotic social battlefield, forced to write their own etiquette for even the most insignificant encounters. And then there are the big questions, like what do you do when your girlfriend suggests sharing a toothbrush? But aside from jokes about masturbation and oral sex, the fundamental difference between *Seinfeld* and *Pride and Prejudice,* say, is that *Seinfeld* in its heart of hearts is concerned with avoiding romantic attachment, with repulsion (and its twin, self-loathing)—the starkest example being George's relief when his fiancée dies licking the envelopes of cheap wedding invitations. —BRUCE HANDY

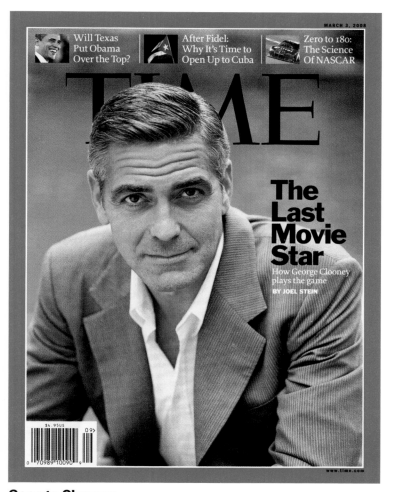

George Clooney
March 3, 2008
Photograph by Sam Jones

After a dozen years in supporting roles on various sitcoms, he was cast as Dr. Doug Ross on ER. *Result: superstardom, Academy Awards and a platform for humanitarian causes.*

It may look as if he is an effortless movie star, but he has actually given the job a lot of thought. He's not manipulative, but he is calculating, following the rules he learned from his family. When his aunt Rosemary Clooney went from being on the cover of this magazine to seeing her fame burst because musical tastes changed, she battled depression and took pills for much of her life. He knows random luck will eventually take fame away, just as random luck made him a star. If NBC had put *ER* on Fridays instead of Thursdays, I might have had Jonathan Silverman over for dinner. And while Clooney didn't get famous until his 30s, when *ER* hit, he had kind of always been famous because of his dad, a popular news anchor in Cincinnati. "From the moment I was born, I was watched by other people. I was taught to use the right fork. I was groomed for that in a weird way," Clooney says. "You give enough. You play completely. You don't say, I don't talk about my personal life. People say they won't talk about their personal life. And then they do. And even when the tabloids say really crappy things and it pisses you off and you know it's not true, you have to at least publicly have a sense of humor about it." —JOEL STEIN

HENRI MATISSE
October 20, 1930

THOMAS HART BENTON
December 24, 1934

Self-Portrait

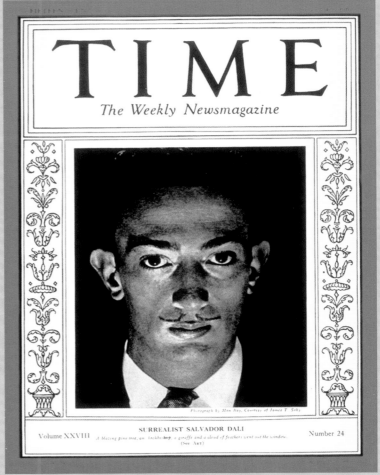

SALVADOR DALÍ | December 14, 1936

Photograph by Man Ray

For Art's Sake, But Mind the Reader Too

The 20th century laid waste to the most basic assumptions that earlier centuries had made about art. Not just what it should look like but what it should draw inspiration from, what it should strive to be and, for that matter, what it was. (A signed urinal, anybody?) Cubism, Surrealism, Abstract Expressionism—the isms whizzed by, soon followed by Pop, minimalism and conceptual art. A magazine coming to grips with this explosion in the early 1920s, when the party was already in full swing, had to calibrate its responses, being open to innovation but skeptical of posturing and novelty.

In the earliest days of TIME, Pablo Picasso and Henri Matisse were already accepted masters—unless you counted a few art-world reactionaries and a great many ordinary people, who still weren't sure what to make of what they did. The magazine stepped gingerly into the cultural maelstrom. The first artist to make the cover was a commercial illustrator, Charles Dana Gibson, whose beautiful and spirited Gibson Girls were a fixture of turn-of-the-century magazines and advertising. The first painter was the swashbuckling but now largely forgotten Welsh portraitist Augustus John, who was admired for having secured "a triple allegiance with fashionable public, ultra-modernists and academicians."

He was anything but ultra-modern, but he appealed sufficiently to the conservative taste of Henry Luce that he made the cover again 20 years later. Though Matisse, Picasso, and Salvador Dalí all appeared inside the red frame—Picasso three times, plus a fourth cover illustrated with one of his paintings—more conventional representational painters, including Thomas Hart Benton, Edward Hopper and Andrew Wyeth were probably a better reflection of TIME's comfort zone. And for that matter, of most people's of those times. —RICHARD LACAYO

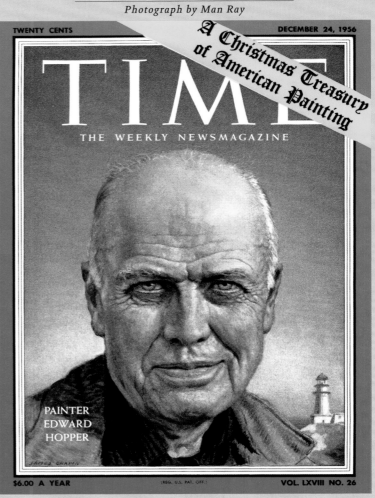

EDWARD HOPPER | December 24, 1956

Portrait by James Chapin

PABLO PICASSO | February 13, 1939

Photograph by Dora Maar

GRANDMA MOSES | December 28, 1953

Portrait by Boris Chaliapin

MARC CHAGALL | July 30, 1965

Self-Portrait

ROBERT RAUSCHENBERG | November 29, 1976

Self-Portrait

JAMES JOYCE
January 29, 1934

Portrait by Marcel Maurel

WILLIAM FAULKNER
July 17, 1964

Portrait by Robert Vickrey

T.S. ELIOT
March 6, 1950

Portrait by Boris Artzybasheff

GEORGE ORWELL
November 28, 1983

Portrait by R.B. Kitaj

J.D. SALINGER | September 15, 1961

Portrait by Robert Vickrey

Getting the Word Out: Author! Author!

A magazine cannot but celebrate the power of words. Even as graphics and photography took up more room in the magazine, TIME remained fascinated with the appeal of literature. The magazine gave over its sixth cover to Joseph Conrad, and though the story itself took up a mere 435 words, in part to herald his upcoming visit to the U.S., the brevity included an evaluation of the novelist's place in the literary pantheon. It was a function the magazine would continue to play for the next nine decades, parsing fiction, poetry and drama to benefit an audience eager to figure what was most profitable to read next. In 1934 the cover story on James Joyce rejoiced that his masterpiece *Ulysses*, "a much-enduring traveler, world-famed but long an outcast, [had] landed safe and sound on U.S. shores" after a court case decided it was not pornographic. Declared TIME: "He will be longest remembered as the man who made 'unprintable' archaic." Words to celebrate, as TIME has done again and again with author after author.

TONI MORRISON | January 19, 1998

Photograph by Deborah Feingold

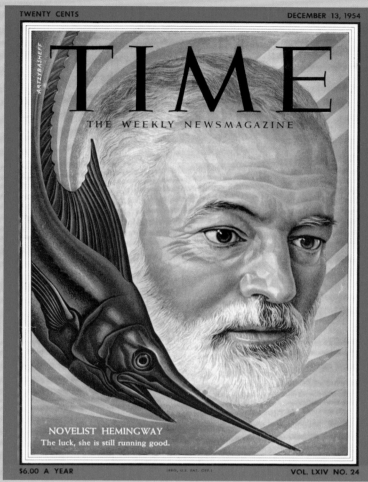

ERNEST HEMINGWAY | December 13, 1954

Portrait by Boris Artzybasheff

JOHN UPDIKE | April 26, 1968

Portrait by Robert Vickrey

TOM WOLFE | November 2, 1998

Photograph by Michael O'Neill

JONATHAN FRANZEN | August 23, 2010

Photograph by Dan Winters

Faith & Religion

John Paul II looking out over his flock during meditations on the Via Crucis, or Stations of the Cross, by Rome's Colosseum

Photograph by Gianni Giansanti

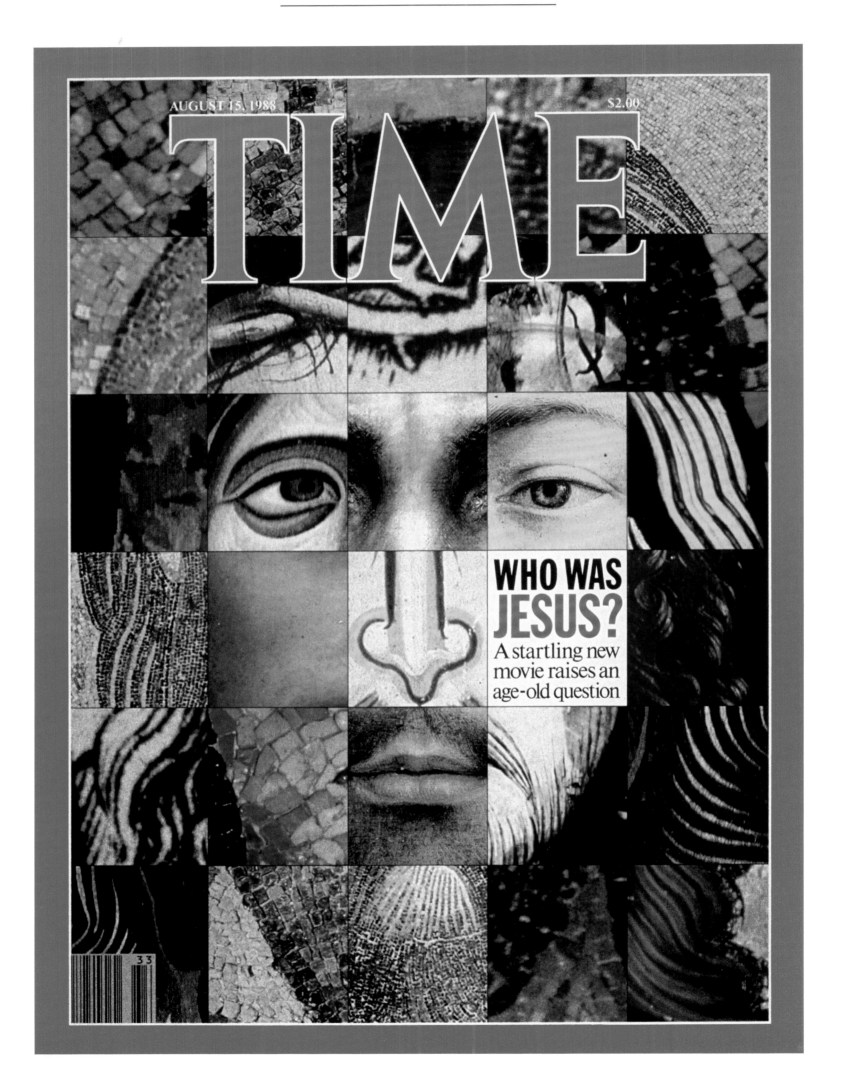

AUGUST 15, 1988

$2.00

TIME

WHO WAS JESUS?

A startling new movie raises an age-old question

A "CHRISTIAN NATION." THE PHRASE STILL RINGS OUT occasionally, polemically or wishfully. But from 1865 to 1920, those words— implying Protestant—accurately described the United States. Presidents saw their service as a Christian enterprise. Prohibition was a Christian project. Writes historian Mark Noll, "The [white] Protestant mainstream ... dictated cultural values, provided standards for private and public morality, assumed primary responsibility for education and powerfully shaped the media." By 1923, however, a war, a flood of immigrants and a

half-century of urbanization had dislocated the lives of millions; diversity and financial-boom hedonism eroded small-town homogeneity and social reinforcement. The nation was primed for a spiritual shift, and over the next 90 years, a huge one would unfold: the Protestant consensus would collapse, Catholicism would mature, and a profusion of borrowed faiths, new faiths and nonfaiths would replace a monoculture with a true religious marketplace.

All this began almost exactly as TIME began publishing. European scholars had long challenged the Bible with insights from modern science, including evolutionary theory. When the debate jumped the Atlantic, outraged conservatives compiled a list of doctrinal "fundamentals," including the Bible's literal truth and the centrality of personal salvation. Liberals, wed to social action rather than inerrancy or soul saving, fought back fiercely, and over a decade Protestant unity ripped. In 1925 open hostilities ceased: the fundamentalists' dramatic drubbing at the Scopes "monkey trial" over teaching evolution resulted in their 25-year retreat from public debate. Over that next quarter-century, victorious mainline churches aided in social progress like the civil rights movement. But with half of white Protestantism still in internal exile in the Bible Belt, a decades-long national vacuum continued.

Roman Catholicism helped fill it. Even in 1923, Catholics populated much of the labor movement and the Democratic Party, but the church was marginalized because of its ethnic divisions and the country's lingering nativist prejudice. As late as 1960, TIME described a tendency to see Catholics as "vaguely alien and as narrow-minded servants of an absolutist theology" based in Rome.

Yet as those words were written, the roadblocks were falling. Bishops had consolidated now well-settled flocks; World War II had exposed no divided Catholic loyalties. Fulton Sheen, whom TIME called "The golden-voiced Msgr.," reached 4 million radio listeners in 1950 and pioneered religious television. John F. Kennedy's 1960 election proved that voters could accept Catholics not just as neighbors but as leaders. And the Second Vatican Council of 1962 to '65 introduced reforms that not only redefined the Church for a modern age but also comported better with the American outlook. By the 1980s the country practically adopted Pope John Paul II, whose life was so eventful, he was on TIME's cover 16 times.

Even John Paul's social conservatism found American resonance—and not just in his contemporary Ronald Reagan. In the '50s the preaching prodigy Billy Graham captivated the country with a less bellicose form of fundamentalism, and he imparted it to a movement dubbed evangelicalism. Its breathtaking progress introduced half the buzzwords of late-20th-century religion headlines—"televangelism," "the Religious Right," "megachurches" and eventually "the faith of George W. Bush." As large as the mainline and far more vital, it re-established Protestant primacy.

Yet the victory meant less than it once would have. In 2012, for the first time in history, Protestants accounted for less than half the U.S. population; white Protestants, just 34%. Besides Catholics, most of the remaining 66% consisted of groups ignored or unborn in 1923. Pentecostalism is one of the world's fastest-growing faiths. Latinos are transforming both Catholicism and evangelicalism; Judaism has produced a nominee for Vice President; Mormonism, for President. Buddhism and Islam are now major American creeds. Equally striking, nearly a fifth of Americans identify as religiously unaffiliated. The media and education are now robustly secular. Defining morality, the old Protestant game, is now everybody's scrimmage. We are no longer a "Christian nation."

The shift pales in comparison with places where national traumas have driven religious change like a pinwheel. Communism nearly killed Russian Orthodoxy; it is now riding high under Vladimir Putin. Post–World War II disillusionment accelerated the emptying of Western European churches, while conservative Christianity now competes, sometimes bloodily, with Islam, for Africa. Islam has undergone the most public changes, re-emerging as a political force in the Middle East; struggling with modernity (very differently) in Afghanistan, Iran and Europe; tarred because of the terrorism of its radical fringe.

We live in a world Henry Luce could not have envisioned. The preferences of Luce, TIME's co-founder and the son of Presbyterian missionaries, are clear in the older covers—dislike of early fundamentalism, admiration for neo-orthodoxy, adoration of Billy Graham. As Luce aged, however, religion reportage shifted, reflecting both the secularization of journalistic practice and the growing diversity of TIME's staff. Today covers featuring Christian theology coexist with ones on Buddhism and Islam, body/spirit, religious scandal and attention to the nonfaithful.

America, in other words, as it is. —DAVID VAN BIEMA

WHO WAS JESUS?
AUGUST 15, 1988 | Collage by Tom Bentkowski

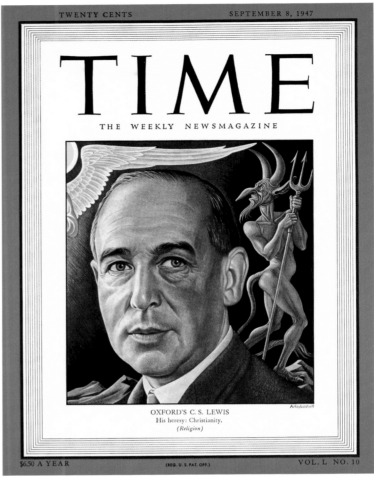

Pope Pius XI
December 29, 1930

Popes at this time were still something of a puzzle to American non-Catholics, regarded as wily European diplomats or exotic potentates. But everyone loved how ancient institutions renewed themselves.

Modernity. Modernization of the Papal State to lead in the modern world has been thoroughgoing. A railway viaduct has been built into Vatican City. The station now is practically completed. Guarding the City (close to the station) are two enormous steel doors, moved by the latest-type electric motor. Senator Guglielmo Marconi, Papal Marquess, built Vatican City a radio station so potent that the Pope could address the entire Western world in person if occasion arose. Hernand Behn, Papal knight of St. Gregory, president of International Telephone & Telegraph Corp., revamped the Vatican's telephone system and made Vatican City's self-contained. It is a dial system. His Holiness' personal instrument is the new American French-type, made of gold and silver. His Holiness, who likes mechanical contraptions, enjoys dialing his own numbers. The Ring of the Fisherman flashes as he manipulates a call. His own number is Vatican City 102. But no one may call him without his prior permission.

C.S. Lewis
September 8, 1947
Portrait by Boris Artzybasheff

When TIME *profiled him, the Oxford don was famous in England for his diabolical satire* The Screwtape Letters. *The* Narnia *books and* Mere Christianity, *his classic Christian primer, lay ahead.*

Lewis (like T.S. Eliot, W.H. Auden, et al.) is one of a growing band of heretics among modern intellectuals: an intellectual who believes in God. It is not a mild and vague belief, for he accepts "all the articles of the Christian faith"—which means that he also believes in sin and in the Devil. After sneezing, he was once heard to murmur that it was "because of the Fall." He was referring, not to the season, but to the Fall of Man, which Christian theology holds responsible for the major disorders of mankind. Lewis is scornful of many modern intellectual and moral fashions: he thinks a Christian can do worse than imagine God as a fatherly ancient with a white beard. —DOUGLAS AUCHINCLOSS

Billy Graham
October 25, 1954
Portrait by Boris Chaliapin

Graham, "God's machine gun," was already a sensation as a preaching prodigy. But this cover explored his appeal to non-fundamentalists, which would make him a seminal religious figure.

He preaches with his shirt collar unbuttoned, so that "my Adam's apple can move up and down." Yet he always looks immaculately pressed and groomed. He is surrounded by electronics—a tiny portable microphone to pick up his voice while he preaches (with a wire clipped to his belt loop), batteries of Dictaphones for dictation, the whole Bible on records. And yet he never sounds mechanical and often seems oldfashioned. He unblushingly applies the hard-sell technique to God ("I am selling," he says, "the greatest product in the world; why shouldn't it be promoted as well as soap?"). And yet such eminently low-pressure, dignity-bound clerics as the Archbishop of Canterbury have given Graham their blessing. A farewell dinner given for him in London this spring included 70 peers and peeresses, and even the austerely intellectual Manchester *Guardian* admitted, "He has a holy simplicity." —DOUGLAS AUCHINCLOSS

The Dalai Lama
April 20, 1959
Portrait by Boris Chaliapin

The Dalai Lama's escape from Chinese-occupied Tibet was primarily a Cold War tale. By the next time he was on the cover, in 2008, he was the leader of a world faith and an Apple icon.

They listened tensely for the sound of gunfire behind them, which would mean that the pursuing Red Chinese had clashed with the rearguard of Khamba tribesmen. Up front, scouts probed carefully to make sure Communist paratroops had not been dropped in the pass to bar their way. All of them—the 35 Khambas of the rearguard, the 75 officials, soldiers and muleteers—were charged with a solemn responsibility: to make good the escape from Tibet of the God-King in their midst ...

When the Dalai Lama this week finally made his way ... to the airfield ... he was welcomed by officials of the Indian government before being flown to a mountain resort at a safe distance from the Tibetan border—so as not to give offense to Red China. He will be inundated by the good wishes of the free world, but for the foreseeable future, the Dalai Lama and 3,000,000 Tibetan patriots can only put their trust—as their ancestors did before them—in the Three Precious Jewels of Tibetan Buddhism: the Buddha, the Doctrine and the Community. —ROBERT MCLAUGHLIN

TWENTY-FIVE CENTS — JANUARY 4, 1963

TIME
THE ... ZINE

MAN of the YEAR

JOHN XXIII

VOL. LXXXI NO. 1

Pope John XXIII

January 4, 1963

Portrait by Bernard Safran

As this Man of the Year cover story intuited, Pope John was not long for this world, but his legacy, Vatican II, was his church's great modern watershed.

Only last week he told a group of cardinals: "Our humble life, like the life of everyone, is in the hands of God …" However soon or late that humble life may end, the world will not be able to ignore or forget the forces that Pope John has unleashed. The importance of the council that he called is already clear. By revealing in Catholicism the deep-seated presence of a new spirit crying out for change and rejuvenation, it shattered the Protestant view of the Catholic Church as a monolithic and absolutist system. It also marked the tacit recognition by the Catholic Church, for the first time, that those who left it in the past may have had good cause. "Even the most agnostic and atheistic people were cheered when they saw those thoughtful people saying those thoughtful things," says one Harvard scientist. —ED JAMIESON

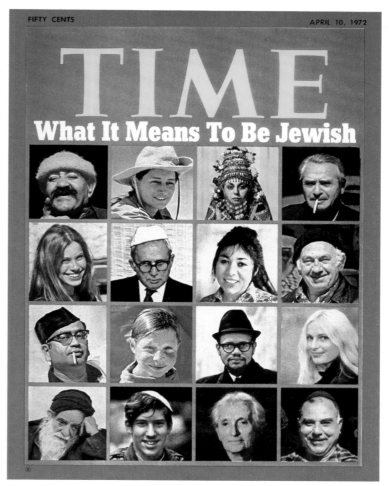

The Jesus Revolution
June 21, 1971
Illustration by Stan Zagorski

It materialized on secular campuses and in Jesus coffeehouses, where teens strummed guitars and quoted Scripture—a foretaste of evangelistic Christianity's move back toward the cultural center.

There are signs that the movement is something quite a bit larger than a theological Hula-Hoop, something more lasting than a religious Woodstock. It cuts across nearly all the social dividing lines, from crew cut to long hair, right to left, rich to poor. It shows considerable staying power: many who were in its faint beginnings in 1967 are still leading it. It has been powerful enough to divert many young people from serious drug addiction. Its appeal is ecumenical, attracting Roman Catholics and Jews, Protestants of every persuasion and many with no religion at all. Catholics visit Protestant churches with a new empathy, and Protestants find themselves chatting with nuns and openly enjoying Mass. "We are all brothers in the body of Christ," says a California Catholic lay leader, and he adds: "We are on the threshold of the greatest spiritual revival the U.S. has ever experienced." —MAYO MOHS

What It Means to Be Jewish
April 10, 1972

With the last great wave of Jewish immigration a generation back, the rich variety of the mature community could be celebrated and analyzed.

The search takes many forms, for Jews—as indicated by their diverse Passover observances—identify themselves with a broad assortment of labels—ethnic, religious and political ... There are Ashkenazic and Sephardic Jews; Orthodox, Conservative, Reform and Reconstructionist Jews; Zionists and anti-Zionists. In the welter of causes and allegiances that vie for the Jew of the '70s, the essence of Judaism sometimes seems hard to find.

Since Judaism is an inextricable mixture of religion and nationhood, a certain ambiguity about Jewish identity will always remain and may ultimately be creative. "We cannot live on borrowed courage," warns Los Angeles Rabbi Leonard Beerman, counseling U.S. Jews to define their identities out of their own roots. But shared courage could well add up to redoubled strength.

In his short story "Monte Sant' Angela," Arthur Miller writes of the Jewish experience: "The whole history is packing bundles and getting away." That may have been. Now the business, Jews hope, is unpacking bundles and settling where they are. —MAYO MOHS

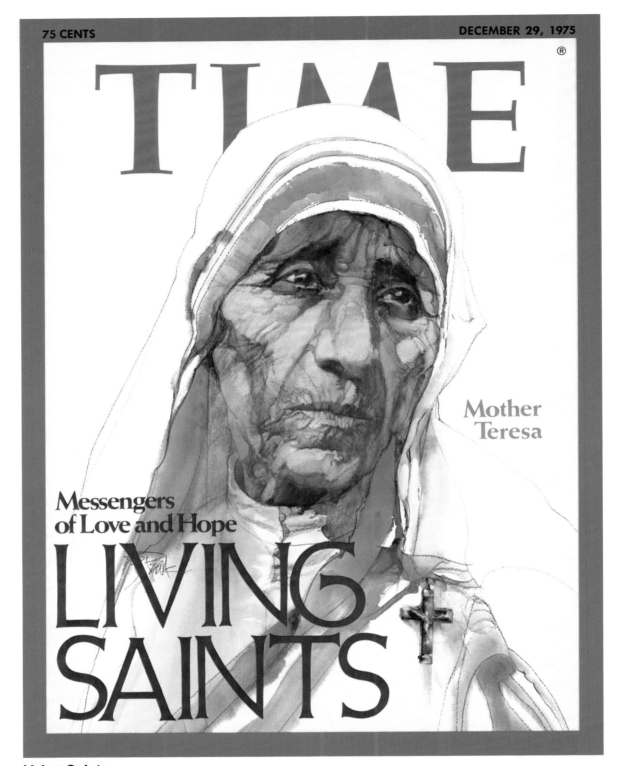

TIME

Mother Teresa

Messengers
of Love and Hope
**LIVING
SAINTS**

Living Saints
December 29, 1975
Portrait by Bob Peak

TIME *simply could have profiled one of the age's most compelling figures. Instead, it included 16 people around the world in addition to Mother Teresa, embracing an extended idea of holiness.*

Not until two years later did the sisters take on one of their harshest and most widely admired tasks, care of the dying. Mother Teresa remembers finding a dying woman on the sidewalk, her feet half chewed away by rats, her wounds alive with maggots. Only with great difficulty did she persuade a hospital to take the woman. Within days the nun was pleading with authorities for "just one room" to which she could take the dying ... The poor, she says, suffer even more from rejection than material want. "If we didn't discard them they would not be poor. An alcoholic in Australia told me that when he is walking along the street he hears the footsteps of everyone coming toward him or passing him becoming faster. Loneliness and the feeling of being unwanted is the most terrible poverty." —MAYO MOHS

Evangelicals
December 26, 1977

Jonestown
December 4, 1978
Photograph by David Hume Kennerly

To some, Jimmy Carter's evangelical faith seemed an exotic outlier. TIME, *identifying and quantifying one of the most important religious changes of the century, explained why it was not.*

A cult, or belief group focused on one living person, is not intrinsically harmful. But Jim Jones' Peoples Temple illustrated how one could go hideously wrong.

The Bible Belt is in fact bursting the bonds of geography and seems on the verge of becoming a national state of mind. Encouraged by the presence of a born-again Southern Baptist in the White House, stirred by the widespread fear that modern man will not be able to make it to the end of the century without some spiritual help, the far-flung residents of the new Bible Belt are loosely lumped together under the name Evangelicals. There are an estimated 45.5 million of them on the U.S. church rolls after a generation of steady growth. They are outnumbered only by the Roman Catholics (49 million). Says Rice University Sociologist William Martin: "The Evangelicals have become the most active and vital aspect of American religion today." He is almost certainly right. —RICHARD N. OSTLING

TIME Correspondent [Don] Neff arrived on the scene in the same Cessna that had flown away from the gunfire at Port Kaituma. He reported: "The first of the bodies was a man by himself, face down, his features bloated, his torso puffed into balloon shape. Then more bodies, lying in a yard. Grotesque in their swollenness but looking relaxed as though comforted in their family togetherness. Nearly all of them were on their faces, eerie figures of slumber.

"I turned a corner, and the whole mass of bodies came into view. The smell was overpowering, the sight unworldly. There were no marks of violence, no blood. Only a few bodies showed the gruesome signs of cyanide rictus. Outside there were three dead dogs, poisoned. Down the road in a large cage was 'Mr. Muggs,' the commune's pet gorilla. He had been shot. In a tree-shaded area was Jones' home, a three-room bungalow. Bodies were scattered through all three rooms, some on beds, others on the floor. The quiet was broken only by the meowing of a cat beyond the porch." —ED MAGNUSON

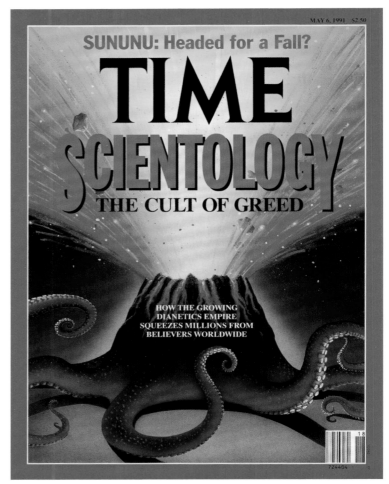

New Age

December 7, 1987

Photograph by Ken Regan

American pop mysticism recurs. A spiritualism vogue beginning in 1850 tailed off only in 1920. The new-age movement is still with us, and this cover caught the crest nicely.

Now come to the ballroom of the New York Hilton, where 1,200 of the faithful have paid $300 apiece to get the word from the New Age's reigning whirling dervish, Shirley MacLaine [who] leads her new acolytes in meditating on the body's various chakras, or energy points ...

"Feel the cleansing power of the stream of life ..." MacLaine purrs. She is wearing a turquoise sweater, violet sweatpants and green ankle-high sneakers, and a sizable crystal dangles from her neck. "There is so much you need to know ... See the outer bubble of white light watching for you ... It is showing you itself, that part of God that you have not recognized."

A woman in the audience complains that she has suffered chronic physical pain since childhood. MacLaine is not fazed ... "Pain is a perception, not a reality ..." The woman in the audience (women outnumber the men two to one) does not feel healed. "No one else goes through what I do," she says ... From the back, another small voice says, "I do." —OTTO FRIEDRICH

Scientology

May 6, 1991

What is a religion? In 1991 TIME asserted that the Church of Scientology was a "racket." Scientology sued for defamation, but a federal appeals court dismissed the suit in 2001.

Harriet Baker learned the hard way about Scientology's business of selling religion. When Baker, 73, lost her husband to cancer, a Scientologist turned up at her Los Angeles home peddling a $1,300 auditing package to cure her grief. Some $15,000 later, the Scientologists discovered that her house was debt free. They arranged a $45,000 mortgage, which they pressured her to tap for more auditing until Baker's children helped their mother snap out of her daze. Last June, Baker demanded a $27,000 refund for unused services, prompting two cult members to show up at her door unannounced with an E-meter to interrogate her. Baker never got the money and, financially strapped, was forced to sell her house in September. —RICHARD BEHAR

The Bible
December 18, 1995

The perceived tension between the Bible and the findings of science (in this case archaeology), which has changed the landscape of American religion, continues to fascinate.

Many professional archaeologists maintain that such questions are irrelevant. Says the British School of Archaeology's Woodhead: "I'm not interested in whether there was a David or a Solomon. I'm interested in reconstructing society: what was traded in clay pots, whether the pots or the contents were traded, where the clay was from ... I don't deal with the Bible at all ..."

Yet for ordinary Jews and Christians, it's impossible to maintain scientific detachment ... Millions of people grew up listening to Bible stories, and even those who haven't set foot in a church or synagogue for years still carry with them the lessons of these stirring tales of great deeds, great evil, great miracles and great belief. Many may be able to accept the proposition that some of the Bible is fictional. But they are still deeply gratified to learn that much of it appears to be based on fact. Says Harvard's [Frank Moore] Cross: "To suggest that many things in the Bible are not historical is not too serious. But to lose biblical history altogether is to lose our tradition." —MICHAEL D. LEMONICK

Ralph Reed
May 15, 1995
Photograph by Nigel Parry

Ralph Reed is the link between the Christian right's contributions to Ronald Reagan's elections and its role more than a decade later in George W. Bush's.

That the religious right could virtually dictate an important part of the congressional agenda was unimaginable when the modern movement began in 1979. Back then, such conservatives as Paul Weyrich and Richard Viguerie helped [Jerry] Falwell set up the Moral Majority. Their idea was to mobilize white Evangelicals in the South and border states ... against Washington's perceived intrusiveness. The Moral Majority gained legitimacy, along with White House access, during the Reagan years, but Falwell neglected to build real foundations at the grass roots. After [Pat] Robertson ran unsuccessfully for the Republican nomination for President in 1988, he converted his huge mailing lists into the Christian Coalition and turned its operations over to Reed, then 27. Reed sought to build ... from the bottom up ... with activists much more involved in local issues. The strategy has paid off.

"The future of America is not [shaped] by who sits in the Oval Office but by who sits in the principal's office," Reed [said]. If the Coalition grows large enough, he advised, "then everyone running for President will be pro-family; they'll have to come to us." —JEFFREY H. BIRNBAUM

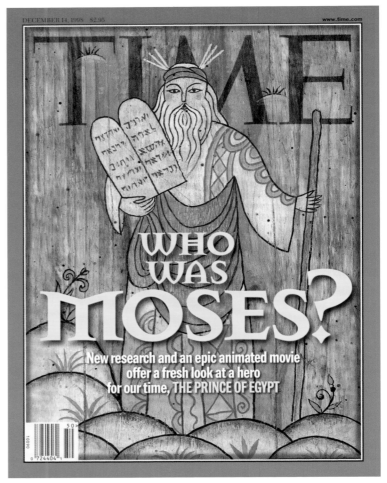

The Mormon Church
August 4, 1997
Photograph by Acey Harper

This Latter-day Saints story was evenly divided between a rare financial assessment of America's most successful homegrown faith and a frank talk with its president-prophet about theology.

The top beef ranch in the world is not the King Ranch in Texas. It is the Deseret Cattle & Citrus Ranch outside Orlando, Fla. ... Its value as real estate alone is estimated at $858 million. It is owned entirely by the Mormons. The largest producer of nuts in America, AgReserves, Inc., in Salt Lake City, is Mormon-owned. So [is] the Beneficial Life Insurance Co., with assets of $1.6 billion. There are richer churches than the one based in Salt Lake City: Roman Catholic holdings dwarf Mormon wealth. But the Catholic Church has 45 times as many members ...

President [Gordon] Hinckley seemed intent on downplaying his faith's distinctiveness. The church's message, he explained, "is a message of Christ. Our church is Christ-centered. He's our leader. He's our head. His name is the name of our church." At first, Hinckley seemed to qualify the idea that men could become gods, suggesting that "it's of course an ideal. It's a hope for a wishful thing," but later affirmed that "yes, of course they can." —DAVID VAN BIEMA

Moses
December 14, 1998
Illustration by Stefano Vitale

Anti-Semitism's wane enabled a more relaxed discussion of Old Testament figures like Moses—in seminaries, from pulpits and in pop retellings like the movie The Prince of Egypt.

What we choose to dwell on in the story of Moses says as much about our dreams and fears as it does about Scripture. Eugene Rivers, a Pentecostal minister in Boston's poor Dorchester neighborhood, has depicted Moses as an African revolutionary (Egypt is in Africa, after all) to teach gang members about throwing off the yoke of slavery to drugs. Norman Cohen, provost of New York City's Hebrew Union College, used the prophet's speech defect to come to terms with his own temporary paralysis. Moses is a universal symbol of liberation, law and leadership, sculpted by Michelangelo, painted by Rembrandt, eulogized by Elie Wiesel as "the most solitary and most powerful hero in biblical history ... After him, nothing else was the same again." Even baseball managers grow eloquent about Moses as paragon: when recounting why Mets star Bobby Bonilla failed to inspire his teammates ... in the early 1990s, Frank Cashen explained, "He was supposed to lead us out of the wilderness, take us to the Red Sea and part the waters. It didn't work that way. He said he couldn't swim." —DAVID VAN BIEMA

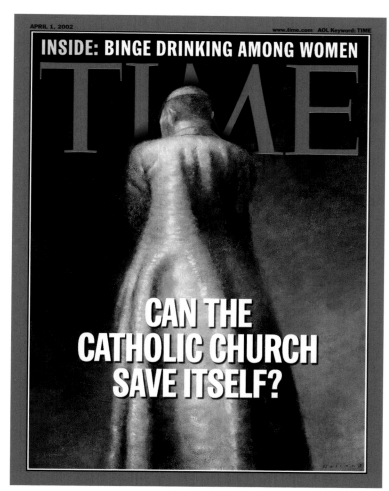

The Catholic Church

April 1, 2002

Illustration by Brad Holland

Predatory priests were not the surprise of the abuse scandal in 2002. It was the complicity or willed ignorance of many of their bishops, almost all of whom remain unsanctioned.

The crisis gathers steam day after day, with perhaps 2,000 priests accused ... It is not just what Boston's Bernard Cardinal Law called "a tragic error" but a spiritual and financial body blow to church authority as well, demoralizing to every man who wears a Roman collar. Lives have been hurt, trust damaged and the credibility of the church to speak on social issues tainted.

How long does it take powerful institutions to learn that it's not just the crime, it's also the cover-up that damns you? The Roman Catholic Church kept silent for decades about the immoral, even criminal betrayal of its children, but in this era of openness, that just won't do. When priests stand in their pulpits this holiest week of the Christian year, what are they going to say to congregations shamed, in pain, frustrated, angry that so much was so hidden for so long? As the Roman Catholic faithful in America are bidden to rejoice that a risen Christ will save their souls, they now want to hear how their church is going to save itself. —JOHANNA MCGEARY

Islamophobia

August 30, 2010

Illustration by Joe Zeff Design

The (ultimately successful) campaign against New York's Park51 Islamic cultural center suggested that a new wave of prejudice may prevent full assimilation of over 2 million law-abiding Muslims.

To be a Muslim in America now is to endure slings and arrows against your faith—not just in the schoolyard and the office but also outside your place of worship and in the public square, where some of the country's most powerful mainstream religious and political leaders unthinkingly (or worse, deliberately) conflate Islam with terrorism and savagery ...

Why has Islamophobia suddenly intensified? ...

Bloggers like Pamela Geller, a New Yorker who runs the website Atlas Shrugs, played a pivotal role in making Park51 a national issue even after mainstream conservative commentators had given it a thumbs-up. In December, Laura Ingraham, sitting in for Bill O'Reilly on Fox News, interviewed [Park51's] Daisy Khan and ended the segment by telling her, "I like what you're trying to do." Geller, however, mounted a concerted campaign against the center. "This is Islamic domination and expansionism," she wrote. "The location is no accident—just as al-Aqsa was built on top of the Temple in Jerusalem." Eventually other bloggers picked up the thread, and the campaign went viral. —BOBBY GHOSH

THIRTY-FIVE CENTS

APRIL 8, 1966

TIME

THE WEEKLY NEWSMAGAZINE

Is God Dead?

What in God's Name Are They Saying?

NEVER BEFORE HAD A TIME COVER APPEARED WITHOUT AN image. Here were just stark, simple letters, spelling out a stunning question. Inside, a richly woven story addressed that question as "a summons to reflect on the meaning of existence." By re-examining the fundamentals of religious faith, this issue elicited one of the biggest reader responses in the magazine's history. The tumultuous 1960s were a time of great upheaval in religion, as in politics, art, sexuality and other areas of life. The Vatican's liberal reforms had rejuvenated the Roman Catholic faithful. Many Protestants were taking their zeal to the streets, fighting for equality and civil rights. A group of radical theologians even argued that the age-old notion of a personal God was defunct and that religion should simply get along without him.

TIME's religion editor John Elson spent a year preparing to take the measure of all this ferment. He read some 40 books, sifted through stacks of research and gathered more than 300 interviews and reports from TIME correspondents around the world.

His 5,000 word article, "Toward a Hidden God," in the April 8, 1966, issue, explored the secularism, science and urbanization that had undermined traditional beliefs and sorted out the various theological approaches to the problem of God. "Is God dead?" Elson wrote, beginning his story with what would be the lines on the cover. "It is a question that tantalizes both believers, who perhaps secretly fear that he is, and atheists, who possibly suspect that the answer is no ... The three words represent a summons to reflect on the meaning of existence. No longer is the question the taunting jest of skeptics for whom unbelief is the text of wisdom and for whom Nietzsche is the prophet who gave the right answer a century ago. Even within Christianity, now confidently renewing itself in spirit as well as form, a small band of radical theologians has seriously argued that the churches must accept the fact of God's death, and get along without him." The story then begins an erudite survey of how humankind came to its conceptions of God—and what the controversial new thinking was all about.

To Elson, the death-of-God theories represented "a new quest for God." He pointed out that some doubt may be necessary to any true faith. "Contemporary worry about God," he concluded, "could be a necessary and healthy antidote to centuries in which faith was too confident and sure."

As he worked on his story, TIME's editors searched for an appropriate cover image. They considered classic works of religious art as well as contemporary paintings like Abraham Rattner's *Window Cleaner,* showing a shadowy figure behind stained glass. They commissioned a work by Pop artist Larry Rivers, who submitted a collage of an old man lying in a sort of foldout coffin, surrounded by symbolic markings and images. Nothing seemed right.

Time Inc. founder Henry Luce wrote to managing editor Otto Fuerbringer, "The only artist who could paint a portrait of God is God." Apparently agreeing, Fuerbringer ultimately opted for the text-only solution.

Editorials and sermons addressed the cover's provocative question. Readers applauded, scorned and rebutted both the cover and the article, in tones from complimentary to pious to fiercely critical. The magazine received 3,500 letters—still one of the largest responses to any cover story TIME has published. —CHRISTOPHER PORTERFIELD

The Pope Who Helped Bring Down An Empire

The Catholic Church was in shock. The new Pope with the double name, John Paul, had died, just 34 days after his election. The faithful—indeed, the world—would be stunned by whom the Cardinal electors chose next: Karol Wojtyla, the charismatic Archbishop of Krakow, the first non-Italian to occupy the throne of St. Peter since 1523. The election of a Polish Pope amid unrest in the Soviet bloc was provocative, and John Paul II would inspire his people to throw off communist rule, a domino in the chain-reaction collapse of Moscow's empire. His papacy would be covered relentlessly on the covers of TIME, from the attempt on his life to the jailhouse visit in which he forgave his assailant to his perpetual peregrinations to increase the influence of his church. His 26-year pontificate was marred toward the end by the scandal of priestly-abuse cover-ups. Nevertheless, he retained his heroic glow and, along with Pope John XXIII, was on schedule for sainthood in late 2013.

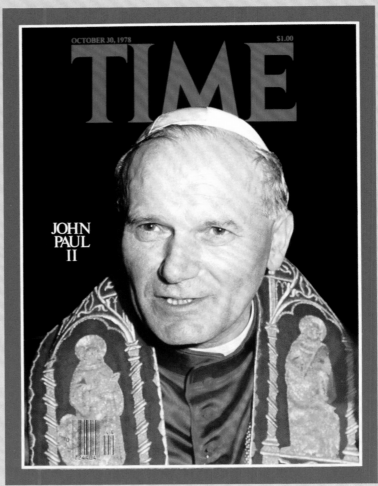

OCTOBER 30, 1978 | *Photograph by Arturo Mari*

MAY 25, 1981

JANUARY 9, 1984 | *Photograph by Arturo Mari*

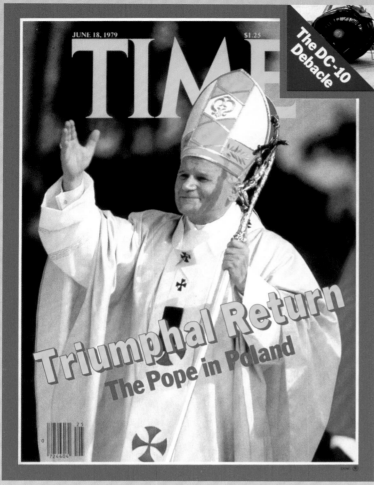

JUNE 18, 1979 | *Photograph by Gianfranco Gorgoni*

OCTOBER 15, 1979 | *Photograph by Neil Leifer*

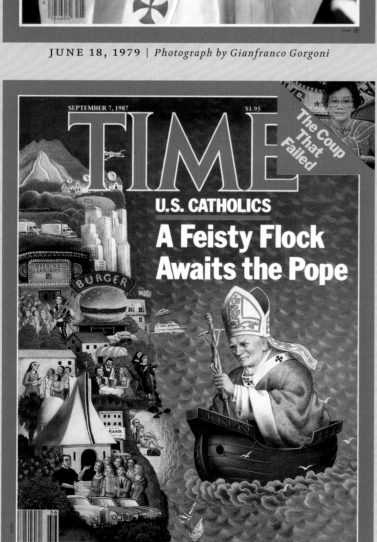

SEPTEMBER 7, 1987 | *Illustration by Kinuko Craft*

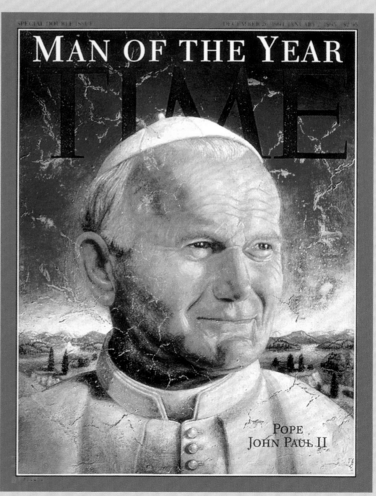

DECEMBER 26, 1994 | *Fresco by Nicholas Kahn and Richard Selesnick*

In the 1980s, Hollywood goddess Jane Fonda became the oracle of the aerobic way to fitness with a series of workout videos and books

Photograph by Steve Schapiro

□ Trends

N THE FALL OF 1959, AS THE NATION'S COLLEGE STUDENTS HEADED back to school, one thing was obvious to them: the great telephone-booth-stuffing craze that swept the country that spring had run out of steam. The kids had to come up with something new, something different. The result: hunkering, which involved squatting on the balls of their feet for as long as they could. Sounds like a wild time, doesn't it? Hunkering didn't last very long, soon taking its place in the tomb of departed fads alongside the zoot suit of the 1940s, the Hula-Hoop from the late '50s and the

Pet Rocks and mood rings of 1975. The Harlem shake is hunkering's energetic 2013 counterpart. That's the fate of fads. But some fads stick around, burrow into the culture and change it in unexpected ways, metamorphosing into trends that reflect subjects and issues that are much more tenacious.

In the 1950s, TIME's cover stories increasingly came to be about how we live, how we would like to live and the obsessions and anxieties that accompany our pleasures. There was, for instance, the subject of sexuality in its various forms. Sex, of course, is neither fad nor trend, but writing about it frankly in a publication like TIME was definitely a new kind of directness. In the article accompanying our 1969 "The Sex Explosion" cover, TIME declared that "an erotic renaissance (or rot, as some would have it) is upon the land. Owing to a growing climate of permissiveness—and the Pill—Americans today have more sexual freedom than any previous generation. Whatever changes have occurred in sex as behavior, the most spectacular are evident in sex as a spectator sport." That obsession lasted about two decades. Then with the spread of, among other things, sexually transmitted diseases like herpes and AIDS, TIME declared an end to the sexual revolution in its April 9, 1984, cover story, which read, "The buzz words these days are 'commitment,' 'intimacy' and 'working at relationships.' There is much talk of pendulum swings, matters coming full circle and a psychic return to prerevolutionary days."

The pendulum swung back and forth with other facets of modern living. In a 1991 cover story, TIME observed that "after a 10-year bender of gaudy dreams and godless consumerism, Americans are starting to trade down. They want to reduce their attachments to status symbols, fast-track careers and great expectations of Having It All. Upscale is out; downscale is in. Yuppies are an ancient civilization. Flaunting money is considered gauche: if you've got it, please keep it to yourself—or give some away!" A lot of that simplification would involve digitizing the way we live—a trend that TIME started spotting in the '60s with "The Computer in Society," its April 2, 1965, cover. At that moment, Steve Jobs had just turned 10, and Bill Gates was 9, and nobody had even dreamed of laptops, smartphones or the Internet. Peeking into this strange new world, TIME wrote, "Arranged row upon row in air-conditioned rooms, waited upon by crisp, young, white-shirted men who move softly among them like priests

serving in a shrine, the computers go about their work quietly and, for the most part, unseen by the public."

Almost everything in that sentence, including the white-shirted men, seems quaintly obsolete now; computers, then barely in their teens, as the story noted, would, however, elbow their way into daily life. But the conveniences afforded by computers would give way to anxieties over their unforeseen influence, from viruses to spam to the extinction of privacy. By 1997, TIME's tech guru Josh Quittner wrote, "If things seem crazy now, think how much crazier they will be when everybody is as wired as I am. We're in the midst of a global interconnection that is happening much faster than electrification did a century ago and is expected to have consequences at least as profound. What would happen if all the information stored on the world's computers were accessible via the Internet to anyone? Who would own it? Who would control it? Who would protect it from abuse?" Clearly, the new civilization-changing technology that made life simpler came with its own problems.

Of course, weightiness had little to do with much of TIME's reporting on trends. Unless it was about weight gain, in which case TIME chronicled America's many diet crazes. We have put fitness regimens and yoga on the cover—and come around to another view. In a 2009 cover article, we wrote, "The basic problem is that while it's true that exercise burns calories and that you must burn calories to lose weight, exercise has another effect: it can stimulate hunger. That causes us to eat more, which in turn can negate the weight-loss benefits we just accrued. Exercise, in other words, isn't necessarily helping us lose weight. It may even be making it harder." But the magazine has never really been against calories. We did a cover on ice cream in 1981.

Always, of course, the editors ponder the question, Is it a trend or just a fad that may disappear before the issue hits the stands? On June 8, 1953, for instance, TIME ran a cover story about 3-D movies. Fad or trend? Would this be the way we enjoy movies from now on? Shortly afterward, 3-D went into hibernation, remembered mainly as a phase your parents went through. It was just a fad.

Or was it? In the 1990s, spurred by new technology, 3-D came roaring back, and its latest, gaudiest incarnation is still with us, making big money for Hollywood. So 60 years ago, someone made the right call. —MIKE NEILL

THE SEX EXPLOSION

JULY 11, 1969 | *Photo-illustration by Dennis Wheeler*

3-D Movies
June 8, 1953
Illustration by Boris Artzybasheff

Hollywood was on the ropes—again. TV, still black and white and flickering, represented the future. Then came a technical innovation that lured audiences back to the theaters. It was fun while it lasted.

One day the movies had been just a mental transom the public was half-tired of peeking through. The next day the movies were a gap in the mind's defenses through which a roaring lion leaped and landed in the delighted moviegoer's lap. Spears and guns threatened his head, spiders walked on his face, beautiful girls reached alluringly from the screen. Then, just when a man's guard was up, came a roar of sound from the balcony, and, caught from behind and before, he was yanked into the screen and taken for a thrilling ride on a roller coaster ...

But even Hollywood admits that audiences in recent years have become more severely selective: It is an era of "the premeditated purchase." Can Hollywood reclaim, and retain, its prodigal audience? Or will the entertainment business settle down into a running fight between TV and the movies? ...

Can the moviemakers match all the technical to-do with some creative excitement, add some psychic dimensions to the physical sense of depth? ... "Revolution?" laughed a onetime Hollywood scriptwriter last week. "The only revolution I hear is the sound of Hollywood turning over in its grave." —HENRY BRADFORD DARRACH JR.

Amateur Photography
November 2, 1953
Illustration by Boris Artzybasheff

Forget the tribes who saw the camera as a soul-stealing demon. If any soul was at risk, it was that of the American determined to reduce all of civilization to an album of out-of-focus vacation shots.

The great Sphinx lay in fleeting twilight. In the background loomed the Pyramid of Cheops, majestic monument to human striving for eternity. Over the entire scene hovered the breath of the silent desert, the hush of ages. Then a voice spoke. "For God's sakes, Betsy, stop wiggling," said the voice. "Hold on a minute while I take another light reading ... Now, smile."

Before the natural wonders of the world and facing its innumerable small mysteries, before Niagara Falls, Mount Rushmore and the Eiffel Tower, in Siamese temples, French cathedrals and New England stores, at the bottom of the Grand Canyon and at the top of the Empire State Building, the U.S. amateur photographer pursues his hobby. His camera's combined clicks (he is taking nearly 2 billion pictures this year) would drown out the loudest thunder, and the combined light from his flashbulbs (he is using 500 million) would make a major planet pale. The sun to him is chiefly a source of light that often calls for a yellow filter and the moon merely an object which is hard to photograph without a tripod; he approaches the highest peaks through a telephoto lens, scans new horizons through his range finder— and if he ever comes across the Blue Bird, he would whip out his color chart. —ALEXANDER ELIOT

Do It Yourself

August 2, 1954
Illustration by Boris Artzybasheff

Awakened by sawing, drilling, hammering, America realized it was all coming from next door, driven by the self-reliant (and sometimes self-deluded), with the motto "Honey, I'll fix that!"

In the postwar decade the do-it-yourself craze has become a national phenomenon. The once indispensable handyman who could fix a chair, hang a door or patch a concrete walk has been replaced by millions of amateur hobbyists who do all his work—and much more—in their spare time and find it wonderful fun. In the process they have turned do-it-yourself into the biggest of all U.S. hobbies and a booming $6 billion-a-year business. The hobbyists, who trudge out of stores with boards balanced on their shoulders, have also added a new phase to retail jargon: "The shoulder trade." —GEORGE DANIELS

The Suburban Wife

June 20, 1960
Illustration by James Chapin

In 1963, Betty Friedan proclaimed, "We can no longer ignore that voice within women that says, 'I want something more than my husband and my children and my home.'" Not yet in 1960.

The key figure in all Suburbia, the thread that weaves between family and community—the keeper of the suburban dream—is the suburban housewife. In the absence of her commuting, city-working husband, she is first of all the manager of home and brood, and beyond that a sort of aproned activist with a penchant for keeping the neighborhood and community kettle whistling. With children on her mind and under her foot, she is breakfast getter ("You can't have ice cream for breakfast because I say you can't"); laundress, house cleaner, dishwasher, shopper, gardener, encyclopedia, arbitrator of children's disputes, policeman ("Tommy, didn't your mother ever tell you that it's not nice to go into people's houses and open their refrigerators?") ...

In Suburbia's pedocracy huge emphasis is placed on activities for the young ... The suburban wife might well be a can-opener cook, but she must have an appointment book and a driver's license and must be able to steer a menagerie of leggy youths through the streets with the coolness of a driver at the Sebring trials ... Beyond the home-centered dinner parties, Kaffeeklatsches and card parties, there is a directory-sized world of organizations devised for husbands as well as for wives (but it is the wife who keeps things organized). —JESSE L. BIRNBAUM

TWENTY-FIVE CENTS

JULY 14, 1961

CAMPING: Call of the Not So Wild

TIME
THE WEEKLY NEWSMAGAZINE

$7.00 A YEAR   (REG. U.S. PAT. OFF.)   VOL. LXXVIII NO. 2

Camping

July 14, 1961

Illustration by Boris Artzybasheff

Three centuries after the first colonial ax blade rang against the first tree trunk, Americans decided that, while they wouldn't want to live in the remaining wilderness, it was a nice place to visit.

Across the whole expanse of the U.S., the wildernesses where once only the hardiest of outdoorsmen trod now shuddered under the invasion of hundreds of thousands of families hungering for a summertime skirmish with nature. Smitten by the call of the not-so-wild, these families were happily engaged in a great and grown-up national pastime—camping …

Why this mass movement into the world of mosquitoes, snakes and burrs? … For a great number of other people, the urge goes deeper than economics: in a sense they still seek what Thoreau looked for at Walden.

The industrialization, urbanization and suburbanization of modern life have sharpened the need for many to rediscover the essential facts of existence … But as their industries, their urbs, suburbs and highways encroach upon the wilderness, that wilderness becomes particularly precious. Where it remains, its symbol has become a disturbingly anthropomorphic grizzly named Smokey the Bear, who wears pants and a hat and speaks …

But even for those who chose the new-style, cocktail-slinging mass encampments that will surely spread from park to park in the years ahead—even for those, there was least some of the flavor of living as the pioneers had lived. —JESSE L. BIRNBAUM

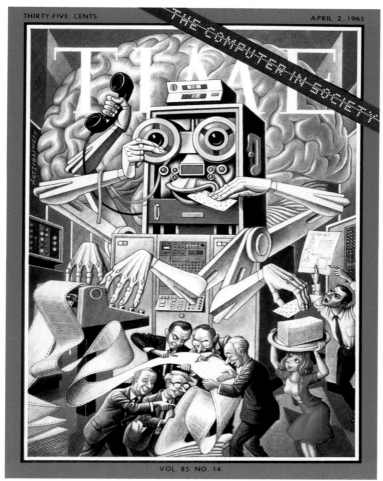

Computers
April 2, 1965
Illustration by Boris Artzybasheff

At the dawn of our digital age, giants ruled the world: room-size machines serviced by armies of programmers and technicians. As their roles in our lives expanded, computers would become smaller.

Just out of its teens, the computer is beginning to affect the very fabric of society, kindling both wonder and widespread apprehension. Is the computer a friend or enemy of man? Will it cause hopeless unemployment by speeding automation, that disquieting term that it has brought to the language? Will it devalue the human brain, or happily free it from drudgery? Will it ever learn to think for itself?

The answers will not be in for quite a while, but one thing is already clear: swept forward by a great wave of technology, of which the computer is the ultimate expression, human society is surely headed for some deep-reaching changes.

"The electronic computer," says Dr. Louis T. Rader, a vice president of General Electric, "may have a more beneficial potential for the human race than any other invention in history ..." Computermen have even been advised to get their machines out to "see life" in that society by setting up communications links between them and other computers in dispersed locations. Says R.M. Bloch, a vice president of Honeywell: "The computer that lacks an ability to communicate with the outside world is in danger of remaining an isolated marvel mumbling to itself in the air-conditioned seclusion of its company's data-processing room." —JOHN NOBLE WILFORD

London
April 15, 1966
Illustration by Geoffrey Dickinson

Britain lost an empire but found an unexpected role. The generation that had withstood the Blitz watched bemused as its children danced in the streets and invited the world to their hip capital.

In this century, every decade has had its city ... Today it is London, a city steeped in tradition, seized by change, liberated by affluence, graced by daffodils and anemones, so green with parks and squares that, as the saying goes, you can walk across it on the grass. In a decade dominated by youth, London has burst into bloom. It swings; it is the scene.

The city is alive with birds (girls) and beatles, buzzing with minicars and telly stars, pulsing with half a dozen separate veins of excitement. The guards now change at Buckingham Palace to a Lennon and McCartney tune, and Prince Charles is firmly in the longhair set ... London is not keeping the good news to itself. From Carnaby Street, the new, way-out fashion in young men's clothes is spreading around the globe, and so are the hairdos, the hairdon'ts and the sound of beat; in Czechoslovakia alone, there are 500 beat groups, all with English names ... It has become the place to go. It has become the latest mecca for Parisians who are tired of Paris ... From the jets that land at its doors pour a swelling cargo of the international set, businessmen, tourists—and just plain scene-makers. —PIRI HALASZ

Hippies

July 7, 1967

Illustration by Group Image

It was the Summer of Love, with the nation awash in love-ins and be-ins and the suddenly ubiquitous bouquet of pot everywhere. Without warning, America's children had turned into exotic aliens.

One sociologist called them "the Freudian proletariat." Another observer sees them as "expatriates living on our shores but beyond our society" ... To their deeply worried parents throughout the country, they seem more like dangerously deluded dropouts, candidates for a very sound spanking and a cram course in civics—if only they would return home to receive either ... Hippies preach altruism and mysticism, honesty, joy and nonviolence. They find an almost childish fascination in beads, blossoms and belts, blinding strobe lights and ear-shattering music, exotic clothing and exotic slogans. Their professed aim is nothing less than the subversion of Western society by "flower power" and force of example. —ROBERT JONES

APRIL 8, 1991 $2.50

Tense Times in Moscow

TIME

THE SIMPLE LIFE

Rejecting the rat race, Americans get back to basics

The Simple Life
April 8, 1991
Photograph by Ken Robbins

Overwhelmed with too much—too much work, too much stress, too much stuff—
some Americans decided to take Thoreau's advice to "simplify, simplify, simplify!"

In a TIME/CNN poll of 500 adults, 69% of the people surveyed said they would like to "slow down and live a more relaxed life" ... Marsha Bristow Bostick of Columbus remembers noticing with alarm last summer that her three-year-old daughter Betsy had memorized an awful lot of TV commercials. The toddler announced that she planned to take ballet lessons, followed by bride lessons. That helped inspire her mother, then 37, to quit her $150,000-a-year job as a marketing executive. She and her husband, Brent, a bank officer, decided that Betsy and their infant son Andrew needed more parental attention ... Marsha explained: "I found myself wondering, How wealthy do we need to be? I don't care if I have a great car, or if people are impressed with what I'm doing for a living. We have everything we need." —JANICE CASTRO

AUGUST 8, 1994 $2.95

TIME

Everybody's Hip
(And That's Not Cool)

724404 1   0

Being Hip
August 8, 1994
Illustration by Bryan Leister

Hepcat. Hipster. Hippie. Square. It was all so clear once. Then the lines began to blur as plain old Middle America embarked on a campaign of hip displacement.

Though it was always a little hard to pin down, hip was a notion roomy enough to describe flower children in tie-dye as well as bikers in black leather, the impeccable cool of John Coltrane's sax as well as the jerky forward thrust of Abbie Hoffman. All of it was admissible on the principle that it represented a heartfelt rejection of the mainstream. The mainstream was understood to be all-powerful and wrong about everything: politics, art, religion, sex, drugs and music. It was deaf to the beat, blind to the truth and dressed by Penney's … In its infinite pliancy, capitalism proved itself well suited to absorb whatever it was in hip that might fascinate consumers, while discarding the uncomfortable parts. For every counterculture, there emerged a corresponding sales counterculture. —RICHARD LACAYO

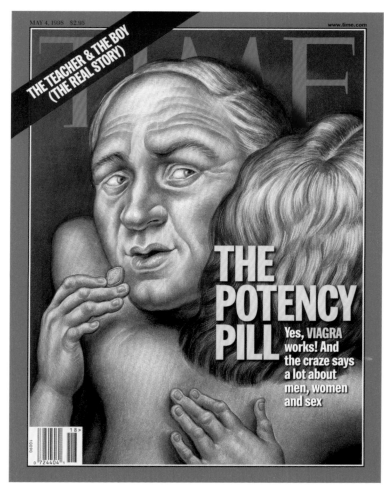

Viagra
May 4, 1998
Illustration by Anita Kunz

It was the Fountain of Youthfulness in pill form. Comedians filled the airwaves with bons mots about the new wonder drug, and American men laughed—but they filled their prescriptions.

"People always want a quick fix," complains Dr. Domeena Renshaw, a psychiatrist who directs the Loyola Sex Therapy Clinic outside Chicago. "They think Viagra is magic, just like they thought the G-spot worked like a garage-door opener ..." Pfizer, leaving nothing to chance, has even requested and received the Vatican's unofficial blessing for Viagra. All in all, a happy ending for American men, their partners and especially Pfizer stockholders, who have seen the value of their shares jump nearly 60% this year alone ...

The promise of Viagra is its discretion and ease of use. Doctors recommend taking the pill an hour before sex, which might lead to some wastage among overly optimistic users but shouldn't otherwise interfere greatly with the normal course of coital events ...

Tom Cannata, a 43-year-old accountant from Springfield, Mass., has been taking Viagra for the past three years as a trial subject ... So pleased has Cannata been with the results that he was inspired, he says, to go out and buy a sports car not long after beginning the drug—indicating, perhaps, a soon-to-boom, Viagra-inspired marketplace for souped-up cars, Aramis, oversize stereo equipment and other accoutrements of the virile life-style. —BRUCE HANDY

Low-Carb Diets
November 1, 1999

America, dreaming it was an M trapped in an XXL body, was looking at the numbers on the bathroom scale again—and realizing it couldn't see them. Naturally, we looked for a solution.

The fat-embracing diets, like so many fads we shouldn't have invited back, are from the '70s, when high-protein plans like the Scarsdale Diet and Dr. Atkins' Diet Revolution made fondue hip. Now the low-carb diets are back and bigger than ever. Low-carb diet books will clog up the top four spots next Sunday's New York *Times* paper best-seller list for advice and how-to books. Dr. Robert Atkins, at 69 still the reigning guru of the movement, is back on the charts with *Dr. Atkins' New Diet Revolution*. Other low-carb diet books jamming the shelves include *The Carbohydrate Addict's Diet* and a plateful of spin-offs by Rachael and Richard Heller, *Protein Power* by Drs. Michael and Mary Eades, *Sugar Busters!*, *The Zone* and *Suzanne Somers' Get Skinny on Fabulous Foods*. Some probably bought the Somers book for the color picture of her licking a butterflied-lamb-slicked finger, but it still became a No. 1 best seller, something her poetry collection (despite Johnny Carson's best efforts) never did. Even bread-loving France has had a best-selling high-protein diet book, *Eat Yourself Slim* by Michel Montignac, and Poland has the Optimal Nourishment plan. Russia would have one too if it had meat. —JOEL STEIN

Yoga

April 23, 2001

Photograph by Ruven Afanador

Seeking longevity, limberness, enlightenment and the chance to rock cool workout outfits, Americans went to the mat as the province of holy men in the East became big business in the West.

Stars do it. Sports do it. Judges in the highest courts do it. Let's do it; that yoga thing. A path to enlightenment that winds back 5,000 years to its native India, yoga has suddenly become so hot, so cool, so very this minute … Yoga now straddles the continent—from Hollywood, where $20 million-a-picture actors queue for a session with their guru du jour, to Washington, where, in the gym of the Supreme Court, Justice Sandra Day O'Connor and 15 others faithfully take their class each Thursday morning …

At each stage, the most persuasive advocates were movie idols and rock stars—salesmen, by example, of countless beguiling or corrosive fashions. If they could make cocaine and tattoos fashionable, perhaps they could goad the masses toward physical and spiritual enlightenment. Today yoga is practiced by so many stars with whom audiences are on a first-name basis—Madonna, Julia, Meg, Ricky, Michelle, Gwyneth, Sting—that it would be shorter work to list the actors who don't assume the asana …

"Madonna found it first, and I'm following in the footsteps of the stars," groans Minneapolis attorney Patricia Bloodgood. "But I don't think you should reject something just because it's trendy." —RICHARD CORLISS

Marijuana

November 4, 2002

Photo-illustration by Arthur Hochstein

With reefer madness well in the nation's rearview mirror, the forces pressing for repeal of marijuana laws were making their case forcefully. Our cover said one could be both all toke and all action.

So instead [pro-pot forces] fight federal policy with initiative after initiative, while also defending local pro-pot laws. Their side got a major media boost in California in September, when federal agents busted Santa Cruz's Wo/Men's Alliance for Medical Marijuana in an early-morning raid. The feds dragged the farm's owners, who were legally growing pot under California law, to a federal building in San Jose for breaking federal law and held a paraplegic resident at the farm for hours. "I opened my eyes to see five federal agents pointing assault rifles at my head. 'Get your hands over your head. Get up. Get up.' I took the respirator off my face, and I explained to them that I'm paralyzed," said Suzanne Pheil, 44, who is disabled by the effects of postpolio syndrome. Her story was broadcast everywhere, since the pro-pot people had basically been waiting for her to be harassed, punching every phone number on their media list minutes after the raid. Pot people, surprisingly, can move pretty fast when they want to. —JOEL STEIN

Jamie Lynne Grumet, 26, and her 3-year-old son

Attachment Parenting

May 21, 2012

Photograph by Martin Schoeller

Inside one of TIME'*s most incendiary covers, readers encountered one of our most controversial subjects: Dr. William Sears, the pediatrician author of the best-selling* The Baby Book.

Attachment parenting says that the more time babies spend in their mothers' arms, the better the chances they will turn out to be well-adjusted children. It's not a big leap from there to an inference that can send anxious moms into guilt-induced panic that any time away from their baby will have lifelong negative consequences. The debate and the anxiety have become a self-perpetuating cycle. So is attachment parenting a misogynist plot to take women out of the workplace and put them back in the home full time? Or is it a way to encourage mothers and babies to form loving bonds, which science has shown is beneficial to long-term emotional health and well-being? —KATE PICKERT

◻People

The 1981 marriage of Prince Charles to Lady Diana Spencer at St. Paul's Cathedral in London was watched by millions around the world

Photograph by Anwar Hussein

TWENTY-FIVE CENTS

APRIL 6, 1962

TIME

R Bouché

SOPHIA
LOREN

$7.50 A YEAR

(REG. U.S. PAT. OFF.)

VOL. LXXIX NO. 14

FROM TWITTER TO TUMBLR TO GAWKER TO BUZZFEED, THE 21st century appears hopelessly addicted to fame and the private lives of celebrities. Day by day, secrets are revealed—or perhaps packaged—for a public wanting to know more and more gossip about their idols. Including whom they are dating, what they are wearing, where they are dining and, of course, the percentage of clay in their feet. But the power of celebrity news—and its insinuations—arose in the 1920s with the emergence of Walter Winchell, the first syndicated gossip columnist, whose dominance of print and radio, the most effective media of the day, made him one of the most feared journalists of his time. He popularized what is now called the blind item, a cryptic bit of mongering written in a way to spur maximum speculation. As TIME wrote in its 1938 cover story on him, "After studying a picture of Winchell's nervous, foxlike face, examining the column and hearing his breathless voice on the radio, a psychiatrist recently classed Winchell as a sufferer from 'sublimated voyeurism,' a man who passionately wants to see, to know, hating a secret, vicariously participating in all the things he sees and learns about and living everybody's life." We may all be sublimated voyeurs.

Winchell was emulated by others: the gossip queens of Hollywood, Louella Parsons and Hedda Hopper (the latter on the cover of TIME herself in 1947), and through the decades, the high-society chronicler Suzy (the nom de plume of Aileen Mehle) and the genial generalist Liz Smith to Richard Johnson of Page Six, Matt Drudge and Nikki Finke. These are the high priests of the mythology of celebrity, propagating the parables of the rich and famous, sinners and sinned against, transforming them from paragons to pariahs or vice versa in the cautionary tales that the public craves.

Princes and princesses, of course, are almost always to these narratives born, royalty being our own ordinary families writ large—bedecked with crowns and jewels, exemplary at times but, just as often, a reason to wag fingers. Thus the fascination with King Edward VIII's decision in 1936 to abdicate the British throne because "I have found it impossible to carry the heavy burden of responsibility and to discharge my duties as King as I would wish to do without the help and support of the woman I love." In the 1990s, there was a similar obsession with the infidelities that led to the breakup of the marriage of his great-nephew Charles and his mediagenic wife Diana Spencer—as there were great expectations for the happiness of their son William and his bride Kate Middleton at their marriage in 2011. Royal families carry the burden of all families, happy and unhappy in every way.

In the U.S., where there are no hereditary titles, the role of royalty is played by a variety of people: the wealthy and the denizens of the make-believe kingdom of Hollywood. And the Kennedys. These stories were sprinkled with heroics, steeped in melodrama and simmered with scandal to provide an irresistible heat. Beginning with its very first issue, on March 3, 1923, TIME had a section called Imaginary Interviews, which declared, "During the past week, the daily press gave extensive publicity to the following men and women. Let each explain to you why his name appeared in the headlines." There followed boldfaced names with statements fabricated from the known facts and placed between quote marks to give the impression that the words had actually been uttered by the celebrities. By Sept. 13, 1926, Imaginary Interviews had become the People section, a legendary department that remained a magazine staple till 2008. (The section would inspire the title of another Time Inc. publication, PEOPLE, which was first published in 1974.)

But the pithy tales of the People section, which quickly involved real reporting as the magazine's resources grew, were not the only stage for celebrities in TIME. The cover itself became a natural niche for their public and private lives. Tragedy would humanize heroic figures but also make them subject to tabloid reflexes. In 1926, Charles Lindbergh became the first person to fly solo across the Atlantic and achieved almost mythic status because Americans saw themselves in his taciturnity. Fascination became near hysteria after his young son was kidnapped and later found dead—a story featured on the cover of TIME on May 2, 1932. More than 60 years later, the country and much of the rest of the world would obsess over the details of a Los Angeles murder case involving O.J. Simpson, transforming him from an affable former football hero to one of America's most unwanted. Perfection, physical or moral, is hardly a requisite for celebrity. Otherwise, most would look like fashion models and live as hermits. There is always a certain oddness about the people whose lives we are drawn to. Hence Julia Child's gangliness was key to her culinary charm, as Cher's crooked teeth were to her sequined sexiness. This was how TIME described the woman on its April 6, 1962, cover: "Her feet are too big. Her nose is too long. Her teeth are uneven. She has the neck, as one of her rivals has put it, of 'a Neapolitan giraffe.' Her waist seems to begin in the middle of her thighs, and she has big, half-bushel hips. She runs like a fullback. Her hands are huge. Her forehead is low. Her mouth is too large. And, *mamma mia,* she is absolutely gorgeous." Who was this? Sophia Loren. Through nine decades of TIME, the rule for celebrities has been this: You're imperfect; don't ever change. —HOWARD CHUA-EOAN

SOPHIA LOREN

APRIL 6, 1962 | *Portrait by R. Bouché*

Charlie Chaplin
July 6, 1925

During a career muddle, the future legend got advice from Roscoe "Fatty" Arbuckle, his comic predecessor in the movie world, who was felled by a sex scandal in 1924.

His first efforts to be funny in celluloid were dismal. Keystone [Film] directors feared that he was overpaid, offered to cancel the contract. Chaplin told Roscoe Arbuckle, the now deposed cinema clown, that he needed a pair of shoes. Arbuckle tossed him a pair of his own enormous brogues. "There you are man," he said. "Perfect fit." Chaplin put them on, cocked his battered derby over his ear, twisted the ends of his prim moustache. His face was very sad. He attempted a jaunty walk which became, inevitably, a heart-breaking waddle. He put his hand on the seat of his trousers, spun on his heel. Arbuckle told him that he was almost funny. Such was the research that led him to "create a figure that would be a living satire on every human vanity" ... His [$40] salary became $1,000, $2,000, $3,000 a week ... He sat down in eggs. He held babies in his lap. His salary became $1,000,000 a year.

Leni Riefenstahl
February 17, 1936
Photograph by Martin Munkácsi

Adolf Hitler's cinematic propagandist was a "cinemactress"—a TIME neologism with a brief lifespan—and a magnet for rumors about the German leader's romantic life.

In 1934 she met Adolf Hitler, who had long admired her work on the screen. He perceived in her a personification of those qualities of health, energy, ambition, good-looks, youth and love of sport which are the German equivalent of female glamour, promptly amazed the German cinema industry by commissioning her to make the official film of last summer's Nuremberg Party Congress in which she directed 800,000 men. When Herr Hitler's crony, Air Minister Göring, married Cinemactress Riefenstahl's crony, Actress Emmy Sonnemann, last year, Hitler was best man. That Realmleader Hitler, a confirmed celibate, has any such intentions concerning Cinemactress Leni Riefenstahl no one suspects for a moment, but that he holds her in high esteem, entertains romantic admiration for her achievements and her character as a prime example of German womanhood, is apparent to everyone. Functioning as an inspiration both to Herr Hitler and her female contemporaries is a job which, for Cinemactress Riefenstahl, is never done.

The Dionne Quintuplets

May 31, 1937

Their third birthday was a moment to remember the miracle of the five little Canadian girls. All other such multiple births had lived no more than a few hours.

Dr. [Allan Roy] Dafoe admits that he could not believe they would live. After baptizing them himself, he left them lying "like rats" under a blanket at the foot of their mother's bed, while he went for a priest to give them a regular Roman Catholic baptism. Later that morning, as a matter of routine, he eye-dropped a little warm water into each shapeless mouth. When the tiny monstrosities continued to breathe, he added rum to the water, later corn syrup ... Next day he weighed the lot in a scoop scale usually used for potatoes. Gross weight of the five: 13 lb. 6 oz. Their average height was only 9 in. ... But then they began to gain and Medicine mobilized. From Chicago and Toronto had come incubators and bottles of mother's milk ... No country doctor ever received such a volume of expert advice as did Dr. Dafoe from foremost pediatricians all over the continent.

Grace Kelly

January 31, 1955
Portrait by Boris Chaliapin

The patrician actress took Hollywood by storm and abandoned it just as dramatically in 1956 to marry Prince Rainier of Monaco. Their offspring remain tabloid fodder.

Said one Hollywood observer: "Most of these dames just suggest Kinsey statistics. But if a guy in a movie theater starts mooning about Grace, there could be nothing squalid about it; his wife would have to be made to understand that it was something fine—and bigger than all of them. Her peculiar talent, you might say, is that she inspires licit passion ..." The well-bred Miss Grace Kelly of Philadelphia has baffled Hollywood. She is a rich girl who has struck it rich. She was not discovered behind a soda fountain or at a drive-in. She is a star who was never a starlet, who never worked up from B pictures, never posed for cheesecake, was never elected, with a press agent's help, Miss Antiaircraft Battery C. She did not gush or twitter or desperately pull wires for a chance to get in the movies. Twice she turned down good Hollywood contracts. When she finally signed on the line, she forced mighty M-G-M itself to grant her special terms. —A.T. BAKER

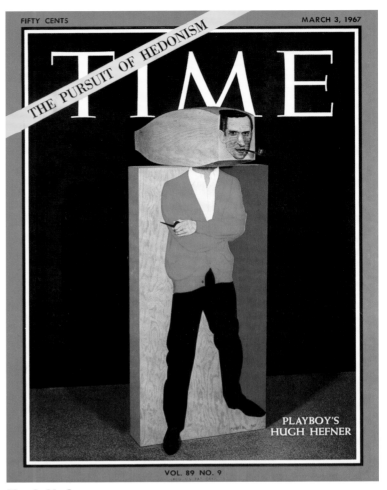

Julia Child
November 25, 1966
Portrait by Boris Chaliapin

The woman who was once a spy became America's tutor in French cooking. Her personality continues to resonate in the culture, with movies and countless impersonations.

The TV camera zooms in for a close-up and focuses on her hands. She may be dicing an onion, mincing a garlic clove, trussing a chicken. Her fingers fly with the speed and dexterity of a concert pianist. Strength counts, too, as she cleaves an ocean catfish with a mighty, two-fisted swipe or, muscles bulging and curls aquiver, whips up egg whites with her wire whisk. She takes every short cut, squeezes lemons through "my ever-clean dish towel," samples sauces with her fingers. No matter if she breaks the rules. Her verve and insouciance will see her through. Even her failures and faux pas are classic. When a potato pancake falls on the worktable, she scoops it back into the pan, bats her big blue eyes at the cameras, and advises: "Remember, you're all alone in the kitchen and no one can see you." —MARSHALL BURCHARD

Hugh Hefner
March 3, 1967
Sculpture by Marisol

The founder and publisher of Playboy *magazine brought the sybaritic life and the joy of sex into the American consumerist mainstream, complete with centerfold. Oh, and thoughtful articles too.*

Dialogue between Art Director Paul and Editor Hefner when choosing pictures for the Playmates-of-the-year feature:
Paul: This is the best shot of her face.
Hef: That shot makes the girl look too Hollywoodish. She doesn't look natural.
Paul: Don't her breasts look somewhat distorted? ... It looks as if the shots were made on a foggy day. We don't want to mix the reader up. You can't really be sure that this is the same girl.
Hef (viewing new layout): There is something wrong with the angle of that shot. Her thighs and hips look awkward. This doesn't do her justice ... There must be other aspects to her personality. —EDWIN G. WARNER

75 CENTS

MARCH 17, 1975

TIME

Glad Rags to Riches
Cher

Cher

March 17, 1975

Photograph by Richard Avedon

The epitome of camp, glam, kitsch and Vegas, she divorced her partner Sonny Bono in 1975 and later won an Oscar as Best Actress for her role in Moonstruck.

Her liberation from Sonny is a personal triumph, but it carries no ideological example for the rest of womankind, so far as Cher can see. As for being a sex symbol for males, that too is mostly in the eye of the beholder. It is true that after leaving Sonny she involved herself for more than 15 months in a much-publicized romance with David Geffen, 31, innovative president of Elektra/Asylum/Nonesuch Records. "Look, I've traded one short, ugly man for another," she zinged—typically—when she and Geffen ran into Singer-Songwriter Paul Simon. Then, a few months ago, she took up with Gregg Allman, lead vocalist in the rock band that bears his name. But these have not been casual affairs. "I'm a one-man-at-a-time woman," she says. "To put it in the vernacular, I'm not an easy lay." —RICHARD SCHICKEL

In the late 1970s,
New York's Studio 54 was
the planet's hottest celeb
hangout. From right: Andy
Warhol, Bianca Jagger and
Interview's Bob Colacello

*Photograph by
Ron Galella*

Elton John
July 7, 1975
Portrait by Don Weller

The singer, knighted by Queen Elizabeth II in 1996, came out as gay in 1988. He and his partner David Furnish are now the parents of two children.

The disaster he was saved from was marriage to a 6-ft. 2-in. girl named Linda. He had been smitten by her when she came to a Christmas Eve bash he was playing ... Terribly insecure then (and now) around women, he may have been encouraged to unwonted boldness by the fact that her escort on that occasion was a midget. In any event, by the following summer she was sharing a pad with Elton and Bernie [Taupin, his music-writing partner]. Elton was miserably going ahead with plans to marry her, despite the fact that "she hated my music. Everything I'd write she'd put down ..." It was not exactly a match made in heaven. Still, when the pair broke up shortly before the wedding day, Elton was bereft. "I tried to commit suicide. It was a very Woody Allen type suicide. I turned on the gas and left all the windows open." He has remained "wary of up-front women getting to know me." There have been very few women in the Elton entourage since. —RICHARD SCHICKEL

John Travolta
April 3, 1978
Photograph by Douglas Kirkland

Catching his big break on the sitcom Welcome Back Kotter, *Travolta swiftly transformed himself from teen idol into a serious actor—with some serious dance moves.*

The movie star Travolta most clearly calls to mind is Montgomery Clift. Travolta may lack the depth of Clift's gifts, but he has much the same quicksilver charm. He too can give an audience the sense of immediate but always fragile intimacy, of shared secrets, of private truths known without speaking.

And sexuality. "Maybe the major thing is how sensual he is," suggests Lily Tomlin, who will star with him this spring in a romance called *Moment to Moment.* "And how sexy too. The sensitivity and the sexuality are very strong. It's as if he has every dichotomy—masculinity, femininity, refinement, crudity. You see him, you fall in love a little bit." Adds *Saturday Night Live* Producer Lorne Michaels ... "John is the perfect star for the '70s. He has this strange androgynous quality, this all-pervasive sexuality. Men don't find him terribly threatening. And women, well ..."

There is a whole future in that ellipsis. —JAY COCKS

The Allure of The Kennedys: An American Saga

The Kennedys are often called America's royal family. But for most of the 20th century, the clan was more of a dynasty on the make than the coroneted one on the other side of the Atlantic. "The Kennedy clan is as handsome and spirited as a meadow full of Irish thoroughbreds, as tough as a blackthorn shillelagh, as ruthless as Cuchulain, the mythical hero who cast up on the hills of Ireland with his sword," declared a TIME cover story on July 11, 1960. The patriarch was old Joe Kennedy, the diplomat and plutocrat who had been on the cover of TIME twice by the time he and 10 other members of the storied Irish-American clan were featured on that cover (including a cameo of his father-in-law, the influential Boston politician John "Honey Fitz" Fitzgerald). Front and center were the family's two most luminous stars: Democratic presidential candidate John F. Kennedy and his wife Jacqueline. Jack and Jackie would occupy the White House for a brief presidency but a long love affair with America—enhanced by glamour, energized by youth and made legendary by tragedy. Jackie Kennedy's life would be a barometer of American sentiment—stoic at the funeral of her husband; emotional as she recalled their life as "Camelot"; despondent when she abandoned the country after her brother-in-law's 1968 murder to marry the Greek shipping magnate Aristotle Onassis, transforming into Jackie O; and then mesmerized by anything that had touched her when, after her death in 1994, much of her estate was auctioned, setting off a frenzy. After JFK's death, the family's hopes moved to his brother Bobby, a crusade that ended with his assassination, then to Teddy, who would serve as one of the country's most influential liberal Senators till his death in 2009. For a few moments, many looked upon young John Kennedy Jr., too, as a family standard bearer. A fatal plane accident in 1999 ended that dream.

THE KENNEDYS | July 11, 1960

Portrait by Bernard Safran

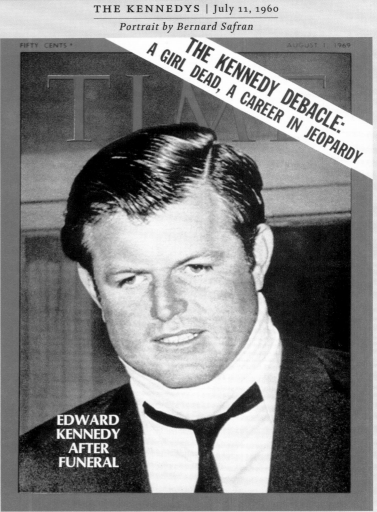

THE CHAPPAQUIDDICK AFFAIR | August 1, 1969

Photograph by Lou La Prade

ROBERT KENNEDY | May 24, 1968

Portrait by Roy Lichtenstein

JACKIE & ARI ONASSIS | October 25, 1968

Portrait by Robert Vickrey

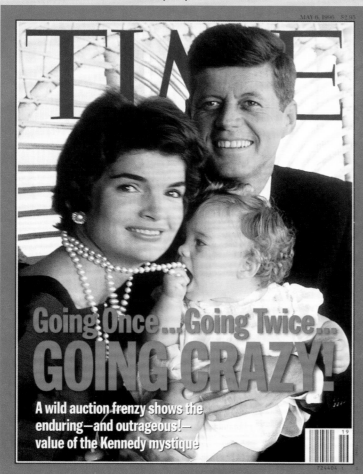

THE KENNEDY AUCTION | May 6, 1996

Photograph by Jacques Lowe

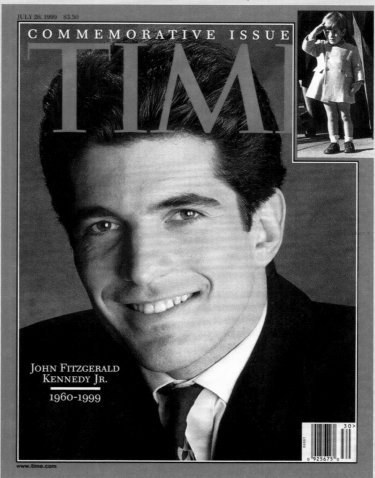

THE DEATH OF JFK JR. | July 26, 1999

Photograph by Ken Regan

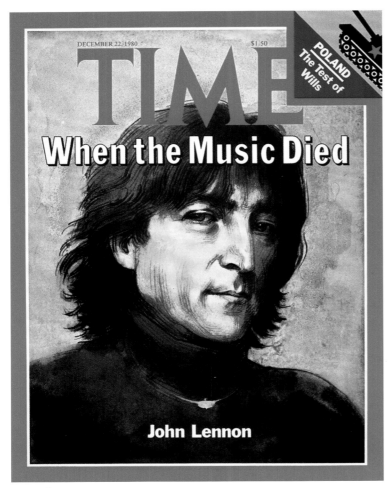

John Lennon
December 22, 1980
Portrait by Daniel Maffia

The Beatle's murder in New York City occurred in the middle of a career comeback. He is commemorated by a circle called Strawberry Fields in Central Park.

The outpouring of grief, wonder and shared devastation that followed Lennon's death had the same breadth and intensity as the reaction to the killing of a world figure: some bold and popular politician, like John or Robert Kennedy, or a spiritual leader, like Martin Luther King Jr. But Lennon was a creature of poetic political metaphor, and his spiritual consciousness was directed inward, as a way of nurturing and widening his creative force. That was what made the impact, and the difference—the shock of his imagination, the penetrating and pervasive traces of his genius—and it was the loss of all that, in so abrupt and awful a way, that was mourned last week, all over the world. The last "Day in the Life," "I read the news today, oh boy ..." —JAY COCKS

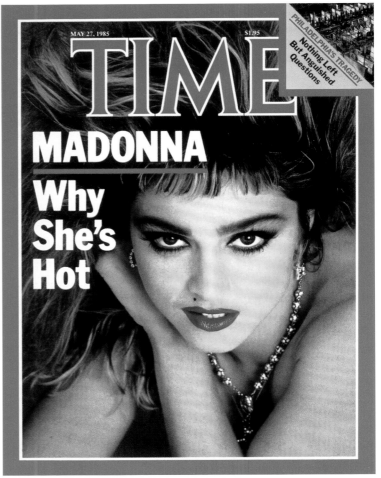

Madonna
May 27, 1985
Photograph by Francesco Scavullo

The Material Girl is also a chameleon—changing personae with each new album and retaining a loyal fan base from the 1980s into the second decade of the 21st century.

She seems to have passed through the lives of a lot of people and to have remained in not many. She sees her father and stepmother only rarely. It can be hard, now, to get her to talk about her scroungy years in New York. She recalls being fired from a long succession of ratty jobs. She resents suggestions that she slept her way to the top. That is not because she didn't learn her trade from a succession of musicians and deejays, some of whom she slept with, but because the idea that she couldn't make it to the top on drive and talent alone is insulting ... Mark Kamins, deejay at the Danceteria, a funky, four-floor Chelsea disco that caters to purple-haired punks in leather and other exotics, is credited with "discovering" Madonna in 1982, although like America before Columbus, she was there all along. "She had this incredible sense of style," says Kamins. "She had an aura." —JOHN SKOW

O.J. Simpson

June 27, 1994

Photo-illustration by Matt Mahurin

The cover caused controversy because Simpson's face appears darker than the original mug shot. TIME *apologized, saying it intended no commentary on race.*

Friends who knew Simpson well understood that he was a creature of careful intention, the natural ease a measure of his discipline. He did not so much change, from the days of his raw, painful childhood, as add layers, coats of polish that only occasionally peeled. One day he was making a television commercial in Oakland, California, and fell into his first language, the street-corner argot of his gang years. Furious with himself, he stopped the shooting, regrouped and then said he wanted to do it again. The second try went perfectly. "That's what happens when I spend too much time with my boys," he said. "I forget how to talk white." It's not that Simpson was a phony; he was just a man who had traveled a long way, accumulating public expectations. When his image was autopsied last week, the story of his life provided evidence to both sides; that he was gentle and generous and violent and mean. —NANCY GIBBS

Ellen DeGeneres

April 14, 1997

Photograph by Firooz Zahedi

When the TV host wed actress Portia de Rossi in California in 2008, People *magazine put them on its cover, with a story that, reflecting changed attitudes, focused on the flowers and food, not sexuality.*

I always thought I could keep my personal life separate from my professional life," says DeGeneres ... "In every interview I ever did ... everyone tried to trap me into saying I was gay. And I learned every way to dodge that. Or if they just blatantly asked me, I would say I don't talk about my personal life. I mean, I really tried to figure out every way to avoid answering that question for as long as I could." That became a lot harder last September when the news leaked ... that DeGeneres wanted to have the character she plays on *Ellen,* her three-year-old ABC sitcom, discover that she—the character, that is—is a lesbian ... For the public, the news was a sensation: a gay lead on TV—that would be a first, and to those who attach importance to these sorts of things, either a long time coming or another way station on the road to moral abandon ... Or maybe it was just something to gossip about. —BRUCE HANDY

KING GEORGE VI | May 15, 1939

Portrait by Ernest Hamlin Baker

The Royal Way Of the Windsors: A Very British Style

Royalty has always been welcome in TIME, even if the appearance is sometimes an excuse to question the practical purpose served by crowned heads of state. The very first iteration of what would become the magazine's People section cited two members of the British royal family: the Prince of Wales—the future King Edward VIII, very briefly—and his brother Prince George, who would become King thereafter and, as father of Elizabeth II, the progenitor of the ruling line of Windsors. The American fascination with British royalty may be a tenacious holdover from the colonial era, but there is something about primogeniture (and the limits imposed even on Kings by the established church) that make such pomp and circumstance exotic and quaint and, indeed, simpler than the messy machinations of democratic political succession. Plus, scandal is much more palatable—and entertaining—when it does not have serious bureaucratic consequences. The Windsors, in this case, have been an epic fairy tale, well worth the distraction from the real world. While the 1936 abdication of Edward VIII was a crisis in the royal family, there was the less charismatic but much more suitable George waiting to become King. Diana Spencer's entry into the Windsor fold was meant to give the old royal firm a new vigor, and with her vivacity and charm, it did. The world fell in love with her. Unfortunately, the Prince she was in love with did not feel the same way, and soon the world was falling out of love with Charles and the Windsors as well. The couple's divorce and her sudden death in a 1997 car accident in Paris sent much of the globe into mourning even as all eyes turned in hope to her son William to try to finally bring the fairy tale to a happy ending. And so it continues.

CHARLES AND DIANA | November 11, 1985

Photograph by Lionel Cherruault

QUEEN ELIZABETH II | January 5, 1953

Portrait by Boris Chaliapin

PRINCE CHARLES | June 27, 1969

Portrait by Peter Max

THE DEATH OF DIANA | September 8, 1997

Photograph by Mark Lennihan

KATE & WILLIAM | May 16, 2011

Photograph by John Stillwell

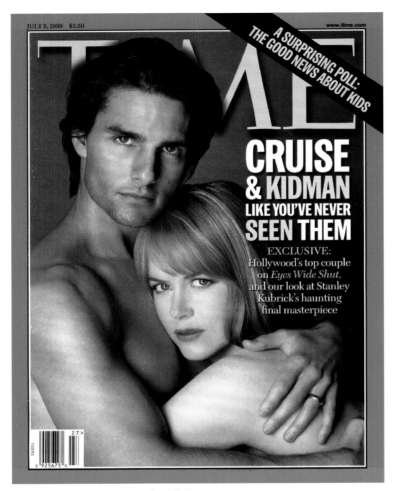

Tom Cruise and Nicole Kidman
July 5, 1999
Photograph by Herb Ritts

The couple, who adopted two children together, had been the subject of many rumors because of his prominent role in the Church of Scientology. They divorced in 2001.

When Warner Bros. ... announced the project in 1995, it merely stated that [director Stanley] Kubrick was making "a story of sexual jealousy and obsession starring Tom Cruise and Nicole Kidman." Officially, no one has added anything substantive to that press release in the years since—which is, of course, why the rumor that Cruise and Kidman play psychiatrists drawn into a web of sexual intrigue with their patients got started. And the one about the mad genius Kubrick making an NC-17-rated blue movie. And the one that has Cruise wearing a dress in one sequence. None of these are remotely true. —RICHARD CORLISS

George Harrison
December 10, 2001
Photograph by Mark Seliger

Of the Fab Four, he was the most given to mysticism and spiritual seaching. After his death from lung cancer, the Beatle's ashes were cast into the rivers that meet at the holy city of Benares in India.

He was the quiet Beatle only in that he was standing alongside two louder-than-life characters and in front of a guy playing drums. He held many strong opinions—on Beatlemania, on global want, on his right to privacy, on his God—and gave firm voice to most of them. But George Harrison was certainly the most reluctant Beatle, wanting out almost as soon as he was in. He often said that his luckiest break was joining the band and his second luckiest was leaving it ... "Being a Beatle was a nightmare, a horror story. I don't even like to think about it." He never really looked comfortable in his tight suit and pudding-basin haircut, not even in the fun-fest *A Hard Day's Night,* and in this he was perhaps the most honest Beatle, the one least convincing when wearing the mask. The standard line is that George Harrison was an enigma, but perhaps he was transparent: a terrific guitarist, a fine songwriter, a wonderer, a seeker and, overriding all, a celebrity who hated and feared celebrity. —ROBERT SULLIVAN

Michael Jackson

July 2009 (special issue)
Photograph by Herb Ritts

Four days after the superstar's death from an overdose of the drug propofol, TIME *published a special issue commemorating his life, his music and the way he changed the world of entertainment.*

Even if he had succeeded in making it back to the top for a while, however, it would have always been difficult to imagine Jackson, the eternal child, in old age. It was hard not to picture him as ever more eccentric and secluded, like Howard Hughes, or Gloria Swanson in *Sunset Boulevard.* The Michael Jackson we prefer to keep in our memories is the man-child at the height of his phenomenal powers, the one with the saw-toothed yelps and the jackhammer moves, the one who flung thunderbolts from the stage. That's the man whom the future, which has a way of putting uncomfortable questions to the side, will take to its heart. —RICHARD LACAYO

Person Of the Year

British Prime Minister
Winston Churchill was
TIME's Man of the Year
in 1941 and was named
TIME's Man of the
Half-Century in 1950

*Photograph by
Hans Wild*

THE YEAR 1927 WAS DRAWING TO A CLOSE, AND WITH THE NEWS fronts quiet for the holidays, TIME's editors were stumped for a cover subject. An inspired idea was needed, and some nameless hero came up with it. Why not Charles Lindbergh? It would make up for the magazine's failure to put him on the cover when he completed his epochal solo flight across the Atlantic earlier that year. To offset the belatedness of Lindy's appearance, TIME could dub him Man of the Year. ¶Thus was born the magazine's most distinctive feature. What began as an afterthought quickly grew into a journalistic institution. Today TIME's annual selection of a Person of the Year is a news event in itself, widely followed and widely imitated. As the end of each year approaches, readers submit nominations by the thousands. The announcement of the choice triggers a flood of comments, second-guessing, cheers and raspberries in forums around the world, from Internet blogs to editorial pages to office water coolers.

When the Lindbergh stopgap was being considered, TIME's co-founder Henry Luce wondered uneasily whether sufficiently prominent people could be found in subsequent years to warrant the designation Man of the Year. He need not have worried. In the decades since, a succession of towering personalities has emerged to claim the title—statesmen and warriors, shapers of nations, Popes and other spiritual leaders, brilliant scientists and thinkers, trailblazing artists and tycoons. By the time such figures were chosen, they usually were already famous. But not always. Occasionally TIME picked relatively obscure people as exemplars of a major field of endeavor, as when it named AIDS researcher Dr. David Ho in 1996.

The Person of the Year is the fullest realization of one of TIME's bedrock principles: its focus on individuals, its penchant for telling stories through representative people. Luce and his partner, Briton Hadden, subscribed to the great-man theory, the notion that powerful individuals influence history more than impersonal political and socioeconomic forces do. TIME's cover subjects, particularly in its earlier decades, were almost always individuals.

After the Man of the Year was launched, it was not long before the magazine had to bend the formula it had devised. In 1936 the unavoidable choice was Wallis Simpson, the American divorcée for whom Edward VIII had renounced the British throne in a drama that captivated the world. And so, for the first time, the Man of the Year temporarily became the Woman of the Year. (Not until 1999 did TIME resolve the gender issue for good by changing the title to Person of the Year.) The following year brought another variation. In 1937 TIME selected a Man and Wife of the Year, Generalissimo and Madame Chiang Kai-Shek, whose quest to unify and rule all of China Luce fervently championed.

In later decades the designation grew ever more flexible. Some leaders, for example, dominate not just a year but an entire era. Acknowledging Winston Churchill's lifetime at the forefront of international affairs, most notably during World War II, TIME named him Man of the Half-Century in 1949. This set the precedent for a Man of the Decade in 1990 (the reformist Soviet leader Mikhail Gorbachev) and a Person of the Century in 1999 (physicist Albert Einstein, a "locksmith of the mysteries of man and the universe").

The choice in 1950 was the U.S. Fighting Man, representing the servicemen at war in Korea. It was the first symbolic figure selected by TIME. The generic G.I. was followed by such other symbols and groups as the Hungarian Freedom Fighter (1957), the Twenty-Five and Under generation (1966) and U.S. Women (1975). Twice the selection was not even human. In 1982 TIME named the computer the Machine of the Year, and in 1988 the environmentally endangered Earth was the Planet of the Year.

Throughout these changes over the years, the criterion for the Person of the Year has stayed the same. It is the individual who, for good or ill, exerted the greatest influence on the year's events. Readers have always had a problem with the "or ill" part of the formulation. They tend to see the designation as an honor, forgetting that it is an impartial news judgment. The key is impact, not merit.

Nevertheless, outrage greeted the choice of Adolf Hitler as Man of the Year in 1938. Even Luce, who was out of town when the issue went to press, was angered by the cover illustration, which he felt abandoned objectivity and lapsed into editorializing. Readers were even more upset by the choice of Iran's Ayatullah Ruhollah Khomeini in 1980 after his radical Islamist followers overpowered the U.S. embassy in Tehran and held 52 Americans hostage. In one of the most impassioned outpourings in the magazine's history, nearly 5,000 readers sent letters about the Khomeini cover—84% of them negative.

It may be that the Person of the Year can never please everyone—nor should it. TIME came close, however, with one of its most audacious and unusual selections. In 2006 the Person of the Year was You, the reader, for "seizing the reins of the global media, for founding and framing the new digital democracy." TIME affixed a piece of reflective Mylar to the cover illustration of a computer screen on each copy, 6.9 million in all. Some questioned whether this was too much of a clever gimmick. But really, who could resist seeing one's own mirrored face gazing out from under that famous rubric? It seemed, for once, a choice that every reader could approve. —CHRISTOPHER PORTERFIELD

Charles Lindbergh

January 2, 1928

Portrait by S.J. Woolf

Lindbergh's pioneering transatlantic flight made him a worldwide hero of almost unequaled dimensions. He did not welcome the fame, but he seized upon a lifelong mission to promote aviation.

Height: 6 ft. 2 in. Age: 25. Eyes: blue. Cheeks: pink. Hair: sandy. Feet: large. (When he arrived at the American embassy in France no shoes big enough were handy.) Habits: smokes not; drinks not. Does not gamble. Eats a thoroughgoing breakfast. Prefers light luncheon and dinner when permitted ... Likes sweets. Characteristics: modesty, taciturnity, diffidence (women make him blush), singleness of purpose, courage, occasional curtness ...

He has flown to France, Belgium, England, Mexico, Canada in the interests (his) of aviation progress and the interests (governmental) of international goodwill ... He climbed into *The Spirit of St. Louis* at Mexico City; nosed upward; set off for Guatemala, British Honduras, Salvador, Honduras, Nicaragua, Costa Rica, Panama.

In Detroit a schoolteacher put aside her pointer and ... journeyed south to meet her son in Mexico City. Mrs. Evangeline Lodge Lindbergh, previously laconic regarding the achievements of her amazing child, expressed herself to the press thus: "He has always been my boy. I have always loved him, been proud of him and thought he was the world's greatest."

Mohandas Gandhi

January 5, 1931

Portrait by V. Perfilioff

Mohandas Gandhi's shrewd, stubborn campaign of civil disobedience galvanized the subcontinent's masses and forced the Raj down the road that would lead to India's independence in 1947.

It was exactly twelve months ago that Mohandas Karamchand Gandhi's Indian National Congress promulgated the Declaration of Indian Independence. It was in March that he marched to the sea to defy Britain's salt tax as some New Englanders once defied a British tea tax. It was in May that Britain jailed Gandhi at Poona. Last week he was still there, and some 30,000 members of his Independence movement were caged elsewhere ...

[British journalist Henry Noel] Brailsford traveled through district after district where the peasants had taken and kept this vow: "We will pay no taxes until Gandhi is released from jail."

For Mr. Gandhi, for the Mahatma, for St. Gandhi, for Jailbird Gandhi, not thousands but millions of individual Indians are taking individual beatings which they could escape by paying what His Majesty's Government call, quite accurately, "normal taxes" ...

Although [the government] have got him in a jail staffed by British jailers, they have not yet stopped him from producing writings which are smuggled out somehow, week after week, to his people.

Wallis Warfield Simpson
January 4, 1937
Portrait by Dorothy Wilding

The world was transfixed by Edward VIII's renunciation of the English throne, and especially by the woman he abdicated for: a commoner, a divorcée—and an American!—Wallis Simpson.

In the entire history of Great Britain there has been only one voluntary royal abdication, and it came about in 1936 solely because of one woman, Mrs. Wallis Simpson ... Mrs. Simpson was an ordinary divorcée of the international set, definitely not rich and seldom or never mentioned in society columns. In the single year 1936 she became the most-talked-about, written-about, headlined and interest-compelling person in the world. In this regard no woman in history has ever equaled Mrs. Simpson, for no press or radio existed to spread the world news they made ...

In England the news that the king, as king, wanted to marry Mrs. Simpson was the culmination of a tide of events sweeping the United Kingdom out of its cozy past and into a more or less hectic and "American" future ... She was first in the news; first in the heart of Edward VIII (who during most of 1936 was first in British hearts); first in that historic British crisis—moral, emotional, political, religious—which aroused all civilization.

Generalissimo and Madame Chiang Kai-shek
January 3, 1938
Portrait by S.J. Woolf

Henry Luce was born in China and favored the Chiangs' cause. When the issue ran, they were in hiding after Japan seized the capital at the time, Nanjing, with the resulting massacre.

Under this man and wife the traditionally disunited Chinese people—millions of whom seldom used the word "China" in the past—have slowly been given national consciousness ...

The material progress of Chiang's China has been phenomenal. He called in a Princeton professor to give China the plan for its first sound currency. Roads and buses to run on them were sent stabbing far into China from her ports. In a land which has existed for centuries in a state of complete disorganization, such elementary progress was revolutionary ...

For the colossal purchases Chiang had to make, he could not afford the normal luxury of graft. The Generalissimo turned ... to his own wife. She it was who pored over aircraft catalogs, dickered with hard-boiled white salesmen, and is reputed to have had several Chinese officials of her Air Ministry shot to reduce thieving.

What China's officialdom needed, the Generalissimo and Mme. Chiang had decided, was a big dose of the castor oil of Puritanism ... and with every ounce of [Nanjing's] authority, they dosed all China.

FIFTEEN CENTS   JANUARY 2, 1939

TIME

THE WEEKLY NEWSMAGAZINE

MAN OF 1938
From the unholy organist, a hymn of hate.
(Foreign News)

Rudolph Charles von Ripper

VOLUME XXXIII   (REG. U. S. PAT. OFF.)   NUMBER 1

Adolf Hitler

January 2, 1939
Illustration by Rudolph Charles von Ripper

With war seemingly inevitable, Germany's Führer, a charismatic but savage dictator, loomed as the most powerful and ominous threat to free democratic nations in Europe and everywhere.

The figure of Adolf Hitler strode over a cringing Europe with all the swagger of a conquerer ... What [he] did to Germany in less than six years was applauded wildly and ecstatically by most Germans. He lifted the nation from postwar defeatism. Under the swastika Germany was unified. His was no ordinary dictatorship, but rather one of great energy and magnificent planning ... The 1,500 miles of magnificent highways built, schemes for cheap cars and simple workers' benefits, grandiose plans for rebuilding German cities made Germans burst with pride ...

But what Adolf Hitler and Co. did to the German people in that time left civilized men and women aghast. Civil rights and liberties have disappeared. Opposition to the Nazi regime has become tantamount to suicide or worse. Free speech and free assembly are anachronisms ... Germany's 700,000 Jews have been tortured physically, robbed of homes and properties, denied a chance to earn a living, chased off the streets ... Meanwhile, Germany has become a nation of uniforms, goose-stepping to Hitler's tune.

Winston Churchill

January 2, 1950
Portrait by Ernest Hamlin Baker

Expanding the franchise, TIME named Winston Churchill Man of the Half-Century for his tireless striving, by word and deed, to preserve Britain and the values of Western civilization.

From 1930 to 1950, Churchill was four men ... The personal Churchill was happy, reveling in the good things of life ... Churchill the journalist maintained a fairly high average of quality. Churchill the historian in the '20s wrote *The World Crisis,* professionally regarded as the best account of World War I. Churchill the politician has the other three, especially the historian, working for him. He uses history as an instrument of prophecy.

Churchill spotted Hitler early as the main enemy of Britain and of civilization ... Churchill's warnings had two effects of transcendant importance: 1) they speeded up expansion of the Royal Air Force to the point that saved Britain; 2) they left Churchill with a clear record, giving the free world a man to trust, a man who then led Britain to victory.

In 1946 he performed one of his greatest services for Western civilization, warning of communism's "Iron Curtain." Out of that speech came the Marshall Plan ... and the spirit of defiance that inspired the great airlift to Berlin. —MARGARET QUIMBY AND LOUIS BANKS

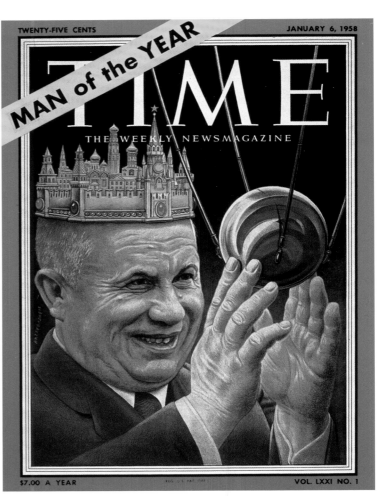

Hungarian Freedom Fighter

January 7, 1957
Illustration by Boris Chaliapin

TIME *evoked a symbolic figure to represent the Hungarian patriots whose revolt against their Soviet masters was doomed but whose courage inspired a new resistance against communist tyranny.*

History would know him by the face, intense, relentless, desperate and determined, that he had worn in the streets of Budapest; history would know him by the name he had chosen for himself during his dauntless contest with Soviet tanks: the Hungarian Freedom Fighter.

The ultimate consequences of his action could only be assessed in the future. But the effect upon European political and military alignments was already stupendous. The Kremlin's current irresolution owes much to him. So does communism's great loss of prestige around the world ... Destroyed also was the *1984* fantasy that a whole generation could be taught to believe that wrong was right, or could be emptied of all integrity and curiosity.

But the Freedom Fighter's greatest triumph was moral: he demonstrated the needful truth that humanity is not necessarily forever bound and gagged by modern terrorist political techniques. Thus he gave to millions, and specifically to the youth of Eastern Europe, the hope for a foreseeable end to the long night of communist dictatorship. —GODFREY BLUNDEN

Nikita Khrushchev

January 6, 1958
Portrait by Boris Artzybasheff

The Soviet Union stunned the world by launching the Sputniks, history's first man-made satellites. The leader behind the feat, Nikita Khrushchev, showed there was more to him than that.

Khrushchev was as extraordinary a dictator as the world has ever seen. Not since Alexander the Great had mankind seen a despot so willingly, so frequently, and so publicly drunk. Not since Adolf Hitler had the world known a braggart so arrogantly able to make good his own boasts. In 1957 Nikita Khrushchev did more than oversee the launching of man's first moons. He made himself undisputed and single master of Russia. Few men had traveled so far so fast ...

He reorganized Soviet industry, laid down the law to Soviet intellectuals, stemmed the tide of desertions from the Western Communist parties, soothed the incipient rebellion in the satellites, and got from China's Mao Tse-tung a showpiece pledge of allegiance ...

He lived and spoke as a man who moves in Communism as a fish in water, oblivious of dialectical debate or moral pang. Drunk or sober, he never seemed to worry about what he said, who was listening, how it might diverge "from the current line." A man in motion, he had the air of a man who never looked nervously back over his shoulder in his life. —CARL SOLBERG

TWENTY-FIVE CENTS

JANUARY 5, 1959

MAN of the YEAR

TIME
THE W...NEWSMAGAZINE

DE GAULLE

$7.00 A YEAR

VOL. LXXIII NO. 1

Charles de Gaulle

January 5, 1959

Portrait by Bernard Buffet

A military hero in World War II and briefly the provisional President of postwar France,
Charles de Gaulle emerged from near obscurity to stave off civil war.

Eight months ago Charles de Gaulle, soldier, scholar and writer, was a recluse, regarded by most of the world—when it thought of him at all—as a man whose role in history had ended a dozen years earlier. Today he is Premier and President-elect of France's Fifth Republic ...

He has all but destroyed the Communist Party as an active factor in French government, has laid the groundwork for a fruitful new relationship between France and her onetime African colonies, and has immensely strengthened France's moral and psychological position in revolt-torn Algeria. Above all, he has given Frenchmen back their pride ... Where most mid–20th century statesmen feel obliged to cloak their extraordinary qualities in a mantle of folksiness, he unabashedly regards himself as a historic figure and comports himself as a man of greatness. —ROBERT C. CHRISTOPHER

THIRTY CENTS JANUARY 3, 1964

TIME
THE WEEKLY NEWSMAGAZINE

MAN of the YEAR

Robert Vickrey

MARTIN
LUTHER
KING JR.

VOL 83 NO. 1

Martin Luther King Jr.
January 3, 1964
Portrait by Robert Vickrey

The magazine's first black Person of the Year eloquently led the civil rights movement, forcing Americans of all colors to confront the meaning of their democratic heritage and core belief in liberty.

The U.S. Negro, shedding the thousand fears that have encumbered his generations, made 1963 the year of his outcry for equality ... There was Birmingham with its bombs and snarling dogs; its shots in the night and death in the streets and in the churches; its lashing fire hoses that washed human beings along slippery avenues without washing away their dignity; its men and women pinned to the ground by officers of the law. All this was the Negro revolution ...

King, the leader of the Negroes in Birmingham, became to millions, black and white, in South and North, the symbol of that revolution ... He has an indescribable capacity for empathy that is the touchstone of leadership. By deed and by preachment, he has stirred in his people a Christian forbearance that nourishes hope and smothers injustice. —JESSE L. BIRNBAUM

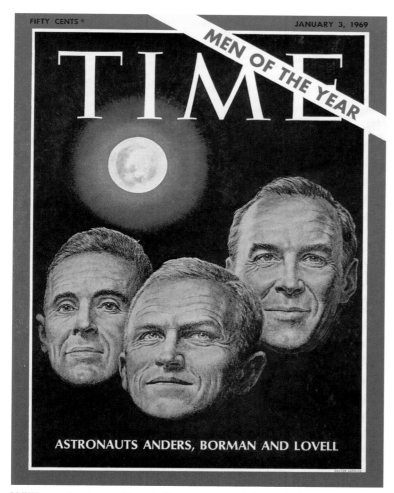

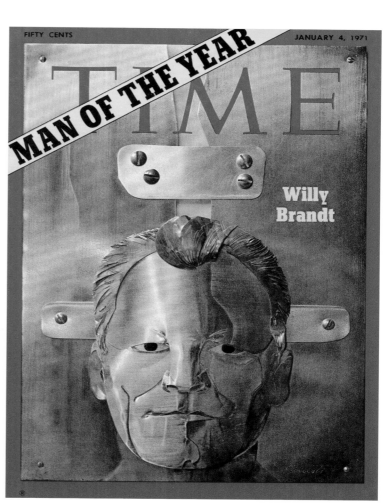

William Anders, Frank Borman and James Lovell
January 3, 1969
Portrait by Héctor Garrido

*After a grim, dispiriting year, Apollo 8's astronauts
lifted the world's spirits as they realized the age-old fantasy
of orbiting the moon.*

Ⅰn Christmas week 1968, the human race glimpsed not a new continent or a new colony, but a new age, one that will inevitably reshape man's view of himself and his destiny. For what must surely rank as one of the greatest physical adventures in history was, unlike the immortal explorations of the past, infinitely more than a reconnaissance of geography or unknown elements. It was a journey into man's future ...

It was three lonely men who risked their lives and made the voyage. And in the course of that first soaring escape from the planet that was no longer the world, it was the courage, grace and cool proficiency of Colonel Frank Borman, Captain James Lovell and Major William Anders that transfixed their fellowmen ...

Below them, less than 70 miles away, lay a desolate, pockmarked landscape. In the black sky above hung a half-disk—the earth ... Thus, incredibly, they were there, precisely where the mission planners had predicted, finally living the dreams of untold generations of their ancestors. —MICHAEL DEMAREST

Willy Brandt
January 4, 1971
Sculpture by George Giusti

*Renowned as a feisty mayor of West Berlin, Willy Brandt became
Chancellor of West Germany on a platform of building new
bridges between Europe's communist East and its democratic West.*

Ｗhile most political leaders in 1970 were reacting to events rather than shaping them, Brandt stood out as an innovator ... Using West Germany's considerable strategic and economic leverage, he is trying to bring about an enlarged and united Western Europe, which would remain closely allied with the U.S. but would also have sufficient self-confidence and independence to form close ties with the Communist nations. It is a daring vision, full of opportunity and danger, rekindling the dreams of unity that have inspired Europeans from Charlemagne to Napoleon ...

Brandt's attempt ... will require astute diplomacy. By personality, background and experience, however, he is uniquely equipped to deal with both East and West. According to Klaus Harpprecht, editor of the intellectual monthly *Monat* and a close friend, Brandt possesses "an Anglo-Saxon sense of fairness, a respect for others and a very clear sympathy for weaker persons." "Of all the politicians I have known," says [Common Market architect Jean] Monnet, "Brandt stands out for one great quality: he is a generous man." —DAVID TINNIN

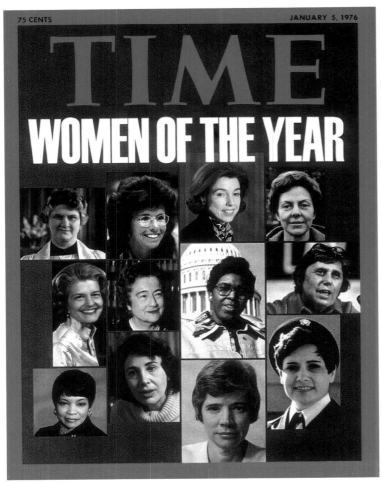

American Women

January 5, 1976

Ruhollah Khomeini

January 7, 1980

Portrait by Brad Holland

Feminism became more than a movement; it became a national transformation. The lives of American women—and their relations with American men—would never be the same.

They have arrived like a new immigrant wave in male America. They may be cops, judges, military officers, telephone linemen, cab drivers, pipefitters, editors, business executives—or mothers and housewives, but not quite the same subordinate creatures they were before. Across the broad range of American life, from suburban tract houses to state legislatures, from church pulpits to Army barracks, women's lives are profoundly changing, and with them, the traditional relationships between the sexes. Few women are unaffected, few are thinking as they did ten years—or even a couple of years—ago ... Says Critic Elizabeth Janeway ... "No maps exist for this enlarged world. We must make them as we explore."

It is difficult to locate the exact moment when the psychological change occurred. A cumulative process, it owes much to the formal feminist movement—the Friedans and Steinems and Abzugs. Yet feminism has transcended the feminist movement. In 1975 the women's drive penetrated every layer of society, matured beyond ideology to a new status of general—and sometimes unconscious—acceptance. —LANCE MORROW

In its most controversial choice ever, TIME named Iran's Ayatullah Khomeini after he had stoked his radical followers in Tehran to imprison Americans in their own embassy.

As the leader of Iran's revolution [Khomeini] gave the 20th century world a frightening lesson in the shattering power of irrationality, of the ease with which terrorism can be adopted as government policy. As the new year neared, 50 of the American hostages seized on Nov. 4 by a mob of students were still inside the captured U.S. embassy in Tehran, facing the prospect of being tried as spies by Khomeini's revolutionary courts. The Ayatullah, who gave his blessing to the capture, has made impossible and even insulting demands for the hostages' release ...

Unifying a nation behind such extremist positions is a remarkable achievement for an austere theologian ... But Khomeini's carefully cultivated air of mystic detachment cloaks an iron will, an inflexible devotion to simple ideas that he has preached for decades, and a finely tuned instinct for articulating the passions and rages of his people ... He possesses the most awesome—and ominous—of political gifts: the ability to rouse millions to both adulation and fury. —GEORGE J. CHURCH

Lech Walesa

January 4, 1982

Portrait and collage by Jim Dine

Though crushed in the end, the unimposing electrician Lech Walesa and the Solidarity movement he led won notable reforms from Poland's government, striking a blow for freedom and dignity.

The beleaguered government of General Wojciech Jaruzelski, pushed to the wall by Walesa's challenging Solidarity union ... struck back in the classic Communist fashion. Its minions came for Walesa at 3 a.m. at his apartment in Gdansk, the gray Baltic seaport whose windswept shipyards had given birth to Solidarity in August 1980. They hustled him aboard a flight to Warsaw and then held him in a government guesthouse ... They cut off communications with the outside world and imposed martial law ...

Walesa and his movement had made a travesty of Communism's pretensions in the eyes of the world. An authentic proletarian revolution had risen, just as Marx had predicted, only to be put down by the guns of the oppressor class: the Communists themselves. However Solidarity's revolution may ultimately run its course, the movement brought the heady taste of a new life to the Poles. That memory will die hard, if at all. Nor will the world forget the lessons in courage displayed by the millions of Polish workers who were inspired by Lech Walesa. —THOMAS A. SANCTON

JANUARY 3, 1983 $1.50

TIME
MACHINE OF THE YEAR
The Computer Moves In

Computers

January 3, 1983
Sculpture by George Segal

*The computer had become commonplace, even necessary,
to many industries, but before the days of the World Wide Web,
it was not an essential part of most households.*

It is easy enough to look at the world around us and conclude that the computer has not changed things all that drastically. But one can conclude from similar observations that the earth is flat, and that the sun circles it every 24 hours. Although everything seems much the same from one day to the next, changes under the surface of life's routines are actually occurring at almost unimaginable speed. Just 100 years ago, parts of New York City were lighted for the first time by a strange new force called electricity; just 100 years ago, the German Engineer Gottlieb Daimler began building a gasoline-fueled internal combustion engine. So it is with the computer ...

[But] many of the programs now being touted are hardly worth the cost, or hardly worth doing at all. Why should a computer be needed to balance a checkbook or to turn off the living-room lights? Or to recommend a dinner menu, particularly when it can consider (as did a $34 item called the Pizza Program) ice cream as an appetizer? ... Even the most impressive information networks may provide the customer with nothing but a large telephone bill. "You cannot rely on being able to find what you want," says Atari's [Alan] Kay. "It's really more useful to go to a library." —OTTO FRIEDRICH

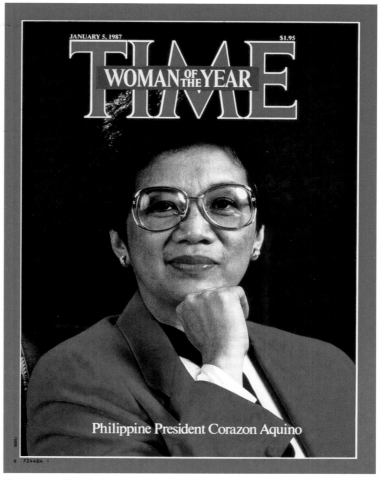

Deng Xiaoping
January 6, 1986
Collage by Robert Rauschenberg

Deng's reforms in the People's Republic of China began the transformation of that nation from a hermetic giant into the economic colossus now challenging the U.S. for primacy.

Marx sits up in heaven, and he is very powerful. He sees what we are doing, and he doesn't like it. So he has punished me by making me deaf," [said Deng]. The leader of 1 billion Chinese was joking, of course; he lost part of the hearing in one ear long before he launched the world's most populous nation on an audacious effort to create what amounts almost to a new form of society. But, as might be expected from the diminutive (4 ft. 11 in.), steel-hard Deng, 81, it was a joke with a sharp point. If in his more solemn moments he still attempts to justify what he often calls his "second revolution" in the name of that patron saint of Communist revolution, Karl Marx, Deng is well aware that the system he is evolving in China either ignores or defies many of the precepts most cherished by traditional Marxists (especially those running the Soviet Union). In the Chinese spirit of balance between yin and yang, Deng's second revolution is an attempt on a monumental scale to blend seemingly irreconcilable elements: state ownership and private property, central planning and competitive markets, political dictatorship and limited economic and cultural freedom. Indeed, it is almost, or so it often seems to skeptics in both the Western and Marxist worlds, an attempt to combine Communism and capitalism. —GEORGE J. CHURCH

Corazon Aquino
January 5, 1987
Photograph by Diana Walker

The downfall of Philippine dictator Ferdinand Marcos at the hands of the widow of his most fearsome political rival was one of the most stirring narratives of the year.

Thousands of volunteer poll watchers, singing hymns and burning candles, formed a human barricade against the armed goons and carried their ballot boxes through the streets to counting stations. Thirty of the government's vote tabulators walked out in protest against the fraud. The country's Catholic bishops publicly condemned the election, and the U.S. Senate echoed the protest ... Soon the implausible turned into the improbable ... As the rebels barricaded themselves inside two military camps, first hundreds, then thousands, then tens of thousands of common citizens poured into the streets to offer food, support and protection, if need be with their bodies, to the maverick soldiers and Aquino backers. As civilians, bearing only flags and flowers, took up positions to defend the military men, the world knew that it was watching more than just an electoral upheaval ... Finally, the improbable became the impossible. Marcos' tanks rolled toward the crowds, only to be stopped by nuns kneeling in their path, saying the rosary. Old women went up to gun-toting marines and disarmed them with motherly hugs. Little girls offered their flowers to hardened combat veterans. In the face of such quiet heroism, thousands of Marcos loyalists defected; many simply broke down in tears. —PICO IYER

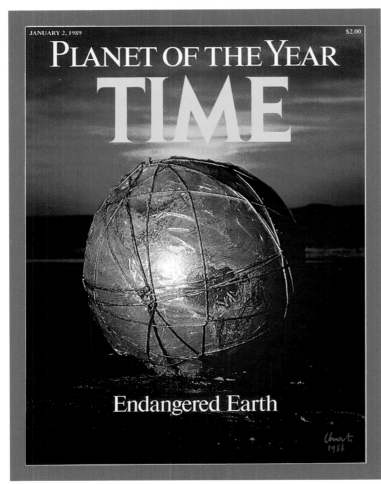

Earth
January 2, 1989
Sculpture by Christo

A year of drought, heat and forest fires—and a prescient concern about what was then usually called the greenhouse effect—led TIME to name its first Planet of the Year.

As man heads into the last decade of the 20th century, he finds himself at a crucial turning point: the actions of those now living will determine the future, and possibly the very survival, of the species. "We do not have generations, we only have years, in which to attempt to turn things around," warns Lester Brown, president of the Washington-based Worldwatch Institute. Every individual on the planet must be made aware of its vulnerability and of the urgent need to preserve it. No attempt to protect the environment will be successful in the long run unless ordinary people—the California housewife, the Mexican peasant, the Soviet factory worker, the Chinese farmer—are willing to adjust their life-styles. Our wasteful, careless ways must become a thing of the past. We must recycle more, procreate less, turn off lights, use mass transit, do a thousand things differently in our everyday lives. We owe this not only to ourselves and our children but also to the unborn generations who will one day inherit the earth.

Mobilizing that sort of mass commitment will take extraordinary leadership, of the kind that has appeared before in times of crisis ... Unless mankind embraces that cause totally, and without delay, it may have no alternative to the bang of nuclear holocaust or the whimper of slow extinction. —THOMAS A. SANCTON

Mikhail Gorbachev
January 1, 1990
Sculpture by Hans Jörg Limbach

The Soviet empire was unsustainable both politically and economically. As Gorbachev attempted to reform his country, he let loose the forces that would bring the Cold War to a close.

The 1980s came to an end in what seemed like a magic act, performed on a world-historical stage. Trapdoors flew open, and whole regimes vanished. The shell of an old world cracked, its iron fragments dropping away, and something new, alive, exploded into the air in a flurry of white wings.

Revolution took on a sort of electronic lightness of being. A crowd of half a million Czechoslovaks in Wenceslas Square would powder into electrons, stream into space at the speed of light, bounce off a satellite and shoot down to recombine in millions of television images around the planet.

The transformation had a giddy, hallucinatory quality, its surprises tumbling out night after night. The wall that divided Berlin and sealed an international order crumbled into souvenirs. The cold war, which seemed for so long part of the permanent order of things, was peacefully deconstructing before the world's eyes. After years of numb changelessness, the communist world has come alive with an energy and turmoil that have taken on a bracing, potentially anarchic life of their own. Not even Stalinist Rumania was immune.

The magician who set loose these forces is a career party functionary, faithful communist, charismatic politician, international celebrity and impresario of calculated disorder named Mikhail Sergeyevich Gorbachev. —LANCE MORROW

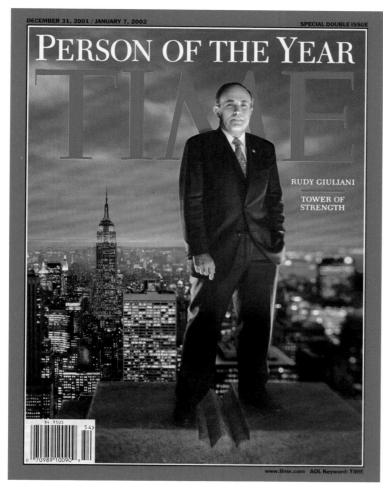

Rudolph Giuliani
December 31, 2001
Photograph by Gregory Heisler

The year that saw Osama bin Laden's assault on America also witnessed the inspiring resilience of New York City, as embodied by its often confrontational and controversial mayor.

"Show me a hero, and I will write you a tragedy," said F. Scott Fitzgerald. On the morning of Sept. 11, primary day in New York City, Rudy Giuliani was paddling along with all the other lame ducks into oblivion. The tower of strength had become an object of pity: the iron man's cancer made him vulnerable, the righteous man's adultery made him hypocritical, the loyal man's passions—for his city and its cops and its streets and its ballplayers—divided the city even as he improved it. After abandoning Gracie Mansion, his marriage in flames, he was camping out with friends on the Upper East Side, and now it was time to choose his successor, and the end was in sight.

The end was, in fact, just a few blocks away. Having raced to the scene at the first news of the attacks, Giuliani was nearly buried alive. In the hours that followed, he had to lock parts of the city down and break others open, create a makeshift command center and a temporary morgue, find a million pairs of gloves and dust masks and respirators, throw up protections against another attack, tame the mobs that might go looking for vengeance and somehow persuade the rest of the city that it had not just been fatally shot through the heart. —NANCY GIBBS

Mark Zuckerberg
December 27, 2010
Photograph by Martin Schoeller

Facebook was seven years old, had 550 million members and was the subject of a recent hit movie, The Social Network, *when its founder was designated Person of the Year.*

Zuckerberg is a warm presence, not a cold one. He has a quick smile and doesn't shy away from eye contact. He thinks fast and talks fast, but he wants you to keep up. He exudes not anger or social anxiety but a weird calm. When you talk to his co-workers, they're so adamant in their avowals of affection for him and in their insistence that you not misconstrue his oddness that you get the impression it's not just because they want to keep their jobs. People really like him ...

He's spent his whole life in tight, supportive, intensely connected social environments: first in the bosom of the Zuckerberg family, then in the dorms at Harvard and now at Facebook, where his best friends are his staff, there are no offices and work is awesome. Zuckerberg loves being around people. He didn't build Facebook so he could have a social life like the rest of us. He built it because he wanted the rest of us to have his. —LEV GROSSMAN

FYI
A dazzling array of trivia about TIME covers

Top-Selling Newsstand Issues

[and the number of copies sold]

1. 9/11 Commemorative
September 14, 2001   **3,397,721**

2. One Nation, Indivisible
September 24, 2001   **2,041,375**

3. The Death of John Kennedy Jr.
July 26, 1999   **1,321,054**

4. Princess Diana Commemorative
September 15, 1997   **1,160,126**

5. Target: Osama bin Laden
October 1, 2001   **841,408**

6. The Death of Princess Diana
September 8, 1997   **823,258**

7. President-Elect Barack Obama
November 17, 2008   **596,032**

8. Michael Jackson Commemorative
July 2009   **570,887**

9. John Kennedy Jr. Commemorative
August 2, 1999   **520,747**

10. Barack Obama: Person of the Year
December 29, 2008   **505,962**

Most Letters

12,191 *Last Tango in Paris,* January 22, 1973
(6,710 cancellations and nonrenewals)

4,938 Man of the Year: Ayatullah Ruhollah Khomeini, January 7, 1980

3,500 Sex in the U.S., January 24, 1964

3,421 Is God Dead? April 8, 1966

Say Who?

There have been many unusual choices for the cover. Below, a gallery of one-shot wonders.

Labor leader Harry Bridges, July 19, 1937

Actress Anita Colby, January 8, 1945

Lt. Col. John Paul Stapp, September 12, 1955

Retailer Eugene Ferkauf, July 6, 1962

Analyst Franklin Spinney, March 7, 1983

754

That's the number of times women have appeared on the cover (compared with men's 4,267) since 1923. Hillary Clinton tops the list at 19; Princess Diana and the Virgin Mary are tied for second with 11 apiece.

November 1, 1990

November 16, 2009

March 11, 1996

October 26, 2009

March 21, 2005

TIME and the English Language

The magazine coined and popularized words and phrases that have become commonplace: *pundit, tycoon, World War II, socialite, kudos* and *cleavage* (as in *bosom*). Neologisms that did not survive: *cinemactor/cinemactress* and *prohibishop.*

Be Afraid! Be Very Afraid!

In a world full of real and hyperreal anxieties, TIME has not been shy about sounding the alarm.

Sharks, July 30, 2001

Guilt and Anxiety March 31, 1961

Crime June 30, 1975

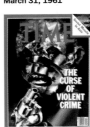

Violent Crime March 23, 1981

Nuclear War March 29, 1982

Air Safety January 12, 1987

Privacy November 11, 1991

The Apocalypse July 1, 2002

Nuclear Trafficking February 14, 2005

Talkin' 'Bout My Generation

From America's teens to ... America's teens, TIME has announced generational shifts.

Today's Teenagers
January 29, 1965

Twenty-Five and Under
January 6, 1967

The Computer Generation
May 3, 1982

Baby Boomers Turn 40
May 19, 1986

Twentysomethings
July 16, 1990

Generation X
June 9, 1997

Twixters
January 24, 2005

World Changers
February 28, 2011

Me, Me, Me Generation
May 20, 2013

2,143 Number of original artworks in "Cover Art: The TIME Collection" in the National Portrait Gallery at the Smithsonian Institution in Washington

Youngest And Oldest

Lisa Harap, 6 months
August 15, 1983

Football coach
Amos Alonzo Stagg, 96,
October 20, 1958

Animal Acts

May 31, 1954

Dogs 7
Horses 6
Tigers 3
Sharks... 3
Insects 2
Cats 1
Pelicans... 1

Told You So ... Oops!

Derivatives
April 11, 1994

A 1994 cover article was prescient about the risks of financial derivatives, but a 2005 cover story celebrating a housing boom failed to notice it was propped up by toxic mortgages, which caused the boom to bust in 2008.

Home Equity
June 13, 2005

55! Most cover appearances by a single person? Nixon's the one!
Second place: Ronald Reagan, with 47.
Third place: Bill Clinton, with 38.

August 25, 1952

November 20, 1972

November 5, 1973

April 2, 1990

What Were We Thinking?

With so many grim and serious events on the cover and in the magazine, TIME has occasionally given readers a break with a focus on not-bad news. Some were pretty silly.

Catalogues, November 8, 1982

Minnesota
August 13, 1973

Soap Operas
January 12, 1976

Ice Cream
August 10, 1981

Cats
December 7, 1981

Cocktails
May 20, 1985

Retirement
February 22, 1988

The Chemistry of Love
February 15, 1993

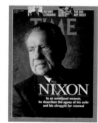

Summer Guide
May 26, 1997

Uncovered: A Look at Ones That Never Ran

The magazine's history-making first all-type cover, "Is God Dead?" came about inadvertently. The artist Larry Rivers had produced a wonderfully eccentric meditation on the subject, but the editors ultimately rejected it. We have reproduced a rare photograph of that painting, whereabouts unknown, on the right. TIME has a long catalog of covers that didn't make the cut at first—losers, junked at the last minute for breaking news or simply set aside for another approach to the subject at hand. Some waited to run another day. Others, however, would never see a newsstand. On these two pages are a broad sampling of those non-runs, finally ready for their close-up.

The Chaliapin Trove

Across three decades, Boris Chaliapin, one of the magazine's favorite portraitists, created more than 400 covers. He also produced several hundred paintings that were never used, including the six below, which are now part of the Smithsonian's National Portrait Gallery in Washington.

The editors did not like this portrait of fashion designer Sophie Gimbel for a 1947 cover, so Chaliapin quickly did another, which did run

Stan Musial of the St. Louis Cardinals appeared on the cover in 1949, but Ernest Hamlin Baker executed that painting

A 1951 cover ended up with a conceptual image of Pentagon bureaucracy instead of this portrait of Defense Secretary George Marshall

TIME planned to do a cover on Gloria Swanson if she won an Oscar for *Sunset Boulevard* in 1951, but she lost out to Judy Holliday

Johnnie Ray's four histrionic 1952 hit singles made him a potential cover subject; it never happened, and all his fans could do was cry

The stage version of J.P. Donleavy's *The Ginger Man* opened the night before JFK was killed—ending plans to put the author on the cover

The legendary radio comic Jack Benny was bumped for Winston Churchill and the eve of WW II

What would have been New York City Mayor Fiorello LaGuardia's third cover was given to Stalin in 1941

His soldiers took Berlin, so a cover on the USSR's Georgy Zhukov gave way to the iconic crossed-out Hitler

Chaliapin prepared this cover in case Barry Goldwater defeated Lyndon Johnson in 1964

The Tiananmen Square massacre in 1989 pre-empted this cover illustration by Frances Jetter

A 1993 Middle East breakthrough inspired this concept, but editors chose to go with photos and a map

Chip Kidd's idea for our 1997 tour of America via Highway 50 was rejected for a mostly type cover

Smarty Jones didn't win the 2004 Triple Crown, then Ronald Reagan died, so this was a moot point

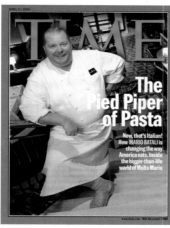

The cult of celebrity chef Mario Batali made way for a 2006 cover on immigration

Instead of this imperiled dove of peace, a 2006 cover depicted rifle barrels twisted in a knot

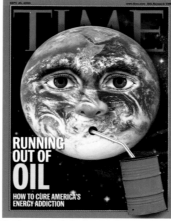

A story on global petroleum shortages made it as far as this proposed September 2006 cover

This take on the U.S. surge in Iraq was set aside for a black-and-white photo of a serviceman's face

The editors opted for a photo-illustration of Obama's head on FDR instead of C.F. Payne's painting

Steve Carell of *The Office* posed, but TIME chose a different route for its 2009 cover on the future of work

The December 2009 cover on a decade from hell produced this idea from designer Chip Kidd

Ai Weiwei had this idea for the 2011 Person of the Year cover; a Shepard Fairey illustration ran instead

A G.I. reads the July 24, 1950, issue with General Omar Bradley on the cover

COURTESY U.S. ARMY

Credits

TIME

Founders Briton Hadden and Henry Luce

The founders of TIME split the management of the magazine. Hadden was the editor, for the most part, until his death in 1929; Luce focused on business but influenced the magazine directly as Time Inc.'s editor in chief until he died in 1967.

Managing Editors
John S. Martin, 1929–33, 1937
John Shaw Billings, 1933–36
Manfred Gottfried, 1937–43
Thomas S. Matthews, 1943–49
Roy Alexander, 1949–60
Otto Fuerbringer, 1960–68
Henry Grunwald, 1968–77
Ray Cave, 1977–85
Jason McManus, 1985–87
Henry Muller, 1987–93
James R. Gaines, 1993–95
Walter Isaacson, 1996–2000
Jim Kelly, 2001–06
Richard Stengel, 2006–present

Inside the Red Border

Editor Howard Chua-Eoan   **Designer** Arthur Hochstein
Picture Editor Crary Pullen
Writers Massimo Calabresi, Jim Frederick, Jeffrey Kluger, Richard Lacayo, Jamie Malanowski, Mike Neill, James Poniewozik, Christopher Porterfield, Michael Scherer, Ishaan Tharoor, Jyoti Thottam, David Van Biema, Claudia Wallis
Reporters Elizabeth L. Bland (Chief), Kathleen Brady, Lina Lofaro
Copy Editor Jose Fidelino
Time Inc. Archivist Bill Hooper
Editorial Production Lionel P. Vargas

Time Home Entertainment

Publisher Jim Childs
Vice President, Brand & Digital Strategy Steven Sandonato
Executive Director, Marketing Services Carol Pittard
Executive Director, Retail & Special Sales Tom Mifsud
Executive Publishing Director Joy Butts
Director, Bookazine Development & Marketing Laura Adam
Finance Director Glenn Buonocore
Associate Publishing Director Megan Pearlman
Associate General Counsel Helen Wan
Assistant Director, Special Sales Ilene Schreider
Brand Manager Bryan Christian
Associate Production Manager Kimberly Marshall
Associate Brand Manager Isata Yansaneh
Associate Prepress Manager Alex Voznesenskiy

Editorial Director Stephen Koepp
Copy Chief Rina Bander
Design Manager Anne-Michelle Gallero

Special Thanks Katherine Barnet, Jeremy Biloon, Susan Chodakiewicz, Rose Cirrincione, Jacqueline Fitzgerald, Christine Font, Diane Francis, Jenna Goldberg, Hillary Hirsch, David Kahn, Amy Mangus, Nina Mistry, Dave Rozzelle, Ricardo Santiago, Gina Scauzillo, Adriana Tierno, Time Inc. Premedia, TIME Research Center, Vanessa Wu

ISBN 10: 1-61893-082-6; ISBN 13: 978-1-61893-082-8
Library of Congress control number: 2013938647
Printed in Mexico

We welcome your comments and suggestions about TIME Books. Please write to us at: TIME Books, Attention: Book Editors, P.O. Box 11016, Des Moines, IA 50336-1016. If you would like to order any of our hardcover Collector's Edition books, please call us at 1-800-327-6388, Monday through Friday, 7 a.m. to 8 p.m., or Saturday, 7 a.m. to 6 p.m., Central Time.